TYRANTS
AND
TYPEWRITERS

By the Same Author

TYRANTS AND TYPEWRITERS

Communiqués From The Struggle For Truth

Robert Conquest

Lexington Books

D.C. Heath and Company/Lexington, Massachusetts/Toronto

Library of Congress Cataloging-in-Publication Data

Conquest, Robert.
    Tyrants and typewriters : communiqués from the struggle for truth
/ by Robert Conquest.
       p.   cm.
    Pieces which appeared in various periodicals, etc. over several
decades.
    ISBN 0-669-21222-9 (alk. paper)
    1. Soviet Union—Politics and government—1985–   2. Soviet Union-
-Intellectual life—1917–   3. Russian literature—20th century-
-History and criticism.   4. Freedom of information—Soviet Union.
I. Title.
DK288.C66   1989
947.084—dc20   89-32022
                                            CIP

Published simultaneously in Canada
Printed in the United States of America
Library of Congress Catalog Card Number: 89-32022
International Standard Book Number: 0-669-21222-9

The paper used in this publication meets the minimum requirements of
American National Standard for Information Sciences—Permanence of
Paper for Printed Library Materials, ANSI Z39.48-1984. ∞™

Year and number of this printing:

89 90 91 92 10 9 8 7 6 5 4 3 2 1

CONTENTS

For
Dennis and Madeleine Enright

PREFACE

These essays, reviews, introductions and so on were written at various times over several decades. Indeed part of the material they discuss goes back further still, to the 1930s and earlier. Together, they amount to a series of communiqués from a long, and often bitterly fought, struggle for truth. They illustrate or register in one way or another its strategies and tactics, its battles and skirmishes. They develop both the general movement of ideas and the particulars of argument; (and they are given in a thematic rather than a temporal order).

At the time of writing, the progress of events could not be predicted: though it always seemed clear that in the long run the lie would rot. I have made some cuts of material now not worth labouring, and I have updated or elaborated a few passages. But nothing has been rewritten retrospectively to pretend a preternatural ability to predict future events. All the hopes, and reasons for hoping, that truth would break through in the Soviet world are as they appeared in the original.

I would acknowledge above all the superlative editing of Kate Mosse, both in meticulous work on textual detail, and in sound and considered advice on the substance of these pieces, and on the book as a whole.

And I owe thanks, once again, to the John Olim Program for the Study of the Soviet Union and Eastern Europe at the Hoover Institution, Stanford University; to Amy Desai's indispensible secretarial assistance; and, as ever, to my wife.

Robert Conquest
Stanford 1989

ACKNOWLEDGEMENTS

Acknowledgements are due to the following, in which these pieces first appeared: *Survey, Commentary, The New Statesman, The New Republic, Problems of Communism, The Listener, The Spectator, The New York Times Magazine, The New York Times Book Review, The Daily Telegraph, Inquiry, Soviet Analyst, The New Criterion, Slavic Review, Russian Review, Solzhenitsyn in Exile* (ed John B. Dunlop, Richard S. Hough and Michael Nicholson), my introduction to an edition of Milovan Djilas' *The New Class*, and my own *Courage of Genius: The Pasternak Affair*.

INTRODUCTORY

On my left, the biggest concentration of brute power the world has ever seen – a tremendous armament, a huge bureaucracy, an enormous police machine, a vast propaganda apparatus. On my right, one man at a typewriter holding a top page and five carbons.

Such were the conditions under which the generation-long struggle for truth was waged in the USSR until the late 1980s. And then the huge edifice of falsehood, built up over sixty years, crumbled. Glasnost, though not as yet complete, means that by and large deception has been declared bankrupt. In this context, it is not to our purpose to consider political, economic and other developments in the USSR, nor to discuss in any detail the possible futures awaiting that country. One of the essentials, nevertheless, has been the collapse of the Stalinist and neo-Stalinist myth which poisoned the Soviet atmosphere and which was, too, the source of deception and dangers for the outside world.

There are profound economic and social, as well as moral and intellectual reasons for this collapse. But it was indeed largely through the efforts of a not very large number of free pens and typewriters that the imposing structure of falsification was eaten away from inside until nothing was left but a hollow shell.

The archetype of the lone figure facing such odds was of course Alexander Solzhenitsyn, before his expulsion from the USSR in 1974. He is today again a key figure in the new moral and intellectual turmoil now taking place in the Soviet Union. His name will arise, and his work be examined, more than once in the pages which follow. In each of the book's divisions he has made a major contribution, and it seems appropriate to end it with a note on his role. But, though he must loom large in any consideration of the contest between force and the human spirit, his exploits are only part of a struggle waged over many years, by many people, and one which continues.

He may remind us, among other things, that one of the major

results of the confrontation was the fact that much of Russian literary creativity was again in exile abroad. The resurgence of independent thought among these writers, but also among those who remained, was a clear indication that the regime had simply failed in one of the main tasks it set itself. The atomisation of the social order and the suppression of all unorthodox thought in the Stalin era was expected to lead to a situation in which the creative minds of the country, having rid themselves of the ideas of the past, would produce a literature wholly in accord with the new form of society in which the ruling party was the admitted leader and inspirer of civilisation. If Marxist-Leninist theory had been correct, something like this might have happened.

When we reflect on the reasons which produce the opposite result, we may yet be surprised at the persistence of unorthodox views. The failures and oppressions of the regime might have been expected to produce hostile moods. But it is a matter of more than mere mood – of profound, sophisticated, philosophical opposition. Its survival underground, at a time when, as the executed writer Isaac Babel put it, 'Today a man only talks freely with his wife – at night, with the blankets pulled over his head', must have deeper sources. One of these, it might seem, was the continued printing of the great literature of Russia – carrying implicitly in every page the alternative values. At the height of Stalin's power, the anarchist Tolstoy, the liberal Turgenev, the humanist Chekhov, continued to be published in large editions; even the 'reactionary' Dostoevsky was never entirely banned. The power of this literature and of the Enlightenment from which it sprang has proved ineradicable.

In a famous phrase the mid-nineteenth century Russian rebel writer Herzen spoke of his fear for the future – the appearance of a 'Genghiz Khan with the telegraph'. In the years that have meanwhile passed his prediction proved well founded. Yet it was not only the tyrants but also those who struggled for freedom who benefited from technical change. He failed to predict Juvenal with a typewriter.

Thus this book is only partly on political themes. It is about writing in general, as the sphere in which the individual asserts autonomy against the power of the state, and truth is established against the falsifications of its propaganda. Today, the average adult life-time has seen a series of devastating changes, and not only in politics and in war. One constant accompaniment has been a struggle for the minds of men and women. It would be incorrect to call this merely a struggle of ideas, for it has often been a struggle over the mere facts.

A Soviet periodical recently and with approval, quoted the present writer as saying in 1973 (in the Introduction to a Western-published Russian edition of *The Great Terror*), 'Of course, it would be better if the history of this period could be written by Soviet specialists. I well understand the difficulties facing a foreigner in such work. Unfortunately, however, in present circumstances objective investigation and serious publication on the period can only be undertaken outside the boundaries of the Soviet Union'.

This is no longer true. There is already a great accumulation of Soviet material: long suppressed facts about the past and present, long unprintable ideas about the Soviet future. It is being admitted that the description of the system given by its enemies and critics was true both in general and in detail; that its apologists, even its partial apologists, were liars or dupes, or a meld of the two.

Perhaps it would be too sanguine to say that the difficult days of the struggle for truth are nearly over. History has seen unexpected revivals of aberrations once thought dead. Moreover, there are regimes outside the Soviet bloc proper where the same techniques of falsification and propaganda are practised, and have some of the same success even abroad. Nevertheless if a victory of truth has been won or is in sight, it must be remembered that it was only possible because the system of lies had exhausted itself. The constant public acceptance of what everyone knew to be not merely falsehoods, but stupid and long-exposed falsehoods – the mere disgrace of it ate into the morale of the Soviet intelligentsia. But this only happened because the ideas of truth and of free opinion were never effectively extirpated.

It has not only been *samizdat* writing which has contributed. A number of legal Soviet writers have published, within the limits allowed them, work which helped keep the spark alive: even *One Day in the Life of Ivan Denisovich* originally appeared with official approbation in the Khrushchev interlude. And we should note the effect of the Western radio stations which, in spite of the immense and expensive jamming effort, was continuous, pervasive and unanswerable, transmitting *samizdat* and other truth back to the USSR. But still, in this long and harrowing struggle the honours go about all to those few thousand active 'dissidents' who, under the most oppressive and dangerous conditions, fanned back to life the spark of truth which a generation of terror had supposedly extinguished.

For the glasnost whose beginnings we now welcome was not a gift. It came as the result of a bitter struggle, and one in which power was able to inflict severe casualties on the defenders of the truth. Of men like the poet Yuri Galanskov and the writer Anatoly Marchenko, dead in labour camp or prison, one can only say more literally what Matthew Arnold wrote in a figurative sense:

> Let the victors, when they come,
> When the forts of folly fall,
> Find thy body by the wall!

This is not to denigrate those who remained silent, or made token obeisance to the imposed outlook. It is not given to everyone – it is not possible for everyone – to show the heroism and self-sacrifice of voluntarily facing persecution, imprisonment and worse. Which of us in the West can know how we would have behaved? But now that the move forward is on a mass scale, we should above all not forget the pioneers who made it possible, nor what some of them suffered.

In the West itself, the Stalinist idea, based in part on theoretical argument in part on factual falsification, gained millions of adherents, more sympathizers. And even apart from these, widespread circles tended to a view which roughly held that the Soviet Union, though flawed and lacking in civil rights, even ruthless as to opponents, had had social and economic achievements not otherwise attainable: (this is, of course, also now admitted in Soviet publications to be quite false). At the same time the notion that, whatever the details, the USSR was on balance no worse than, or better than, the West became fairly common. Not all typewriters were on the side of liberty. There were ambiguous or servile voices in the Soviet bloc, and pseudo-historians in the West intent to prove their own culture wrong. They too are represented in this book.

If their ideas never fully prevailed, it was not for want of a vast investment in them by the Stalin and post-Stalin r͏ꞏ ͏ꞏ.ies. And, again, it can be said with reasonable confidence that the Soviet view on the benign and peaceable attitudes of these regimes might have disarmed the West, or at least key countries in the West, but for the testimonies recorded in these pages. (And that the West, whatever its vacillations, blocked the further advance of Stalinism was, in turn, one of the conditions necessary for the voices of truth in and to the Soviet Union itself to be able to rout their formidable adversaries.)

It has been a hard fight, and one without precedent. And it is a broad field we cover in this conspectus of literary, historical, economic and philosophical writing central to the understanding of the culture of tyranny which has for so long confronted all free pens, all free people.

PART I WITNESSES

Arthur Koestler's *Darkness at Noon*

The death of Arthur Koestler sends us back to a reconsideration of his masterpiece.

In August 1936, January 1937 and March 1938, the three great 'Moscow Trials' were staged in the florid October Hall of the Trade Union House, with its white Corinthian columns and light blue walls, formerly one of the ballrooms of what had been the Nobles' Club. To an immense publicity and in the presence of the world's press and members of the diplomatic corps, many of the leading veterans of Lenin's Bolshevik Party confessed in turn to assassination, espionage, sabotage, treason, in the service of Trotsky and on behalf of Hitler in particular and other foreign rulers. Their crimes had ranged from putting broken glass in Soviet butter to procuring the murder of the writer Maxim Gorky through his doctors.

The world found it hard to know what to make of all this. Though the charges sounded incredible, and most of them out of character too, the public confessions were baffling, at least at first sight. The accused did not seem to exhibit any signs of having been tortured, or of being in any obviously abnormal physical or mental state. All the same there were plenty of indications even then that, as is now beyond dispute, the trials were monstrous frauds, that the 'conspiracy' did not exist, and that the Soviet secret police had found methods of getting their victims to co-operate. But at the time, though to their lasting discredit, many on the left in the West found it possible to accept the Stalinist thesis that these great shows represented the truth. Not everybody, even on the left, did so. One who did not was Arthur Koestler. The result was *Darkness at Noon* – one of a handful of books which has powerfully affected the political, intellectual and moral climate of our times.

Darkness at Noon is marked by an extraordinary elegance and economy. The balance of factual incident or visual detail on the one hand and the development of the argument on the other is little short of perfect, and it is hard to think of any other book which matches it.

Its internal logic is so strict that it by no means excludes a reader from taking the view that it provides, for those who care to accept it, a franker and truer justification of Stalinism than is to be found in any official communist literature. Indeed, Koestler tells us that he had a letter from a young Frenchman informing him that the book had actually converted him to the Stalinist cause. This was not the natural or normal reaction, but it may be thought to show that Koestler, from a deep involvement in the early communist movement, had fairly represented the ways of thought, or at least the self-justificatory pleadings, of both Stalin and his communist opponents.

Koestler tells us that his central figure, Rubashov, is modelled on Bukharin in his thinking and Trotsky and Radek in his personality and physical appearance. But in fact the resemblance seems closer to Christian Rakovsky, who, sixty-five years old at the time of his sentence, resisted interrogation for eight months, but who at the trial was made to proclaim that his surrender was due to hearing, in the summer of 1937, of the Japanese attack on China and the extent of Nazi and Italian intervention in Spain. This, he said, 'had a stunning effect on me. Rancour and ambition fell from me.' He added that he now felt that his 'duty was to help in this struggle with the aggressor' and that 'I would go and expose myself fully and entirely, and I told the investigator that on the following day I would begin to give complete, exhaustive testimony.'

Of course, from the knowledge we have of the physical and mental state to which victims of these trials had been brought, we need not take Rakovsky's way of putting it as representing his own true assessment, in the abstract. It was clearly the result of mental and physical pressures of a variety of types. And yet it is perfectly plausible that it represented his own rationalization of surrender, and in that sense was a true expression of his feelings at the time, even if primarily induced by the brainwashing techniques of the 'conveyor' system of continuous interrogation. We are told by several survivors of the confession trials – for example, the Czechoslovak Evzen Loebl (sentenced to life imprisonment in the Slansky trial of 1952) – that sheer exhaustion finally reduced him to the stage where it did not occur to him to repudiate his confessions even after he was allowed food and rest: 'I was quite a normal person – only I was no longer a person.'

Koestler is far too subtle and experienced not to see this point.

Rubashov is worn down by exhaustion and toothache – if not to the degree of those who became semi-automata – so this component of his surrender is not neglected. In some genuine cases, it seems probable that prisoners were put under no greater physical pressure than Rubashov was: several, indeed, such as Bukharin, Ivan Smirnov, and others, were so much wanted on show by Stalin that they were able to get away with incomplete confessions, so that they failed to come up to Rubashov's final acceptance of the view that it was the duty of the accused to discredit themselves and their political attitudes as much as possible. With some, on the other hand, torture, combined with threats of death against relatives down to infant children, proved effective.

It is one of Koestler's strengths that in *Darkness at Noon* the horrors are not overdone. Another is that the incidents he narrates all have close parallels in the factual literature. For example, the scene when a tortured prisoner is dragged screaming to his execution past Rubashov's cell, in order to weaken the latter's resolve, is firmly based on evidence.

If one had a substantial criticism, or rather reservation, to make about *Darkness at Noon* it is in fact that the moral and intellectual questions are argued out at too high a level. In the first place, the Old Bolsheviks, including those slaughtered by Stalin, were neither morally nor intellectually up to the level of Rubashov. And as to the interrogators who argue with Rubashov about his duty to history and to the party, they too are superior to the real operatives of the NKVD in the 1930s. Even 'Gletkin' would be a remarkably high-level figure of the pre-1937 secret police period, and those who came up thereafter were incomparably lower-grade, both intellectually and morally.

Yet the fact that Koestler has thus given the arguments both of Rubashov and of his Stalinist opponents at their highest level is no disadvantage, in what is essentially a moral fable. For a case can only effectively be answered when put at its strongest.

The Stalinist position, which Rubashov is finally led to accept the logic of, is that the party is always right, that its interests far transcend matters of truth or individual ethics. The comparison is made by one of the interrogators between the 'vivisection' and the 'anti-vivisection' ethic, the implication being that a humanist or moderate desire to spare individuals or even generations of human beings suffering and oppression is in the long run harmful, since it happens to be the case that only such means can lead to the just society. What Rubashov and his persecutors share is, in fact, the view that there is an infallible science of society; and, though Koestler is in one sense branding the Stalinists, in another he is making clear that anyone who accepts such a thesis has no moral defence against Stalinism. It is only in some of Rubashov's memories and moods, and finally in his death, that the probability of a universal ethic transcending such fallible theorizing really emerges.

When Solzhenitsyn remarked that, particularly in our time, literature constitutes the last and strongest line of defence of the truth against forces attempting to destroy it, he was putting things in a way which is unfamiliar to the West. In the ordinary course of events, our imaginative literature seems to subsist on its own – no doubt representing in some general way aspiration to the truth and to true understanding, but seldom involved directly in the political. Or, at least, such work as is overtly political has usually been the result of neither experience nor insight, those essentials to any true creation, but rather of the frigid projection on to unsuitable material of opinions learnt in the abstract, ideologies accepted on trust. But, unlike British and American work in particular, Koestler's reflects what may seem to us to be an almost supererogatory accumulation of real experience – as a communist in the Soviet Union in the early thirties, in the death cell of Seville prison in the Spanish War, in an internment camp in Vichy France. And such experiences, unfamiliar to many of us, were long a commonplace of the vast territories of the Soviet bloc.

It was against such a background that Koestler was able, with *Darkness at Noon*, to effect one of the first major penetrations of the Western consciousness by a true feeling for the element of vast and ruthless deception in the Stalinist scheme of things.

1983

Milovan Djilas 1: *The New Class*

Milovan Djilas, formerly one of the four main leaders of the Yugoslav Communist Party both underground and in power, abandoned communism simply on principle. He saw that its actions were not producing the promised social results, that socialist democracy was absent – that socialist dictatorship, even, was not accurate description if by 'socialist' the absence of a privileged class was implied. He saw everywhere – and among a party which had gained control, and recently, as a result of its own bravery and skill – the political corruption of power and the economic corruption of the perquisites of power.

There can be few men with so much experience of the movement. He had known Stalin, and many of his successors. He had lived in the highest echelons for years. Probably no one, not even Imre Nagy, had seen international communism so intimately from the inside, while retaining his critical sense. Neither power, nor habit, nor all the apologetic apparatus of communist theory could blur the clear mind, nor blunt the sharp idealism, of this revolutionary intellectual from the Montenegrin mountains. And in his classic, *The New Class*, he gives us the ripe fruit of his long political experience and his knowledge of political theory.

Djilas sees the matter in Marxist terms up to a point, but also in the broader perspective. For there are two ways of looking at the new phenomena of Soviet, and Soviet-style, society – that of the Marxist and that of the uncommitted observer. From a simply empirical, commonsensical viewpoint, we can conclude without difficulty that there is in fact a privileged stratum, comparable to and in practice more oppressive than the economic 'ruling classes' of the rest of the world. We can simply treat as irrelevant and absurd the official answer – which is that, by definition, there cannot be an economic ruling 'class' where there is no private ownership of the means of production. Indeed, this is on the face of it a silly scholasticism hardly worth bothering with. Once it is clear that exploitation takes place, and that there is a minority which benefits from it at the expense of a majority, the question of whether or not to use the word 'class' does not seem very important.

Nevertheless, this point has to be given more attention than it may appear to deserve. For the Marxist scheme, because of its apparent success in analysing the layout of other societies, has proved attractive to many. And, as a result, the mere fact of the abolition of 'private' ownership of the means of production is not uncommonly taken, even in the West, as meaning 'socialism' – a social order juster than any other in existence.

Time and again, we see 'progressive' people hypnotized, as it were, by this idea. Though the actual, or at least the earlier, tyrannies and failures of the Soviet order are admitted by them, they nevertheless find it impossible not to make allowances. They continue to treat the communist states as somehow more progressive, or if not more progressive in reality then in some curious fashion more promising, than the mixed economies and democratic politics of the West.

But Marx's categories of society do not necessarily include all forms of possible exploitation, any more than his system of 'classes' is automatically an exhaustive description of all exploiting groups. Indeed, he had traced, already in existence, a form of society which was despotic and exploitative without containing 'classes' in the ordinary Marxian sense: this was the 'Asiatic' type of society, which he defined as consisting of village communes on the one hand and a despotic state machine on the other. In it, the exploiting role was taken by the mandarins and officials of the emperor or pharaoh, that is, of the state machine – an interesting parallel with the Soviet system.

However, it is worth noting that he did not include the 'Asiatic' society in his original scheme. It does not appear, for example, in the Communist Manifesto. He was led to postulating it by his actual studies of oriental history and economics. This is a clear enough indication that he did not regard his theoretical layouts as automatically comprehending all conceivable forms of society, but was prepared to admit the existence of new forms if given the empirical evidence. There can be little doubt that he would have seen in the modern communist states a social form he had previously made not much provision for, and would have adjusted his thinking accordingly.

I say 'not much provision', because, in fact, he had sketchily adumbrated a communism containing the faults he noted of previous societies.

His ethical objection to capitalism was that it produced 'alienation' between man and society. The communism he hoped for was 'the positive abolition of private property as human self-alienation'. He foresaw, however, that there were styles of communism in which all the alienating evils he attributed to capital were simply taken over, in a 'barbaric and stupid' fashion, by the community itself. This would act as 'the general capitalist' and 'by systematically denying man's personality be no more than the expression of private property.' This 'Raw Communism' was merely 'an aspect of the infamy of private property which wants to present itself as the positive community'.[1] The Marxist objections to the Soviet revolution were, in any case, quite basic. Marx's central statement of his philosophy of history (in his *Critique of Political Economy*) states flatly, 'No form of society can perish before all the forces of production which it is large enough to contain are developed, and at no time will outworn conditions be replaced by new higher conditions as long as the material necessities of their existence have not been hatched in the womb of the old Society itself.' He interpreted this, frequently and explicitly, in the sense that capitalism in the advanced countries would so industrialize the economy and proletarianize the non-capitalist masses that the coming to power of socialism would require a political and administrative change.

As Djilas points out, everything in Russia happened differently from how the leaders expected. The communists came to power in a state in which the proletariat formed a minority, and were in any case considerably less experienced politically, or even 'proletarianized' psychologically, than the great working classes of the industrial West. Lenin knew this, and excused his revolution as a temporary tactical seizure of a weak area which could only be justified when the imminently expected revolution took place in the West, and came to Russia's aid. When the Western revolution failed to mature, the communists continued in power, and gradually switched to the idea that their highly centralized party, now alienated (as Lenin conceded) even from the Russian working class, could 'build socialism' – an expression which would have been meaningless to Marx. The idea was that by forced industrialization the conditions could be created *ex post*

---

[1] (Marx and Engels Collected Works, Ryazanov's edition, Moscow 1932 vol. I, section 3).

facto which should have been in existence in the first place to justify the taking of power.

There were a number of objections to this aberration. Above all, the economic transformations which had elsewhere taken place under capitalism were more, not less, inhumanly conducted under the rule of the 'workers' party'. For the party, viewing itself as the sole legitimate representative of the proletariat, allowed no form of free trade union or other resistance to its methods, and the workers had no recourse against the dictatorship. How could they strike, it was asked, 'against themselves'?

Acknowledging all this, sympathisers could nevertheless hope that when this harsh transitional period was over, and a new working class created, the party might renew its links with the people and become in the old Marxist sense a reflection of the working majority. And there the fatal flaw in the ends-and-means argument became apparent. The party had long since become an established interest, with its own mystique and a certainty of its own right to rule. Of the revolutionary idealism of the communists just come to power, Djilas says that it is sincere and genuine, but nevertheless 'the morals of a sect'. Moreover, the party and the doctrinal loyalty which is its main component automatically 'fades, disintegrates and drowns during the course of the climb to complete power and to ownership . . . only the bare forms and observances which have no real substance remain.' A self-perpetuating bureaucracy, it has no thought whatever of restoring the rights of those over whom it has ruled so long.

And this political privilege soon spilled over into the economic field. Marx had written that, in certain circumstances, 'The bureaucracy possesses the State as private property', and this was extended to the perquisites of state-owned production. As early as 1930, the old communist Rakovsky, later to be executed by Stalin, had noticed this development in action when he wrote from Siberia that 'the element which unites this original class is a form . . . of private property, to wit, the State power'. He was not the last to recognise a New Class in control. Even the Chinese of the Maoist epoch often referred to 'the dictatorship of the privileged bourgeois stratum in the Soviet Union': their own solution, indeed, was equally unhuman (and equally un-Marxist), being the equivalent of a militarized theocracy.

But one can gain an equally clear impression of the alienation of the worker and peasant classes from the owning priviligentsia in the press of the countries directly concerned. We may look at two examples printed in the communist countries in periods of 'thaw'. On the Polish worker:

Workers, as a result of obstructions in the development of workers' self-government, among other things have not felt their social advancement to the full. They are not sufficiently aware that they are effectively participating in managing the economy. They have the impression that they are on the lowest rung in the social hierarchy of the factory.[2]

Or again, on the Russian peasant:

We have collective farmers who are careless about common property. Once I reproached one of them for squandering the collective farm harvest, and I reminded him that he was a part-owner of the common property. He grinned sarcastically and sneered: 'Nice lot of owners! It is all empty talk. They just call us owners to keep us quiet, but they fix everything themselves . . .'

A real collective farmer won't cry, when he sees the chairman drive past in his car, 'Here am I, part-owner of the collective farm, tramping along on foot, while he takes his ease in a Pobeda.' Any collective farmer who really cares for his collective farm will agitate to see that the chairman should have his own car! The collective farmer, like the Soviet worker, is interested in strengthening the management of his economy.[3]

As Djilas says, the 'anti-Stalinism' even of the Khrushchev leadership in the Soviet Union was concerned to renounce only Stalin's methods and, more particularly, his actions against the party elite itself. What it showed no sign of doing was relinquishing any privilege over the masses which it gained as a result of Stalin's measures.

Nevertheless, this oldest and most powerful of the communist states was already entering upon its decadence. It retained its power, but its dogmas sounded tired. They ceased to have much appeal even in Russia itself. As Djilas says of the New Class, 'It is at the height of its power and wealth, but it is without new ideas. It has nothing more to tell the people.'

The other communist states were in various different stages of intellectual or moral decay. Djilas sees his own Yugoslavia's regime as much preferable to Stalinist or post-Stalinist Russia, and yet still a backward, narrow-minded, stagnant dictatorship. Djilas himself, serving in a gloomy cell in Sremska Mitrovica jail the latest of a series of sentences for freely expressing his views, seemed a negligible figure compared with the vast and powerful parties and states he was

[2] Professor Oskar Lange, in *Samorzad Robotniczy*, November 1965.
[3] *Party Life*, December 1957.

attacking. But in them the life principle was moribund. In him, the human mind and spirit flourished indomitably. In the long run, we may feel, it was a duel in which the antagonists were not as ill matched as appearances suggested.

1966

Milovan Djilas 2: Mountain Marxism

Djilas's great-grandfather, both his grandfathers, and his father and uncle all perished in the blood feuds of the mountain clans: 'the land was never one to reward virtue, but it was always strong in taking revenge.' The quality that makes Land Without Justice, an account of his Montenegrin youth and childhood, so outstanding is a cool yet 'poetic' humanity, rather as in some of the great Russian novelists. It is a particularly astonishing thing to find in the writing of an old party man; understanding and charity are extended even to villains and enemies – as, after all, human beings. And the reflections are those of a fine mind that has made trial, as few men have, of political solutions, found them wanting and transcended them.

We are all used to reading the speeches of communist and other foreign politicians, couched in a cosmopolitan phraseology. And this has certainly strengthened in their convictions people here who are inclined anyhow to think of all nations as really much alike. A book like Djilas's reminds us that even those who have attempted to sink themselves in the most international ideas, the most unlocalized ideologies, really have deep roots in some area whose every custom and outlook may differ, in a way that determines their whole life, from those of other countries.

I do not think that Djilas is a profound thinker, but he is a fearless one, and one not possessed by the cramps of envy or malice. We sometimes think that what will help democratic ideas in such parts of the world as the Balkans is the Western culture, the Western 'way of life'. That there are natural sympathies between these peoples and ourselves is quite true, but they are based on something quite different. I have spoken with writers from the Balkan peasantry, with knowledge of only Russian literature (and with peasants themselves, if it comes to that), and come across the same common ground. What they turn to in theWesterner is not his culture or his politics as such, but respect for the individual. Djilas's Montenegrins, with their pride in and jealousy of their individuality, are only extreme examples of what is found in many other races. In the Balkans you never got the *moujik* accepting the whims of the Little Father: you got Djilas's father on his few acres, plotting a blood feud against the royal family. What they share with us (what indeed the Russian intelligentsia yearns for too) is rejection of the notion that the collective is a higher thing than the individual.

Djilas fought for collectivism as a convenience for producing arrangements which would make him humanly equal, in a just peace, with everyone he felt equal to – that is, the whole population, high and low, from the village halfwits to the passionate and bloody chieftains. When he found himself at the top of a new hierarchical system, he forswore it, with utter consistency, and returned to the same prison cell he had occupied under the monarchy. It was only then that he concluded that what Marxism lacked was a theory of political liberty. He now says that what he had chiefly sought since childhood, respect for the personal dignity of everyone, was after all impossible without it. Nor is this the lowest compliment that democracy has received.

1958

Milovan Djilas 3: Implacable Conscience

Though the observation is much sharper, and many minor details are added, on the face of it Djilas's account in *Conversations with Stalin* of the political troubles between Yugoslavia and the Soviet Union differs little from that given in Dedijer's semi-official *Tito Speaks*, published here in 1953.

Yet one's impression that one has read all Djilas says before is a superficial one. He uses the same framework of facts. But his emphasis is elsewhere – on the nature of Stalin himself and of the system which sprang up around him. The lessons he draws from his experience of Stalin and the Stalinist milieu are powerfully and effectively argued in a 'conclusion'. This is not specifically critical of the Yugoslav regime, but it is of the Soviet regime, and by condemning all 'ideological conformity and so-called monolithic structure of the party' can be taken amiss by anyone whom the cap fits, including the rulers in Belgrade.

Djilas's courage and honesty have never been in doubt. One of the most extraordinary things about the book is its very starting point – that a man like Djilas, tough-minded, highly educated, brave and independent, should have in the first place found himself accepting the Stalin myth. The lesson of Djilas's whole career is that political liberty is not something which can be sacrificed for larger aims with any hope of genuine results. He stands as a warning to any who may fall into the same temptation. And he continues, at the cost of his own freedom, lucidly and strikingly to press the point home.

As to his prison sentence in connection with this book, some reviewers implied that it was Djilas's revelation that two Yugoslav divisions were about to march into Albania early in 1948 which constituted his 'betrayal of State secrets'. In fact, Dedijer has already mentioned this in the following form:

The Albanian government asked the Yugoslav government to send two Yugoslav divisions to southern Albania, because Enver Hoxha was afraid that the Greeks might occupy some areas of Albanian territory which, they claimed, were inhabited by Greeks.

Djilas's account is almost identical: he speaks of the troops' movement as part of 'an agreement between the Yugoslav and Albanian governments'.

This incident is certainly the most sensitive thing in the book from Belgrade's point of view. But Djilas also reveals, in his description of the suicide of Naku Spiru, that a strong and 'honest' element in the Albanian party was entirely opposed to all Yugoslav penetration. In effect, while Djilas himself is more opposed to Hoxha's Stalinism than anyone, his regard for truth is so great that he supports the Albanian version of the trouble between the parties in 1947–8. Strictly speaking, he does not do so by mentioning new facts, let alone secret ones; but his virtual acceptance of the anti-Yugoslav story, coming from one who was very much in a position to know, is an unpleasant blow to those in Belgrade who may still think that history is 'politics projected back into the past'.

In the same way, he treats even Stalin fairly in connection with the war, where Khrushchev evidently slandered him. Such objectivity makes it all the more devastating when he concludes:

> All in all, Stalin was a monster who, while adhering to abstract, absolute, and fundamentally utopian ideas, in practice had no criterion but success – and this meant violence, and physical and spiritual extermination.

His own view of politics is different: 'I am, of course, far from thinking that success in political struggles is the only criterion.' And he emphasises that even Khrushchev's 'cheap theatrical' de-Stalinization showed that, in spite of temporary failures, 'the human conscience is implacable and indestructible'. In fact, in or out of jail, he still stands in the long run for forces which have already damaged, and should in the end destroy, individuals and organisations on the face of it immeasurably stronger than themselves.

1962

Svetlana Alliluyeva

Miss Alliluyeva's *Twenty Letters to a Friend* is not, as the blurb absurdly remarks, in the class of Tolstoy, Turgenev, Chekhov and Pasternak, and Miss Alliluyeva herself has been more modest. But still, it is well written, and it is of striking interest for a variety of reasons.

First of all, it is a moving personal record of a troubled life. She saw her father's agonized death; she learned of her mother's suicide; her relations went to the execution cellars or the labour camps. Even her own love brought tragedy: she touchingly describes her schoolgirl idyll with Alexei Kapler, the filmscript writer, which eventually led to his serving ten years in a camp on a charge of being a British spy. It was no doubt partly as a result of such things that by the time she was thirty-five this woman brought up in a traditionalist atheism had turned to religion.

She writes most movingly of the feeling she, and most Russians, have for the country as such, and how she is unable to conceive of leaving it. But even she, a few years after penning these pages, found herself unable to stand the disappointment of all hopes of increased liberty which had marked the post-Khrushchev regime. It remains an extremely Russian book. Her feelings for the countryside, for her home and relations, for the sufferings of her country, for the realities of death and love among her family, are in the tone of the classics, of the impulse toward complete candour and complete sympathy which has always characterized the literature of Russia.

The scene is enormously Russian too. When she writes of her childhood and youth it is hard to remember that these families with their nurses and governesses and villas and their intense personal preoccupations are former professional revolutionaries and not the characters of Chekhov. Russian coarseness and brutality come out strongly. So do Russian sentimentality and sensitivity – a pot-pourri whose unmistakable odour clings to an unexpected lot of characters: the dreadful NKVD Commissar First Class Stanislav Redens, Miss Alliluyeva's 'Uncle Stakh', being high-spirited and kind to children; Khrushchev and the boozy bully Vasily Stalin embracing, both in tears, as they plan the young man's rehabilitation from alcoholism.

The author provides us, too, with insights, all the more striking for being incidental, about the way Russia moved in the post-Revolutionary period. Before the Revolution, Sergei Alliluyev, her maternal grandfather, was a mechanic. 'He and his family had a four-room apartment in St Petersburg. It wasn't large, but it would be as much as a Soviet professor could dream of today.' This sort of thing shows more powerfully than any argument the frequently neglected fact that in all the basic necessities of life – food, housing, clothing – the Russian standard of living has if anything deteriorated in the next fifty years.

Svetlana adds that her worker-grandfather's children went to high school. The pre-revolutionary school system in Russia was excellent, and in general surprisingly democratic. It was, indeed, not on a mass scale by modern standards. But it is worth recalling that tsardom's greatest educational blemish, the mass illiteracy in the countryside, was also under serious attack at the end of the first decade of the century, when a programme for liquidating it was in preparation which planned to do away with it entirely by the early thirties. That is, revolution or no revolution, the results here would probably have been much the same.

Again, we learn much when she tells us that when she was young, her uncle, then stationed in Berlin, would occasionally bring or send European clothes. For reasons of Soviet piety, however, the children were told that they had been bought in Leningrad. She has other interesting criticisms of the regime of a type not often heard – for example, her strong condemnation of the extraordinary laxness in preserving the country's architectural heritage. Occasional much-publicised exceptions give the opposite impression. But what has been done to the old quarter of Moscow alone is enough to justify her point of view. Again, when the doctors at Stalin's deathbed apply leeches to his neck, an idea of the backwardness, or rather the mixture of modernity and backwardness, in Soviet medicine emerges (leeches are still used in Russia).

And above and behind all this we note the extraordinarily slapdash and absurd ways of despotism, as when the uncouth and illiterate head of her father's guard somehow takes on himself the role of arbiter of films, operas and even the shapes of buildings, putting his views out as 'Comrade Stalin's tastes'. As for general party attitudes, take the following remark: 'In those days, before the war, it wasn't yet the custom for the Party to criticise films and insist that they be re-made.' We see, too, the awful combination in the families of the leaders of 'this mixture of Party bigotry and the complacency of the bourgeois woman'. (Svetlana's old nurse, when she visited her and her little son, found this new bourgeoisie was worse than the old. She had been treated as a member of the family by the pre-revolutionary rich, but not by the Zhdanovs.)

These vivid flashes are no more than passing observations, to which Miss Alliluyeva gives little space and probably no conscious attention. But, even without her special position as Stalin's daughter, one can see why the book presented itself as, to some extent, the centre of a political storm, and why the bureaucratic elite in the Soviet Union, and their defenders everywhere, conducted such a remarkable campaign, and made so many attempts to divert public attention to various other sensational matters.

Still, it was inevitably her account of her father which attracted the greatest remark. She is continually illuminating about the physical and mental surroundings in which the most powerful and dangerous man in the world had his being. She is too clear-minded and honest to exculpate him from the horrible deeds of his ascendancy. But she is also filial and full of sincere feeling for him, and to a certain degree this leads her into misapprehension. In particular, she allots Beria a far greater share of the blame for the horrors of the Stalin period than is at all plausible.

Beria personally made a very bad impression on Miss Alliluyeva, and on her mother before her. She tells us, 'I won't presume to judge what I don't remember and didn't see with my own eyes.' Thus the personal effect on her of the people she met carries more weight with her than their public activities. Political credibility is lost when she compares the 'odious' Beria with her fine Uncle 'Stakh' Redens, one of the group she describes as 'gifted and fascinating' but not able to live his 'talented and interesting life to the end'.

Redens, however charming in the family circle, was one of the most brutal of the NKVD chiefs over a long period. He was head of the Ukrainian secret police during the frightful collectivisation period, in which millions died – men, women and children. During the Yezhov terror, Redens (the 'man in yellow' of the critic Ivanov-Razumnik's *Memoirs*) was in charge of the secret police in Moscow, and oversaw the imprisonment or execution of tens of thousands of innocent people, many of them his own comrades.

Miss Alliluyeva's rumours about Beria's 'treachery' in 1920 were much bruited in the party right up to the time they were voiced by Health Commissar Kaminsky at a Central Committee meeting in 1937. The latter's arrest the following day muted them considerably. But they were raised again in 1953 among the charges against Beria after he had fallen. In the confused underground intrigues of Caucasian politics in 1918–21, he doubtless had ambiguous contact with the local nationalist agencies. But his selection within months to high office in the Cheka is proof enough that no stigma whatever attached to him in knowledgeable party circles.

Miss Alliluyeva seeks to implicate Beria in the Kirov murder of December 1934. She 'cannot imagine' Kirov's allowing Beria's election to the Central Committee: but Beria became a member during Kirov's lifetime. She maintains that it was after Kirov's murder that Beria began to climb to prominence and power; but, while it is true that he could scarcely hope to reach the Politburo while its then membership continued to flourish, there were eleven more members to be removed before he got his chance, five years later, and with most of their fates it is clear that he had nothing to do. She mentions the 'transparent hints' of Stalin's responsibility for Kirov's death being given in the Soviet press at the time she was writing (1963). But, if Beria had been in any way concerned, the Khrushchev regime would happily have incriminated him as well as Stalin. In fact it is practically certain that Beria, then still in Georgia, was in no way concerned with the Kirov case. There is no longer any serious ground for doubting that it was arranged by the Leningrad NKVD on instructions from Stalin.

In the dramatic scene of her father's death, with which the author starts her *Letters*, Beria is set out in all his hatefulness, a scheming, heartless monster. In general Miss Alliluyeva's account of Stalin's successors round the deathbed reminds one of Saint-Simon's description of the courtiers of the Bourbons in similar circumstances a quarter of a millennium earlier. For such scenes must always be repeated in an autocracy: the combination of sorrow and relief, of the appearance of mourning and the reality of hopes and calculations.

Malenkov, Bulganin, Khrushchev, Kaganovich and Voroshilov are described as being in tears at the death of their patron. These emotions from coarse men with long careers of ruthless death-dealing may strike many of us as mawkish gangster sentimentalism, resembling the scenes in Hitler's bunker. Beria, in contrast, showed nothing but triumph when all was over – just as (Khrushchev tells us) he was unable to conceal his joy at the funeral later on. As he had been an intended victim of Stalin's projected purge, his attitude may not seem unforgivable. Mikoyan, who was present as well, is also not mentioned as being in tears. He too was due for execution. Moreover, as another non-Russian, he perhaps did not subscribe to the same tradition of emotionalism. (We cannot, incidentally, take it as certain that Stalin's death was natural. We do not know who had access to his medicine cupboard. At any rate, communist sources have officially reported a plot to kill him – the Albanian Enver Hoxha publicly stated that Mikoyan told him that there had been such a conspiracy.)

Miss Alliluyeva attributes the tears of the other leaders to the fact that they 'were under the spell of his extraordinary personality which carried people away and was utterly impossible to resist'. It is not necessarily a fault in Beria that he evidently did find it possible to resist. Not only did he nourish a natural resentment at the idea of being shot, but he had also (as it turned out) developed strong political qualms about Stalin's current reversion to raw terror. For – paradoxically enough – in 1953 Beria genuinely represented some sort of attempt to break out of the impasse of Stalinism. Even the brutal dispersal of Stalin's household and abandonment of his dacha after his death, of which Miss Alliluyeva complains, was, in its typical crude fashion, symbolic of an effort to destroy the Stalin image.

Miss Alliluyeva is doubtless right when she says that Beria was 'more single-minded than Stalin', but that 'he was more practised in perfidy and cunning' is hard to credit. To transfer as much odium as possiblé to Beria has been the general practice of post-Stalin leaderships in Russia. Miss Alliluyeva's reasons are quite different. Moreover, she faces up as far as possible to her father's own culpability. But, even so, she apportions the blame in a notably inequitable way. If this had been a work of political history or analysis, this would be a fatal blemish. But since the author is above all giving us an honest subjective account, a tale of her own feelings, it is of no great significance. And her book has, on the whole, been warmly received in spite of such things.

One exception was a reviewer in the London *Times Literary Supplement*, a periodical whose reviews of books on Soviet matters at this time often fell into the hands of one or more anonymous contributors noted for uncontrollable distaste for any non-Marxist criticism of Soviet affairs, a readiness to accept the Leninist myth and a testy, though inaccurate, pedantry. This particular piece, riddled with these accustomed faults, made heavy weather over her exaggerated view of Beria's evildoing, while itself getting point after point wrong. (Khrushchev, it maintained, 'alleged' that Stalin was directly responsible for Kirov's death: he did not, he hinted it, and it has never yet been openly stated. While Miss Alliluyeva blames Beria for Ord-zhonikidze's death, Khrushchev – the reviewer says – blamed only Stalin: he did not, he incriminated Beria as well.)

But then, the reviewer takes Isaac Deutscher as his authority for the circumstances of the death of Miss Alliluyeva's mother. Deutscher, whatever his virtues, is not reliable on such points during this period – even in the last edition of his *Stalin* he maintained, against the virtually unanimous voice of opinion and evidence, that there was a Tukhachevsky Plot, citing unspecified reliable evidence in his own possession - like Hochhuth! On the other hand, the *TLS* reviewer described Djilas's book on Stalin (which Svetlana, writing without knowledge of it, so powerfully confirms) as 'not always reliable'. The only previous criticism of its reliability was in an earlier anonymous review in the *TLS* written in the same tone, which stated that Djilas's first hand account of some mildly coarse behaviour by Molotov could hardly be true because, in effect, it did not fit in with the opinion the reviewer had formed of Molotov's character. (Djilas, then in prison, was unable to reply to this reckless and impudent imputation against his credibility.)

Against Svetlana, the *TLS* set those of Stalin's victims who were 'devoting themselves heart and soul to the Five Year Plan' and were felled by the party purge after March 1937 when Stalin started attacking his own followers. That these men so suffered is doubtless deplorable. Nevertheless, they had themselves killed and condoned killing by the million in the Revolution and the collectivisation. I am afraid that many of us are going to feel that the Russian people, the millions of non-political sufferers, deserve the greater sympathy. And it is with them, in spite of her background, that Svetlana Alliluyeva must be seen as aligning herself, and in her way representing the voice of common humanity triumphing over the bloody aridities of Leninism.

Although Miss Alliluyeva's is, as we have said, essentially a human document rather than a contribution to political history, a number of historical points inevitably emerge. For example, Stalin's relations with the Zhdanov family strongly imply that he did not after all have Zhdanov poisoned, in spite of his mass execution of the Zhdanovite faction over the years immediately following.

It is interesting that the MVD defector Deriabin, who had earlier given the same opinion, is here shown to be accurate in describing the dismissal in 1952 of the oafish Vlasik from the command of Stalin's bodyguard. And in general Miss Alliluyeva's story, written in Moscow without access to such sources, strikingly confirms those defector books which had always been regarded as the most reliable. Her account of her mother's suicide confirms that given by Alexander Barmine. And, as she says in a footnote added after she had come West, and read Djilas's *Conversations with Stalin*, the Yugoslav gives a thoroughly sound picture of the clumsy squalor of Politburo life.

Even apart from this, it is of course wildly untrue that Miss Alliluyeva's book is of little use to the historian. For, above all, she makes a very large contribution to our knowledge of Stalin's character. She may have been somewhat estranged from him for a number of years, but she still knew him incomparably better than anyone else who has spoken freely. Her personal feeling toward him, her affection and her revulsion, naturally colour the picture. But they do so in a clear and honest way, and it is perfectly easy to make the necessary allowances for them.

Stalin seems genuinely to have shared the modest lifestyle of the Old Bolsheviks, and to have greatly disapproved of the new party bourgeoisie. For example, when he hears of a special school set up in Kuibyshev for the children of evacuated officials during the war, he shouts, 'Ah, you damned caste!' (Svetlana comments that he was quite right. These party and government officials evicted thousands and thousands of citizens so that they themselves would have as much space as they were used to in their Moscow apartments.)

But the main impression is of the coarseness and narrowness of the leaders' life, with their dull potations and duller jokes, night after night. His daughter gives many examples of Stalin's own crudity, of which one of the most striking is his sneer at his elder son Yakov's attempt to commit suicide: 'Ha! He couldn't even shoot straight.' She recounts his fondness, standing under Repin's picture *The Reply of the Zaporozhe Cossacks to the Sultan*, for reciting the actual reply – long and tediously obscene (and most easily available to Westerners in a free rendering incorporated into Guillaume Apollinaire's 'La Chanson du Mal-aimé').

Going deeper, Miss Alliluyeva develops certain tragic qualities in that coarse and inhuman character – in particular his baffled rage and horror at his wife's suicide, which she believes to have been decisive in warping his already unphilanthropic mind. All the same, Russia's tragedy, suffered at his hands, must far overshadow the petty unhappiness of the tyrant.

1967

Marxist Disillusion: Nagy and Leonhard

After the suppression of the Hungarian Revolution in 1956 its leader, Imre Nagy, was seized when under a guarantee of safe conduct and was later hanged. Wolfgang Leonhard escaped from East Germany via a transition, both spatial and ideological, in Titoite Yugoslavia, and eventually became a Professor at Yale. Both had passed long years in official circles in Stalin's Soviet Union, and had accepted the Stalinist ideology not as mere laymen, but as true adepts. Their cases illustrate how such minds may change, at first slowly and reluctantly, when faced with contradictions between Communist doctrine and Communist reality.

Imre Nagy, writing in 1955–56, was defending his views during the period of his earlier disgrace after his brief Premiership following Stalin's death, and defending them before the Party and its Central Committee. *Imre Nagy on Communism* is a *tour de force* of a very peculiar kind. For Nagy remained convinced at that time that the Kremlin leadership meant what it said, or at least meant something rather like it on the whole. On these assumptions he has no difficulty whatever in showing that the Rakosi dictatorship was entirely contrary to Marxist teaching. Ably though this is argued it may seem naive. For it misses one major point – in modern Communist teaching Marxist argument is simply a way of giving nice names to nasty things. Nagy's accusations are single-think run mad, the ideologists must have said as they went through the routine of interpreting the runes against him; something one might expect in a bright young Komsomol, but scarcely from a man with years of experience in the heart of the Inner Party. Yet Nagy's sincerity is not in doubt. And as for his naivete, the semi-literate Machiavellians were soon laughing on the other side of their faces, as the collapse he had predicted took place. For, as he saw, Communism had reached an impasse. To maintain terrorism meant that the populations would reject it in the long run. To ease it meant that the population would reject it at once. Nagy and his supporters had the courage to face the issue. They held that to make amends to the people, to accept removal from power even, might in the long run give them the opportunity to rebuild confidence in Communist theory. That men of honesty and patriotism still existed in the parties of Eastern Europe is a remarkable thing. That the Kremlin was not prepared to let them get away with it is much less remarkable.

Wolfgang Leonhard's *Child of the Revolution* is in its way just as significant as Nagy's work. With Leonhard we get an actual case history. He was brought up in Russia from puberty on the strictest principles not only of double-think but of double-feel as well. His motives remained inhuman to the end. When he was reunited with his mother after she had served nine and a half years of an entirely unjustified five year sentence in a labour camp in the Arctic, he says, 'I was determined in no circumstances to allow my mother's fate to influence my political reasoning.' He had, however, already become doctrinally disaffected. So 'Both of us were now in opposition to Stalinism, but our opposition had different roots and turned on different questions. She had before her eyes the sufferings and deprivations of her fellow prisoners . . . of the millions of slave labourers . . . My opposition still turned only on the question of an independent road to socialism and equality among socialist countries'.

This attitude is a difficult one for most of us to understand. And Leonhard's account of the long training aimed at making party officials incapable of thinking outside such narrow intellectual formulae, and at reducing them to moral and emotional morons, is particularly interesting. But even more striking is the fact, illustrated in different ways by the careers of both Leonhard and Nagy, that even those deeply indoctrinated right in the heart of the Stalinist apparatus may yet break free. And both books are written, moreover, not after the break, but during the process, and thus contribute in a special way to our understanding of the difficulties of the struggle between truth and dogma.

1959

A Conspectus of Victims

Joseph Berger, former Secretary General of the Communist Party of Palestine and later a high official in the Comintern, is much the senior political figure to have emerged alive from Stalin's camps and to have got abroad afterwards. In *Shipwreck of a Generation* he proves himself also (not a necessary concatenation) one of the most thoughtful.

Most of us in the West have, by now, a reasonable enough idea of the unpleasantness of Stalin's Russia, in particular of the system of false confession, execution and labour camps. The literature, already impressive but still widely disbelieved in the 1940s, has long since been more than confirmed in every horrible detail by such writers as Evgenia Ginzburg, still in the USSR. Dr Berger is concerned much less to provide further 'documentation' of this massive and dreadful phenomenon (though some of his evidence is valuable from that point of view also) than to consider the thing as a whole. From his experiences in a whole series of prisons and labour camps he has selected the comments and conversations of a varied cross-section of the prison population – writers, communists, Trotskyites, Mensheviks, Christians, 'Young Rebels' and others; and he also traces the evolution of the camp system through the years he spent in it.

His own experiences are fairly typical. In the autumn of 1950, for example, special orders were received in his camp to maltreat prisoners. Some were shot, others, like Berger himself, beaten up and made to stand in the ice-choked river. He recounts how he and his fellow inmates helped the ten-year-old son of Kapustin (executed Second Secretary of the Leningrad Provincial Committee) to put in petitions that, being under twelve, he was being illegally held in a 'general' prison – unsuccessfully, however. He confirms the massacres which took place in the camps during periods of Soviet defeats in 1941–2. And so on.

His hitherto unknown pieces of information about the period include an account, from an eyewitness, of the trial of the 1934 'Leningrad Centre' which had allegedly killed Kirov. We learn, too, of the fate of the officers of the armies of the Baltic states, incorporated into the Soviet army in 1940 (all arrested, but only about a third shot out of hand).

Of his categories of prison conversation, those with communist purgees are on the whole the least interesting. As he points out, the Old Bolsheviks 'were not of outstanding intellectual calibre'. Thus they were continually bogged down with the two Russian words for truth, *pravda* and *istina* – the former a 'higher' ideal concept, and the latter corresponding to objective reality. The struggle in the party, he points out, was by no means between adherents of the two concepts, but between those who had no use at all for *istina*, and those who, while bowing to the superior merits of *pravda*, wished to keep a little bit of *istina* as well.

On the motives for the terror, Berger is equally persuasive. He quotes, for instance, a senior 'cultural' police official to the effect that with writers it was necessary to arrest more or less at random. If they were imprisoned or shot merely for things they had really said and done, then those still at liberty would have an undesirable sense of security, feeling that they need merely avoid such offences. 'This incomprehensible element, the fact that punishment fell at unexpected times and on unexpected victims . . . was an incomparably stronger deterrent.' One might add that the principle applies to terror as a whole, against the general population.

As Berger puts it, and the point is one not perhaps adequately realized, that terror was so intense, lengthy and dreadful that in effect 'after Stalin, Russia is like a country devastated by nuclear warfare. The destruction is not only physical but also moral and intellectual. To prove this one has only to read the leading Soviet philosophical and economic journals. In these the lack of originality, the low level of thought and the incapacity to understand the problems treated is agonisingly apparent.' It is sometimes said that the German consciousness never really recovered from the Thirty Years War. At any rate, it is with some such massive and profound catastrophe that the period should be compared. The way back to civilization is slow and difficult; and so far progress has not been quick. The best one can say is that, however powerless at present, the forces of Russian humanism were not wholly eradicated: given time, the loss may yet be recouped.

During the 22 years Dr Berger spent 'outside society' he very often heard it said that once the truth about conditions in the USSR became known abroad the idea of saving humanity by revolution would be 'discredited for ever'. When he came out he was horrified and astonished to find that for far too many in the West the conclusions which were 'obvious and inescapable' in Siberia had not been reached. He concludes that while New Left critics of Western society are plunged in 'confusion and absurdity' the equivalent of the thinking minority among the new generation in the Eastern bloc is of incomparably higher quality (as can, indeed, be seen in the writing of Czechoslovak and Polish students), and that they may yet contribute far more to a decent future for the world.

1971

Andrei Sakharov

Academician Sakharov, from the heart of the Soviet scientific establishment, the country's leading physicist, creator of its hydrogen bomb, confidant of its political leaders, has searched his conscience and written his testimony about world problems, but in particular those of the Soviet Union. Not, of course published in the Soviet Union, his extraordinary essay *Progress, Coexistence and Intellectual Freedom* has been expanded into a small book by the addition of an introduction, notes and an afterword by Harrison D. Salisbury.

Its briefness should not mislead us into thinking that it represents a mere skirmish in the struggle for truth, liberty and peace. It should be seen as a major offensive, even though launched by one small David against, not Goliath, but a whole Philistia of Goliaths.

No such enterprise can be free of minor defects.

As Mr Salisbury points out, there is a certain tinge of Utopianism divorced from, in particular, economic reality in this essay – as not uncommonly in the thought of well-known scientists. But this is almost entirely on such questions as Sakharov's urging enormous financial subsidies to the backward countries: as even Gunnar Myrdal lately has been pointing out, this is probably not the right way of looking at the problem. And, of course, it is of little appeal to the average citizen of the advanced countries: in Russia the one subject which causes unreserved ill-feeling among the workers is Soviet aid to Asia and Africa. And when Sakharov says 'it is necessary to change the psychology of the American citizens, so that they will approve such measures', the rather important question 'how?' remains unanswered. (Mr Salisbury suggests that in American conditions the pouring out of vast wealth into the backward countries might well produce a boom and greater wealth for the American worker too, which, whether true or not, is at least an argument more likely to appeal.)

But, if some of Sakharov's points, particularly as regards the future, may seem a little trite to us, we must remember the enormous pressures of falsehood to which the Russian intelligentsia has been submitted over such a long period. And in Sakharov's case the touch of unreality applies only to those distant worlds with whose details he is unlikely to be fully familiar. When it comes to internal Soviet affairs – and to the question of atomic warfare – every word counts.

Economically he shows that the USSR is only catching up on the USA in traditional industries such as coal and steel, which are no longer as important as they were to the Americans, while lagging in most of the newer fields. He adds that it is simply untrue to say 'that the capitalist mode of production leads the economy into a blind alley'. Nor is he deluded about other American essentials. He says that 'the ruling group in the United States' wishes to solve the Negro problem, the difficulty being rather the white workers. He says that the millionaires are not a serious problem, that a revolution to eliminate the rich would be more expensive than keeping them on, even apart from the dangers of Stalinism. He adds that the Soviet priviligentsia are just as exploitative as any bourgeois, and that the numbers below the poverty line in Russia are far greater than in America.

He speaks of 'cruel dictatorial regimes' – those of 'Stalin, Hitler and Mao Tse Tung'. Similarly he lumps together 'Eichmann, Himmler, Yezhov and Beria'. The only distinction he makes is that 'Stalinism exhibited a much more subtle kind of hypocrisy and demagogy, with reliance not on an openly cannibalistic programme like Hitler's but on a progressive, scientific and popular socialist ideology. This served as a convenient screen for deceiving the working class, for weakening the vigilance of the intellectuals.'

On the labour camps and the executions in Stalin's time he is of particular interest to myself, as one who has examined the casualty figures of that period. My rough estimate of party arrests in the purge was about one million. Sakharov, certainly working from official material, says that it was in fact over 1.2 million, half the total membership. Of these he reveals that 600,000 were shot: my own figures for *total* executions (including non-party men) was about one million. Of his other 600,000 plus, who went to camps and prisons, only 50,000 survived: my own estimate of the outside figures for camp survival was 10 per cent. He affirms that sentence to a camp 'without the right of correspondence' meant in fact a concealed death sentence. He adds that 'at least 10–15 million people perished' by torture or execution, or in camps during the whole Stalin period: my estimate of about 20 million total casualties, including those from other actions such as the collectivization famine, brings us into accord. And for the first time he gives a figure for the casualties for the national deportations in the 1940s – 46 per cent for the Crimean Tartars.

He clears up many of the illusions fostered in the West by those obsessed by verbalisms. For example, the comparison of Stalin with McCarthy is of course ridiculous, and Sakharov feels it is the Brezhnev regime in Russia which can to some degree be said to resemble McCarthyism.

And here he is on collectivization: 'a policy of unlimited exploitation and predatory forced deliveries at "symbolic" prices, an almost serflike enslavement of the peasantry . . . and the appointment of collective-farm chairmen on the basis of their cunning and obsequiousness. The results are evident – a profound and hard-to-correct destruction of the economy and way of life in the countryside, which by the law of interconnected vessels, damaged industry as well.'

On more immediate Soviet issues he protests against the Brezhnevite articles of the Criminal Code brought in with the obvious purpose of crushing intellectual revolt. He flatly condemns the trials of intellectuals and the maltreatment in camps which followed. He mentions, in passing, that the numbers in the camp group of the Mordvin Republic where they are held are about 50,000 – that is, in this area alone, about half the absolute maximum held by Hitler in peacetime. He gives examples of disgraceful pressures on ordinary intellectuals. He condemns the anti-Semitism to be found among the apparatchiks.

The boldness of all this hardly needs to be laboured. And it is important to note a joint effort of the highest Soviet scientific circles: the solidarity extended, as Sakharov points out, to an actual refusal (repeated in 1979) to elect Trapeznikov, head of the Science and Education Department of the Central Committee of the party, to the Academy of Sciences. In the same way the literary intelligentsia have been almost unanimous in their condemnation of the trials of their colleagues, and at least some historians stood up so firmly against the censoring of Nekrich's book on Stalin that their Institute had to be dissolved. Sakharov sums up coolly that, when people demand that the intelligentsia subordinate itself to the working class, what they 'really mean is subordination to the will of the party or, even more specifically, to the party's central apparatus and its officials. Who will guarantee that these officials always express the genuine interests of the working class as a whole and the genuine interests of progress rather than their own caste interest?'

It is sometimes said, too sanguinely, that any modern society must develop in a rational and democratic direction, because of the extent to which it relies on science and education. This idea of a more or less automatic 'convergence' of Russia towards the Western system is indeed a comfortable doctrine. But we must remember that, as Orwell remarked of Hitlerism, a most advanced science may be readily at the disposal of political ideas suited to the Stone Age. All the same, when a totalitarian system of thought loses its dynamism and becomes thoroughly moribund, the traditional values of reason emerge once more. Sakharov scarcely bothers to argue against the dead idiocies of Soviet orthodoxy. He treats it, rather, with cold contempt. He restates truths long forbidden. He shows that the system is morally and intellectually bankrupt. It remains to be seen whether the great revulsion of the Russian educated classes, who are still almost powerless, will be able to translate itself into political action.

1968

Alternative Russia: *The Chronicle of Current Events*

Though printing and duplicating without a licence and without passing through the Glavlit censorship has long been illegal in the Soviet Union, there is no technical provision against simply typing as many copies as one wishes of a manuscript. The *samizdat* periodicals circulate by constant multiplication on carbon paper. What is more extraordinary is that information from all over the country and all spheres of life gets back to the editors, and that they are able to check it and counter-check it – so that *The Chronicle of Current Events* has been virtually free from factual error. This is important, as the major charge brought against someone for possessing or circulating a mere typescript is anti-Soviet slander, and to establish slander it should be necessary to prove a statement untrue. This obvious point has not, of course, prevented the imprisonment of *samizdat* writers, but at least it makes it more difficult. Similarly, since the court cases reported in the *samizdat* are, technically, public, it cannot be an offence to give factual reports of them. But these legalisms are a paper-thin defence.

A fair amount has now been published in this country about the actions and fate of various members of the movement in Russia. In *Uncensored Russia*, edited and translated by Peter Reddaway, we come across the familiar names and the demonstrations and illicit publications, the victimizations and 'psychiatric' persecutions, which have been reported in the West seriatim. But what the book conveys in a way which has not previously been seen in this country is the day-to-day struggles and suffering of scores of the more obscure members of the rank and file. The cumulative effect is a revelation.

One of the many unpleasant facts to emerge (which has, incidentally, been confirmed by former labour camp inmates now in Israel or the West) is the continuance today of the ration scale of Stalin's time in the labour camps:

> The daily camp ration contains 2,400 calories (enough for a seven to eleven year old child), and has to suffice for an adult doing physical work, day after day for many years. Those calories are supplied mainly by black bread (700 gm a day). The convicts never even set eyes on fresh vegetables, butter and many other indispensable products. To punish a prisoner for 'violating the camp regime', e.g. for failure to fulfil the work quota, he may be put on the 'severe' food ration – 1,300 calories (enough for an infant of one to three years). This was the case, for example, with the writer Daniel.

As an editorial note points out, the ration in the Japanese POW camps on the River Kwai in 1942–3 was 700 g of rice, 600 g of vegetables, 100 g of meat, 20 g of sugar, 20 g of salt and 15 g of oil, amounting to about 3,400 calories.

The Chronicle of Current Events is a unique phenomenon. It owes its standing, in part, to being quite consciously the representative of all trends within the democratic movement and to making one of its main themes the defence of the civil rights of all types of dissident, from 'Leninist' to Christian. In its early days, Semichastny, then head of the KGB, is reported as telling the Soviet leadership that if he were allowed to arrest a couple of thousand people he could destroy the whole movement. The leadership did not take such action. In·part, this seems to be because such arrests might after all have a contrary effect, and involve in protests against them large numbers of other and even more important intellectuals. At the same time, the effect outside Russia would constitute a huge ideological deficit.

Paradoxically, the Soviet Union is less popular in the West than in Stalin's time, when things were very much worse. This is in accordance with the general rule that the very worst regimes of our time have on the whole been able to suppress the truth about their activities precisely owing to the extreme rigour of their control – just as, round the world today, the countries which are most broadly featured in the media as the leading centres of atrocity are not necessarily those which are really the worst. Of course, Stalinism did not in fact prevent a good deal of information coming out; but those determined to be duped in the West were able to reject or (in psychological terms) repress this bad news, because they were offered in competition a clear-cut alternative story, and no way of checking the hostile information except through émigrés (naturally labelled as anti-Soviet and therefore unreliable) could be found.

Orwell suggested that British intellectuals swarmed to the support of the Stalinist system precisely when it reached its worst period, and that part of their motive was a perverse and not publicly admitted admiration for the panache of despotism and cruelty – an admiration not likely to be extended to the pettifogging, faceless persecutors of Brezhnev's Moscow.

One is still occasionally told, it is true, that for a Westerner to register any fact or utter any opinion displeasing to (or insufficiently adulatory of) the Soviet official line is an act of 'Cold War'. The Cold War, it is alleged, is long since over, so that such activity is as obsolete as it is reprehensible. From the official Soviet side, of course, no amount of political détente ever meant any relaxation of the vast barrage of violent criticism of the Western system, Western ideas and Western actions. In fact, it has been laid down as a central principle that 'peaceful co-existence' in no way implies relaxation of the 'ideological' struggle. In fact, the struggle of the regime against these intellectuals is a reflection, or rather an instance, of its permanent struggle against Western concepts.

All the thought in Russia has long been in intellectual opposition; and most of the feeling too. By most standards, the regime has long since lost the mantle of heaven. It is not merely ripe, but greatly over-ripe, for major change. Basically the trouble seems to be that the technical and administrative organization possible in the modern epoch enables regimes quite obsolete from the point of view of their citizenry and of their countries' international interests to persist long past what would once have been a breaking-point.

If the present condition of international truce is ever to be turned into a genuine world peace, it must be as the result of a Russia resumed into the civilized community. The dissident movement is weak, and is faced with a political machine of immense strength. But it constitutes a growing point for the eventual peaceful, democratic Russia we must all hope for.

1972

Alexander Solzhenitsyn's Gulag

On the publication of *Gulag Archipelago* in 1973, a well-known American left-wing journalist, noted for the frequency, the variety and the righteousness of his public interventions on every conceivable matter in the field of foreign affairs, remarked on his horror at what he read in it. For he learned from it facts hitherto unknown to him: for example, that in the Soviet Union large numbers of people had been executed or sent to labour camps during the period when Joseph Stalin held the post of General Secretary of the Communist Party. Now, of course, to any but the most purblind or fanatical admirers of the Soviet system, all this had been established and documented at the very latest with the publication in 1948 of D. J. Dallin and B. I. Nicolaevsky's *Forced Labour in the Soviet Union* (which Solzhenitsyn quotes). And even those compulsive ignoramuses had almost all come to learn of such facts when they were revealed by the then leader of the Communist Party of the Soviet Union, Nikita Khrushchev, in February 1956. In the meantime, much further documentation of these horrors has taken place, including my own *The Great Terror* (1968), in which several thousand references, half of them from Soviet sources, established pretty firmly, I had thought, that all had not been well. And since then there have been such books as *Let History Judge*, (1971) by Roy Medvedev, with further details, almost all of them highly unpleasant.

But, for all that, this journalist's reaction is, if in exaggerated form, something of a very significant portent about the importance of Solzhenitsyn's book. Even if the book had registered no more than we know already, it is written by a man whose courage, whose integrity and whose experience will give it overwhelming authority throughout the world. It is a truly exceptional work; for in it literature transcends history, without distorting it.

It is indeed an important aspect of Solzhenitsyn's book, though by no means the only one, that he confirms and further details many horrors that have been reported (Medvedev, an ideological opponent of Solzhenitsyn, has, incidentally, gone on record as saying that all the factual material in *Gulag Archipelago* is true).

Solzhenitsyn exposes, for example, the full frightfulness of the highly secret Sukhanovka prison, which (in my first edition) I was only able to mention from the evidence of a single prisoner personally known to me, but which Solzhenitsyn has meanwhile spoken of in *The First Circle*. He confirms the summary execution of those serving prison sentences as the advancing Germans approached their camps; the obscure massacre of air force generals in 1941; the incredible crowding in prisons; the notorious 'lists' under which the accused were sentenced under various categories, such as 'Anti-Soviet Agitation'. One of the categories I had noted was 'Suspicion of Espionage', saying that this was a crime perhaps unique in the annals of world justice. Solzhenitsyn (once again) demonstrates my inadequate incredulity; for, in addition to listing that, he names the even more extravagant charge of 'Connections Leading to Suspicion of Espionage'. He notes the groupings most liable to arrest, including the Esperantists, people connected with the Red Cross, Austrian socialist refugees from the 1934 uprising in Vienna, etc. He confirms that in 1949 everyone who had previously been in camp and had managed to survive to the end of his sentence was rearrested and resentenced without further charges.

The post-war categories of individuals sentenced on new charges – as against simply being dragged back to camp – are listed as: spies, believers, geneticists; and there were three special categories of intellectuals insufficiently hostile to the West, against whom the charges were:

VAT – Praising American technique
VAD – Praising American democracy
PZ   – Abasement before the West (a more general charge)

Other war and post-war victims included those who had escaped from German prisoner-of-war camps (all classed as spies), those children of certain victims of the earlier purges who had been too young – even under Stalin's twelve-year-old law – to be charged at the time, and the children of Spanish refugees from the Civil War (as Anglo-American spies).

There is, in addition, useful material for the historian on important political cruxes in the USSR. For example, he gives us what appears to be entirely new information about the notorious 'Doctors' Plot'. This was planned, had Stalin not died, to have been the culmination of the great anti-Semitic campaign of the time. All the Yiddish writers and cultural figures had already been shot secretly in the 'Crimean case' in August 1952, and it was only in January 1953 that a great public propaganda campaign was mounted around the arrest of the 'murderers in white coats' – leading Soviet physicians, mainly Jewish, accused of the medical murders (or attempted murders) of various Soviet personalities. After Stalin's death, Beria repudiated it and released the doctors. There has always been a mystery concerning two of the doctors, who, though cleared, were not available to be released after Stalin's death. About one of these, Dr Etinger, a strange tale now emerges, obtained, moreover, from an excellent source – a member of the prosecutor's office who conducted the interrogation of various guilty police officials after Stalin's death. Abakumov, the Minister of State Security (who figures prominently in Solzhenitsyn's novel *The First Circle*), was arrested near the end of 1951. We now learn that he and Ryumin, Deputy Minister of State Security, had a dispute. Dr Etinger was already under arrest, and Ryumin came to Abakumov and suggested a 'Doctors' Plot'. Abakumov for some reason rejected this. Shortly afterwards Etinger was found dead in his cell. It seems that either Abakumov had killed him to avoid proceeding with the case or that Ryumin haddd interrogated him to death. Stalin went along with Ryumin, and Abakumov himself was jailed with a number of his closest associates. Then came Stalin's death. Ryummin was arrested, but Abakumov was not released by Beria. Beria was then arrested and shot. The following summer Ryumin was shot, and Abakumov took the view that he had been vindicated and would now doubtless be released. However, he too was shot in December 1954, on a charge of faking the earlier 'Leningrad case', in which Politburo member Voznesensky and others had been executed. Solzhenitsyn says that the reason is not quite clear, but that rumour has it that Khrushchev had a non-political objection to Abakumov, since he had beaten Khrushchev's own daughter-in-law before she was sent to die in a labour camp. Such motives need not be discounted, though there is no sign that Khrushchev intervened in her favour at the time, any more than Molotov or Kuusinen or President Kalinin did for their own arrested wives while they themselves were continuing to serve in high positions, or Kaganovich for his brother, a fellow member of the Central Committee, who was lucky enough to get the chance to commit suicide – when accused (though a Jew) of being Hitler's nominee for president of a fascist

Russia. Nevertheless, there were also political motives for Abakumov's execution, in that the men he had shot in Leningrad had been Malenkov's enemies and that Khrushchev was now working to remove Malenkov from the premiership.

So far, then, there are movingly presented accounts of the terror and certain material of great interest to historians of an obscure and gloomy period. But the Soviet leaders of the Khrushchev era themselves (as in speeches at the 1961 party congress) told similar stories. And even though the later policy was to sweep them under the carpet, to condemn harping on the 'errors' of the past, these things were not entirely denied. Other writers on them, like Roy Medvedev and Evgenia Ginzburg, though unpublished in Russia, were not arrested. What is there about *Gulag Archipelago* that made it a kind of last straw and that drove the Politburo to its reckless and arbitrary arrest and expulsion of the author?

First of all, Solzhenitsyn does not put the blame solely on Stalin and the 'personality cult'. He traces the long evolution of terror, showing that the labour camp system, the frame-up trials, the mass shootings, the secret disappearances – all go back to early Soviet times. His brief description of the 'trials' of the early twenties, for example, would be regarded by any humane standards as the sign of a far worse regime, already, than most of the 'reactionary' dictatorships of modern times. He departs from reasonable and orthodox criticism of Soviet terror by failing to restrict his complaints to the frame-up and execution of innocent communists. He actually urges that it was wrong to do the same to non-communist revolutionary socialists and even liberals. Since these were mainly wiped out in the earlier years, his 'fifty-year-old' (as he puts it) juggernaut is the Soviet regime from its beginnings – he was writing in 1967. That is to say, a major aspect of Solzhenitsyn's book is that it breaks totally with the myth that has corrupted and deluded so many commentators on the Russian Revolution and the Soviet regime: the myth of a liberal Lenin.

Solzhenitsyn compounds this 'blasphemy' by a comparison between Soviet standards of terror and those of tsardom. Tsarist Russia was the most backward and despotic regime in Europe. Solzhenitsyn notes that the number of those executed between 1826 and 1906 in Russia amounted to 894. In the revolutionary days of 1905–8, 2200 executions took place. In Lenin's time, very incomplete figures for the central provinces alone estimate that 16,000 were shot in eighteen months. Even in December 1932, before the Stalin terror proper, Solzhenitsyn notes the shooting of 265 people at one time in the Kresty prison in Leningrad. And, in peacetime, at the height of the terror, a minimum of about a million were executed in two years – that is, a rate about 50,000 times as great as that of sixty years of tsardom back to Nicholas I!

Moreover, the tsars' victims had actually plotted against the state; their relatives were not also sentenced; the non-capital prisoners were not starved and sweated to death. (Indeed, Solzhenitsyn is inclined to attribute the collapse of Bukharin and other veterans in the hands of Stalin's police to the comparative softness of their previous treatment in tsarist jails, which they had boasted of, and even thought of, as the utmost hardship possible.) These are comparisons that give offence to the beneficiaries of the Stalin system.

Solzhenitsyn has previously – as in his Nobel Prize speech – also pointed out that, if we are to judge regimes by a calculus of murder and terror, the Stalinist style state is, apart from Hitler's, in a unique category. To compare the sufferings under the Greek colonels and other right-wing governments with those of the Soviet Union is something in the nature of saying that a gross assault, such as punching someone on the nose, is the same as boiling him in oil.

Solzhenitsyn is particularly disgusted at the notion of the ruling group that, if they describe the Stalin terror as a series of 'mistakes' which they have apologized for once and for all and do not wish to be referred to again, that settles the matter. During Khrushchev's ascendancy, the humorous Soviet paper *Krokodil* (20 July 1956) once printed a picture of a mean-looking little boy saying to his teacher, 'Why did you give me a failing mark? I have admitted my mistakes, haven't I?'

Solzhenitsyn compares de-Stalinization with de-Nazification. He points out that in Western Germany de-Nazification tribunals, up till 1966, in one way or another penalized 86,000 Nazis. In Russia a handful of high police officials – and only those who took the wrong side in the struggle for power in the fifties – were shot, while the vast bulk of accomplices, large and small, in the criminal regime of Stalin survived unharmed. This applied even to major criminals like Kaganovich and Molotov, who had actually been openly denounced by the public prosecutor in person as having been responsible for millions of murders. They were removed from power, having happened to lose a round in the struggle. But they were pensioned off quietly. Terror operatives on the winning side kept their jobs. So the Soviet taxpayers still secured a serene old age for those who had murdered their fathers and uncles – and, come to think of it, their mothers and aunts.

Then again, Solzhenitsyn, it is true, denounces the terror with passion; but even more intolerable from the point of view of the *apparat* is the stinging contempt that he expresses for all concerned. They do not appear as men of a certain horrible grandeur, like Robespierre or Genghis Khan, but as vile little pygmies, bird-brained, sniggering torturers.

Perhaps the most important lesson, indeed, is how difficult it is for us in the Western political culture really to make the effort of imagination, as well as that of intellect, to conceive what the other lot are really like, what their background really is. I myself, as a student of Soviet politics for many years, and one not inclined to grant them unproven virtues, have found myself still tending, if I do not make that effort, to grant more common sense in the Western style, to make 'natural' assumptions of conduct, however evil, in ways that do not necessarily apply. I remember once asking that profound student of Russia, the late Tibor Szamuely, himself a former inmate of the camps, a question about the military purges. I could see, I said, why Stalin shot Marshal Tukhachevsky, but I did not see why he shot Marshal Yegorov. Tibor's answer was simple: 'Why not?'

That effort of imagination is made much easier for all of us by the power of Solzhenitsyn's writing in this book. Pasternak breaks off his *Sketch for an Autobiography* before the frightful years of the Yezhovshchina with the words 'to continue it would be immeasurably difficult . . . one would have to talk in a manner which would grip the heart and make the hair stand on end'. This Solzhenitsyn (in some sense Pasternak's successor) has done in *Gulag Archipelago*.

1974

2

How are we to sum it all up? First, no doubt, that it has had an almost unprecedented, worldwide impact on the minds of men. When Solzhenitsyn started assembling the material in Russia, secretly but with the collaboration of scores of confidants, it was simply a matter of undertaking a devoted duty. And this without any guarantee at all that the result would ever appear. At any point, the manuscript or much of it could have been confiscated, and destroyed in the furnaces of the Lubyanka. At any point, Solzhenitsyn himself could have been arrested and been unable to finish his work. In pursuit of this uncertain hope, he nevertheless undertook the immense toil which has resulted in these three huge volumes. And it is the world's good fortune that his toil was not fruitless.

The main result has been that it is now no longer possible in any country with reasonably free publication for the Soviet system to find serious defenders. It is not that some of the offences of Stalinism were not well known in a general way much earlier. But it has been this vast human canvas with its myriad details and its single sweep which has provided the white-hot catharsis, at every level, needed finally to purge most of the clinging remnants of false ideas, inappropriate sentiments, stubborn partisanship about the USSR. The word 'Gulag' has entered the language – every language.

In France, the effect has been particularly striking. We have seen, for the first time, the crumbling of the old delusions of the intellectuals. The incredible deceptions and self-deceptions by which Sartre and all the others indoctrinated the intelligentsia had been impervious to the presentation of facts, and to the advancing of logical arguments by a handful of distinguished analysts like Raymond Aron or polemical attacks on their whole way of thinking by independent men like Jean-François Revel. It remained true that a climate of conformity pervaded the intellectual classes, that every *bien pensant* professor, student, journalist, writer held, in a way too automatic to be called a belief, that even if the USSR or similar systems had their faults they were nevertheless imbued with a central virtue which made them superior to the wicked West.

The sudden disintegration of this new Age of Faith, the swift dissipation of the tenacious miasmas which had hung over the French mind, have been truly astonishing. This has largely been the work of a group of young philosophers whose starting point had been the great left-wing protest of May 1968, but who had meanwhile been subjected to the immense shock of Solzhenitsyn and the *Gulag Archipelago*: that and that alone, as they themselves make absolutely clear, produced their change of heart and mind. For this single achievement in one country alone, its testimony to truth would have justified itself.

Meanwhile his last instalment retains its interest, and fills in new elements in the story. Solzhenitsyn tells of the resistance within the camps: first, the individual escapers, and finally after Stalin's death, in 1953–4, the great wave of camp mutinies. It was now, for a couple of years, that the Archipelago experienced its one period of relaxation. During this brief interlude the prisoners were actually addressed as 'men'. But the morale of the secret police, temporarily shaken by the terror maestro's death and the shooting of his Lord High Executioner Lavrenti Beria, soon returned.

It is an ironic fact that by the time of Khrushchev's open political attacks on Stalinism, from 1956, this great bastion of the Stalin system had already been restored to its old rigour. Solzhenitsyn tells us that even he thought that the system he described in *One Day in the Life of Ivan Denisovich* was coming to an end.

He was horrified to find that among the letters which started to reach him after its publication in 1962, 'on crumpled scraps of paper, in a blurred pencil scrawl, in stray envelopes often addressed and posted by free employees, in other words on the sly, today's Archipelago sent me its criticisms, and sometimes its angry protests. "What do you mean, never again happen? We're here inside now, and our conditions are just the same! Nothing has changed since Ivan Denisovich's time . . .".'

Camp conditions were in fact getting steadily worse – a process marked by an attack in the official *Sovetskaya Rossiya*, 27 August 1960, on any relaxation, and calling for 'hard and strict conditions' for prisoners. But a façade of reasonableness and even liberalism was preserved in Khrushchevian circles proper. One of the most fascinating sections is Solzhenitsyn's account of the time when he was in good odour and under Khrushchev's personal protection, and was actually asked to make suggestions for the improvement of labour camp regulations. The bureaucrats had to be polite, but still managed to reveal the petty nastiness of the whole police interest and effectively argued against every relaxation.

Nevertheless there had been many releases and rehabilitations. The return of survivors who started trickling back from the death camps is described in a fine ironic passage – with such scenes as their meeting with the men who had denounced them, the false witnesses, former camp guards and commandants, even their interrogators, flourishing in good jobs or on comfortable pensions.

In some cases, attempts were made to see that notorious denouncers – such as members of the Writers' Union who had sent scores of their colleagues to death – should be punished. But it was not even possible to get them removed from the union, let alone fired from their jobs or expelled from the Communist Party, even though the Criminal Code provides a short term of imprisonment for false denunciation. Meanwhile a project for paying compensation for the years of imprisonment to the admittedly innocent had to be abandoned when it was found that it would cost the state. They settled instead for two months' compensation.

Solzhenitsyn reminds us in an afterword that he was completing his work on a double anniversary, fifty years after the Revolution and a hundred since the invention of barbed wire. He argues that, above all, it is necessary to understand of the Archipelago 'how closely akin it is to the state, and how necessary to it'. At any rate, though so many of the murders and falsifications have long since been exposed publicly in the Soviet Union itself, so far the 'de-Stalinization' of which so much has been said failed to take. Solzhenitsyn is a guarantee that it will remain on the agenda.

1978

PART II LITERATURE

The Issue

Of course we are dealing with a struggle of ideas. But also, and further, the mere existence of imaginative literature, however apolitical, tends to undermine dogmatic views on the nature of man and society.

One extraordinary example of this was the appearance in 1979 in *samizdat* of the literary almanac *Metropol*, in which such writers as Vasily Aksyonov and Andrei Voznesensky were represented. The authors sought proper publication in print, and had sent copies to the Union of Writers with this in mind – without success. Most of the pieces in the collection had already been submitted, in fact, to various periodicals. The editors' introduction made the issue plain:

> Being engaged in literature, we affirm that there is for us nothing more joyful and wholesome than composition and making public what has been composed; and the birth of a new miscellany, one might think, is a red-letter day for all.
>
> Yet why should it be precisely this form that has emerged? Such a question comes naturally to the lips of a person who is not fully conversant with certain peculiarities of our cultural life. It will not be too impertinent to say that this life suffers from something like a chronic ailment that can be defined perhaps as 'hostility to differentness', or more simply as 'a fear of literature'. The dreary inertia that exists in journals and publishing houses is leading to the emergence of an inflated universal feeling of responsibility for 'a piece' of a literature that is incapable not only of being what it should be, but even what it was yesterday.
>
> This universal 'feeling of responsibility' induces a condition of stagnant quiet panic, a craving to force a literary 'piece' into line. Literature that does not fit into the mould is sometimes doomed to years of vagrancy and homelessness. Only a blind man can fail to see that writings of this sort are multiplying from year to year, that they already form an entire forbid-

den seam, as it were, of our literature. (Our miscellany consists primarily of manuscripts that are no strangers to editorial offices.)

The authors of *Metropol* are writers who are independent (one of another). The only thing that wholly unites them under one roof is the awareness that the author alone is responsible for his work; the right to such a responsibility we consider sacred. It cannot be excluded that the strengthening of this awareness will benefit our entire culture.

In this section of *Tyrants and Typewriters* I examine the works and actions of a number of writers, starting with a consideration of Pasternak from a fundamentally literary point of view. It will be seen that political implications are, at some stage, unavoidable – because the position of the authorities was as much opposed to literature properly speaking as to free human activity in any other sphere.

Pasternak and *Doctor Zhivago*

It is very noticeable that the critics who had qualms about *Doctor Zhivago* were almost entirely the ones who tried to fit it into certain preconceived categories. The logical fallacy is plain enough. For example, a minor source of misunderstanding about the novel is that we have all received our most powerful impressions of the Russian character from the strong and lucid pens of the novelists. For this has the single disadvantage that actions and personalities of the utmost naturalness in the Russian context may appear not as real, but as bookish scenes. Thus Philip Toynbee complained that Lara in *Doctor Zhivago* was nothing more than a blend of two earlier feminine characters in Russian literature. The more natural, and truer, conclusion would be that all the three writers concerned were observing real Russian women, and that these may have something, though not everything, in common!

The main 'faults' (ie departures from received practice) to have been alleged in this way are interestingly dealt with by Pasternak himself, in a passage in which he strikingly develops his general view of art. Most hostile criticism of *Doctor Zhivago* spoke of insufficient characterization and of the use of improbable coincidence. This was sometimes put in such a way as to imply that Pasternak had been trying to write a conventional novel, but had failed through some lack of skill.

His own comment is decisive (his own English):

For this characterization of reality of the being as a substratum, as a common background, the nineteenth century applied the incontestable doctrine of causality, the belief that the objectivity was determined and ruled by an iron chain of causes and effects, that all appearances of the moral and material world were subordinate to the law of sequels and retributions. And the severer the author in showing such consequences (or characters and conducts) the greater a realist he was esteemed. The tragic bewitching spell of Flaubert's style or Maupassant's manner roots in the fact that their narratives are irrevocable like verdicts or sentences, beyond recall.

I also from my earliest years have been struck by the observation that existence was more original, extraordinary, and inexplicable than any of its separate astonishing incidents and facts . . . for the purpose of evoking the same sensations through art's expressive attempts I come to results if not diametrically opposed to the tendencies of the named masterpieces, at least to quite different observations than those of our predecessors and teachers.

If I had to represent a broad, a large picture of living reality, I would not hope to heighten its sense of *extant objectivity* by accentuating the fixed statics of ananke; of natural laws, of settled moral regularity.

There is an effort in the novel to represent the whole sequence of facts and beings and happenings like some moving entireness, like a developing, passing by, rolling and rushing inspiration, as if reality itself had freedom and choice and was composing itself out of numberless variants and versions.

Hence the not sufficient tracing of characters I was reproached with (more than to delineate them I tried to efface them); hence the frank arbitrariness of the 'coincidences' (through this means I wanted to show the liberty of being, its verisimilitude touching, adjoining improbability).

If this is the essential of his view of art, it is also, far more than the mysticism and 'God-seeking' in terms of which it is sometimes expressed, the essential view of his life. When he speaks of religion, basically he means a development of this feeling, rather than the interpretations by which he tentatively tried to capture and fix it.

To say that Pasternak seems to consider art as a technique of producing such individual affective results and, in the case of the greatest art, of generalizing them until they seem to transfer the inexplicable glow to life in general, does not, of course, mean that he has a hit-or-miss attitude to artistic method. On the contrary, the passage just quoted shows his extremely conscious attention to the way in which low characterization and high coincidence are utilized in *Doctor Zhivago*. In his poetry, too, the formal, structural aspect receives the utmost stress. He commonly observes his own dictum that rhyme is 'the entrance ticket' to poetry. Enjambement, even, is rare. And above all, with all the novelty, complexity and allusiveness of some of his poetry, it is almost never ambiguous; it very seldom allows several possible interpretations.

Yet if he does not fall into the traps which await the striver after novelty at all costs, and which have produced so many casualties among the poems of the post-symbolist period throughout the world, neither does he fall into the traditionalist error of cliché. His language is never 'poetical': it has been well characterized as 'impassioned chat'. This is one point in which he is, on the whole, ill served in translation – and, it seems, in his own English, on occasion. This is a natural enough difficulty in translation, and in using a language to which one is not native. The differences between, let us say, 'enchanted', 'bewitched' and 'spellbound' from this point of view could only be adequately grasped, let alone explained, by a limited number even of native English speakers.

These would be those equipped to appreciate their own language's poetry. Applying such criteria to the poetry of another language, we can see in what a difficult position an English writer is when it comes to making any real assessment of Pasternak's poetry. We can perhaps say that at the level of rhythm and sound at least we are not in such trouble as with French. Yet, even here, the traditions of Russian are different from ours in certain ways. George Reavey says, for instance, 'the richest letter in Russian is *p*, just as *s* is the richest in English.' And Henry Lanz tells us in his *The Physical Basis of Rime* that 'In Russian poetry assonance is more easily perceived than in English'. The same author makes a careful comparison between the departures from strict iambics in the first thirty-two lines of *Paradise Lost* and *Boris Godunov* respectively – showing far greater eccentricity on Milton's part than on Pushkin's, though the latter was, comparatively speaking, a rhythmic innovator. Nor is metre a question to be taken for granted, or regarded as minor, as is too often done by those concerned not with poetry as such so much as with its supposedly detachable content. Even poets concerned principally with fresh expression have not failed to consider rhythm vigilantly, as Andrey Bely does in his *Symbolism*. Much, therefore, is lost when we consider Pasternak's poetry. That much is left is a measure of his quality.

Pasternak wrote on poetry in August 1958 (in English, in a letter to Eugene Kayden):

Each art, especially that of poetry, means a great deal more than it comprises. Its essence and values are symbolic. This does in no manner signify that we possess the key by which we can discover behind every word or condition some other hidden sense – mystical, occult, or providential – as was erroneously believed of the dramatic works of Ibsen, Maeterlinck, or Leonid Andreyev. Nor does it mean that each true, creative poetical text ought to be a parable or an allegory. What I want to say is that besides and above the separate tropes and metaphorical turns of a poem there exists a figurative tendency, a drift in the poetry

itself and in art as a whole – and that is its chief significance – to relate
the general, summary purport of a composition to broader and more
fundamental ideas – in order to reveal the sublimity of life and the
unfathomable values of human existence. I am tempted to say that art
does not equal itself, does not mean itself alone, but that it means tangibly
something beyond itself. In this way we call art symbolic in essence.

Just as a certain face in a certain light, a certain landscape from
a certain viewpoint, may make any one of us catch his breath – not
with some easily analysed effect of 'beauty', but with the feeling
that the sources of meaning have somehow been touched in us, so
(Pasternak seems to say) poetry should arrange its material – and to
touch not one, but all, or many, of us.

He does not urge that poetry should be more complex, more
indirect, more 'symbolist', but simply that it should, whatever its
method, attain that feeling of further, of universal, significance.

It will be seen that such an approach, by which the essential of
art is, as it were, the reproduction of 'the light that never was on sea
or land', is comprehensive. By not relying on the normal recourses
of 'symbolism', by seeing the successful discovery of the illuminating
angle of vision as not depending on any particular technique, it
broadens the scope of poetry to include everything from direct statement, or abstract reflection, to the wildest obliquity. Since no
manoeuvrable criteria for determining how to obtain success in the
attempt at illumination have ever been found, this is, as is usual
with the pronouncements of powerful writers, totally destructive of
criticism as we know it. It is also interesting that he directly demol-
ishes the idea of 'explication', which was for so long a widespread
critical industry.

Not that Pasternak was ever much influenced by critics. He has
the real writer's attitude to reputations as manufactured by them. In
'Wind', from the sequence *Some Fragments about Blok*, he starts:

> Who will survive and be accepted,
> Who censured and accounted dead,
> Such is the province of our toadies.

going on to argue that academics arrogate to themselves the right to
say if Pushkin should be honoured or not, and that one welcome
thing about Blok is that 'No one thrusts him down our throats'.

In all his later pronouncements, Pasternak criticizes his earlier
work. His prose he came to regard as 'trivial' and mannered; in *I
Remember* he claims that he no longer likes the style of his verses
written before 1940. This working from a rich complexity to a rich

simplicity, as George Reavey so happily puts it, has led in his last poems to a putting off of the new techniques, the obvious novelties which, in Russia as elsewhere, had for some decades seemed the inevitable accompaniment of a fresh voice, but were now appearing as little more than fashions.

He told Mrs Carlisle in 1960: 'All this writing of the 'twenties has terribly aged.' And he developed the point further by saying: 'Our success in the 'twenties was partly due to chance. My generation found itself in the focal point of history. Our works were dictated by the times. They lacked universality; now they have aged.' Of the theoretical basis of this experimentation he commented:

> I have never understood those dreams of a new language, of a completely original form of expression. Because of this dream much of the work of the 'twenties which was stylistic experimentation has ceased to exist. The most extraordinary discoveries are made when the artist is overwhelmed by what he has to say. Then he uses the old language in his urgency and the old language is transformed from within.

In a late letter to Reavey he writes: 'the support has been taken out from under that modern trend . . . This striving, though true and original in its source, was not self-dependent enough to stand up to the trials of the changed years.'

Such were the intentions, moral and technical, with which he approached *Doctor Zhivago*. It will be seen that his concerns are deeper, though less insistent, than the procrustean generalizations of ideology. After the Revolution it was writers like Mayakovsky, ignorant of politics, yet addicted to literary extremisms and simplifications, who catastrophically sought in the Communist Party and its theories the crude guidance of myth, just as the Italian futurists welcomed fascism. Writers with political training, like the Marxist Zamyatin, were incorrigibly sceptical. But Pasternak felt and thought at a more profound level yet. In him, simplicity is due to generality, not to simplification. He was never tempted to impose finalities on life, only to find in it its natural flow.

Pasternak, as a man of great sensitivity who has lived through periods of unexampled horror, is qualified to speak to us about suffering. He sees, not grand abstractions, but the real human being in his agony. And yet he is qualified too, as in the Epilogue to *Doctor Zhivago*, to tell us that even horrible suffering is actually more tolerable to the human being than 'the reign of the lie':

> It isn't only in comparison with your life as a convict, but compared to everything in the 'thirties, even to my easy situation at the university in

the midst of books and comfort, that the war came as a breath of deliverance . . . its real horrors, its real dangers, its menace of real death, were a blessing compared with the inhuman reign of the lie.

It is from the standpoint of one who has really understood and felt large-scale suffering that he considers the dangerous present. It is perhaps self-centredness generalized which makes us feel that our own, contemporary, troubles are the worst. Pasternak wrote to Eugene Kayden in 1958, almost in passing: 'Many forgotten periods of history were once thought to be the end of the world, like our present nuclear situation.' This may seem a hard saying to many people. Yet it is not only that Pasternak lived among death by the tens of millions in war, famine and purge. It is not only, even, that he saw the human experience more *sub specie aeternitatis* than is possible to most of us.

We do not feel that Chaucer, writing his urbane sketches while a third of the population were dead of the Black Death and worse was expected, was being inhumane. Rather, he gives the impression that his human sympathies can be taken for granted, and perhaps that hysteria would help no one. And, on the contrary, the literature that we still read which concerns itself with the end of the world – the Revelation of St John the Divine, the *Dies Irae*, the *Voluspa* – may impress by grandeurs, but does not give any strong impression of human sympathy.

At a time when it was thought that a conventional bombardment from the air would totally destroy cities and their inhabitants, Yeats could start a poem:

I have heard that hysterical women say

that poets should worry about such issues. Yeats, though he had seen violence and felt revulsion from it, was not a humane man in the sense that Pasternak was. In him one can detect a certain hardness, a feeling that violence is justified if it can be dramatized into great art. It might be said that he sees it from the point of view of eternity, but his eternal is art; he does not see the real human under the tragic mask.

In Pasternak, on the contrary, we have no feeling that his long view, his deep art, has in any way hardened his human sensibility. We feel, on the contrary, that his attitude is based on a sounder compassion, a more encompassing humanity than is possible to weaker nerves.

Though Pasternak was in a sense apolitical, his attachment to Russia is not simply based on his unrivalled feeling for nature. It is no archaic attachment to the land merely. He says also, in the last chapter of *Doctor Zhivago*: 'It has often happened in history that a lofty ideal has degenerated into crude materialism. Thus Greece gave way to Rome, and the Russian Enlightenment became the Russian Revolution.'

It is of that Enlightenment that Pasternak was the heir. He maintained its values in the most difficult times, against the most powerful opponents, and he foresaw its eventual triumph. He told Mrs Olga Carlisle in 1960: 'There will be no return to those days or to those of our fathers and forefathers, but in the great blossoming of the future I foresee their values will revive.'

For Pasternak, as for the whole of the intelligentsia, tsardom was an alien, and largely a hostile, phenomenon. The Enlightenment had found it a permanent obstacle, slow, stupid, ossified, bureaucratic, and in certain circumstances violently and viciously inclined. Yet, though a weight on the chest of Russia, it was not quite a stifling one. It had been possible to breathe. Sometimes the state intervened against a writer, as when Gorky was expelled from the Academy, an event curiously paralleling Pasternak's own later expulsion from the Union of Soviet Writers (one difference lay in the uncensored protests of Gorky's colleagues, and the public resignation of Chekhov and others in sympathy). But, on the whole, cultural freedom was almost untrammelled.

Not that this was a sign of the autocracy's good will or good sense. Nor did it lead to any feeling of sympathy toward tsarism. It is only in retrospect that the good, or harmless, aspects of the time appear. The intelligentsia sympathized, however inactively, with the revolutionaries, who were, indeed, its product. In Soviet times Pasternak (in *The Year 1905*) writes nostalgically of the early revolutionaries – 'The Perovsky girl, the Populist Freedom Party . . . Students pedantic in specs, nihilists smug in their smocks' – as being as remote as Jason.

It was only in the last years of tsardom that the intellectual rebels began to give way to professional technicians of power like those earlier Russian revolutionaries of whom Pushkin had written that 'they care little for their own skins, and still less for those of others'.

The political and intellectual circumstances of the Russia of Pasternak's youth were very different from ours. It is necessary in dealing with Russian literature to make some very important distinctions between its general conditions and background and those which apply to certain countries of the West. In English, the great writers have been men like Dickens and Fielding, strongly connected with the more philistine sections of their society, and having the virtues of scope, humour and power rather than those of subtlety, depth and self-consciousness. In the English-speaking countries no separate 'intelligentsia' developed, alienated from society as a whole: the very word we use for such rudiments and imitations as we have is Russian. The forces which split Russia into a vast militarized bureaucracy with a single official view on the one hand, and the ways of thought of humanism and of revolution on the other, never made much progress with us. The result is that when, mainly in the present century, some of our writers have set up as great alienated martyrs and messiahs of art, they have usually appeared ridiculously pretentious, and their works boringly inflated, to our educated classes.

The point is that it is wrong to transfer such estimates to the Russian writers. The political and social circumstances of nineteenth-century Russia produced as a natural development what was later artificially and unsuccessfully transplanted to soils where it could not take root. And in the great Russian writers and thinkers we find seriousness without portentousness, high aims without egotism, an unselfconscious, unselfregarding effort to attain complete candour and complete charity about the human being.

The power of this enterprise is not spent. Its effect on the educated, and through them on the less educated, classes in Russia has been enormous, and persists, apparently ineradicably. Pasternak regards the Englightenment, rather than any political event, as the great achievement of Russia, and he expects its spirit, in spite of being temporarily silenced, to prove an anvil which will break all hammers. The epochs of tyranny, he seems to feel, must eventually give way to this less ephemeral power. This may be thought the great context of his life and work.

1961

Mayakovsky

In the renaissance of Russian literature which began in the 1960s the influence of Vladimir Mayakovsky (1893–1930) was hardly to be seen. The young spoke of Bely, Zabolotsky, Pasternak, Tsvetaeva. In part this is of course due to natural revulsion against the Establishment Poet whose work, in Pasternak's words (typically denounced as 'sacrilegious'), was beginning to be propagated compulsorily, 'like potatoes in the reign of Catherine the Great'.

Yet, as Pasternak added, 'That was his second death. For that he is not responsible.' And up to a point literary fashions mean almost as little in Russia as they do in the West. Among actual writers and poets, Mayakovsky has never been unread – just as, in the West, Kipling's verse has always been accepted in spite of frequent denunciation by critics, sociologists and other hangers-on.

Herbert Marshall's translation[1] is the product of years of devotion to Mayakovsky. Translations without such motives are seldom of much value. But it is equally natural that the devotee overrates his subject. He has reproduced, as far as possible, the structure and rhyme scheme of the original. In an age which, perhaps for the first time in history, actively demands mistranslation and misrepresentation, this is admirable.

He has largely caught the vigorous and the idiomatic tone of the original. But if, inevitably, a translation cannot give us the whole Mayakovsky, it is also true that the faults of the poet stand out more clearly in the comparative pallor of its English reflection; the original often, if by no means always, conceals vapidity of content behind technical incandescences.

There is an extreme period air to much of Mayakovsky's verse –

[1] *Mayakovsky*, trans. Herbert Marshall (New York).

and this collection, with its sampling of collages of the twenties with their 'modern' manner, rubs this in even further. There is no denying that, as with the art nouveau cathedral at Barcelona, a special effect of sorts has been obtained; and yet Pasternak was surely right when he said that the writing of the twenties had 'terribly aged' because it lacked 'universality', that the attempt to secure a completely original form of expression had been a failure.

Even so, Mayakovsky's earlier, more obscure work stands up better than his later work because its coarse and vigorous rhetoric is balanced by a verbal (and actual) tenderness; partly also because its content – love and animal spirits – is more universal, less dated, than the rant of the later period. Mr Marshall, an English biographer, theatre and film man, rightly defends in principle the poet's freedom to compose simple agitational rhymes. The objection is not against these, but against the fact that none of his supposedly more serious political verse goes much deeper.

His long poem on Lenin is quite embarrassingly silly, and not to be compared, as a poem about revolution, with Pasternak's '1905', or (in prose) with such things as Isaac Babel's 'Cavalry Army'. For example, he claims that Soviet children were asking 'What is a policeman?' In this he is merely versifying the cant of an era: the word 'policeman' had been abolished, not the thing. (Mayakovsky himself descended to an ode to the OGPU.) He lapses, moreover, into self-righteous nastiness, as when he attacks the Social Revolutionaries, then a suffering remnant in Soviet jails. Perhaps, as the men who had actually gained the suffrages of the great Russian majority, they were an unpleasant reminder to the poet that the 'masses' he thought of himself as reaching were an untypical minority. He had cheapened his poetry to reach the people, and he had not reached them. Lenin's comment, 'This is quite interesting literature. It's a peculiar kind of communism, it's hooligan communism', is very penetrating.

As so often with the brashly positive, Mayakovsky was not really the Strong Man of his declamations (had he never read in Lermontov's *A Hero of Our Own Times* that 'fullness and depth of feeling are incompatible with wild outbursts'?). His self-abasing identification with 'the party' bears a tone, vulgar in every sense, of romantic masochism. If, in spite of all this, a good portion of his work persists, it is because he was, after all, not just some sort of loud-mouthed proto-Beat, but 'a cloud in trousers', an awkward fit – and finally a suicide.

1965

Ehrenburg

The Soviet writer Ilya Ehrenburg (1891–1967) has long seemed a
significant, or at least a symptomatic, figure. But significant or symptomatic of what? It is not merely that his career spanned from the
first to the seventh decades of our century, with so many changes of
fortune or direction, but also that he does not seem to have pulled
the contradictions of his own personality together until the comparative and partial success of his last years. The late Anatol Goldberg's
quirky but often fascinating *Ilya Ehrenburg* reflects a rather similar
disjunction, in a way which is helpful, if sometimes distracting, to
our understanding of the issues involved.

Ehrenburg was, above all, a representative of the literary-political
intelligentsia that is to be found in continental Europe, particularly
eastern and central Europe. He started in extreme youth as almost
a caricature of the most avant-garde section of this intelligentsia and
was known among the Bolsheviks as 'shaggy Ilya'. Recruited into the
party in 1907 by Bukharin at the age of sixteen, he was soon arrested
and spent some months in jail before rich parents got him abroad.
There he left the party as a result of listening to Trotsky's dogmatic
views on literature. He never rejoined, but was later to pay at least
lip-service to aesthetic attitudes incomparably more dogmatic than
Trotsky's.

His exile was in Paris, where he nearly became a Benedictine monk
but soon settled down to the Closerie des Lilas and the Rotonde.
After some work as a war correspondent, he was back in Russia in
1917, opposing the Bolshevik Revolution. Over the next few years he
became reconciled, up to a point, with his old comrades. They join
others in what seems a fair characterization – he was a 'sceptic',
'sardonic towards both Red and White', a 'nihilist'. But Bukharin
helped get his first well-known work, *Julio Jurenito*, published; and for

the next decade he moved between Moscow, Berlin and Paris in somewhat distrait fashion, without really committing himself. In 1932, however, he made a definite decision to serve the Soviet regime – initially as *Izvestia* correspondent in Paris.

Ehrenburg seems to have realized that his country's political despotism would become even worse but to have hoped that literary liberties could be preserved. And from now on he exemplifies one of the great moral dilemmas which have faced so many Europeans and others: to what extent is it permissible to collaborate with a tyranny with a view to limiting, however slightly, its excesses? It is the question which faced not Quisling but Laval, who, by his own lights, worked to save what he could of French liberty in case of a Nazi victory. To do so he had to acquiesce or participate in many dubious actions; the same is true of the members of the United Fronts who collaborated with communist governments in the post-war period. The criterion is, presumably, how far they succeed, which is usually not very far. In Ehrenburg's case, twenty years followed in which he had almost no effect, beyond sometimes preserving a little elbow room for himself, at the same time performing services, some of them disgraceful, to the despot. If Ehrenburg had died in 1953, there would be no more to say. But, as we shall see, he was able to defend literature to some extent after Stalin's death.

By the thirties he had become a brilliant journalist. Goldberg quotes some of his pieces, taking them at face value. I remember myself being much struck by his reports on the Asturias rebellion and the *Schutzbund* rising. But the only time I met him, after the war, he wrote his vivid descriptions of the honest Bulgarian peasantry from the bar of the Bulgaria Hotel in Sofia. Such phenomena are not unknown in Western reporting; but in this case it was a matter of fiction decking out Stalinist disinformation.

This is not to imply total dishonesty. The rise of Hitler and the Spanish War engaged his real feelings, and his reports from Madrid, even if unreliable as fact, were powerful and stimulating. He contrived briefly to defend, not anarchism as such, but at least the ordinary anarchist workers; and, although he went along with the virulent attacks on Trotskyism, he never made them his main theme, sticking mainly to the horrors of Francoism. Goldberg notes that some of his books were to be published in Spain while Franco was still in power, and wonders if Ehrenburg knew of this.

On returning to Moscow late in 1937, the question of his being sent back to Spain was unresolved, so he wrote directly to Stalin, who refused permission. Thereupon Ehrenburg wrote again, urging

Stalin to reconsider, and was then let out. Such a request to the dictator to admit that he had made a mistake was totally out of harmony with the spirit of the times. Stalin's response will remind us that there was another strange personality besides Ehrenburg's involved in Ehrenburg's survival – Stalin's own.

Stalin was responsible for the slaughter of a great number of Soviet writers. It was later revealed that of the 700 writers who attended the first Writers' Congress in 1934 (at which Ehrenburg made a mild defence of non-tractor-meets-girl novels) only fifty survived to see the second in 1954, though the average age had been under forty. The victims included Babel, Pilnyak, Mandelshtam, Vasilev, Tabidze – a whole roster of Russian and other genius. Nevertheless, Stalin was not predictable in this sphere. In fact, on the whole he seems to have preferred those not deeply concerned with party matters, even those of wholly 'alien' backgrounds, to communists like Babel and Koltsov. *The Days of the Turbins*, notably heterodox, had been allowed on the Moscow stage. Pasternak (to Ehrenburg's own surprise) had been allowed to work while abject party hacks had perished. The real leftists of RAPP had been condemned. And, though 'socialist realism' was formalized in 1934, Stalin allowed himself the caprice of making exceptions. When it came to individual decisions, like that on allowing Ehrenburg to go back to Spain (rather than face the normal sanction against indiscipline – death), Ehrenburg's rival, Konstantin Simonov, provides a penetrating analysis in one of his novels. A character, 'General Serpilin', approaches Stalin to release a colleague, whose civil war services he recounts. But

> Serpilin's recalling of past services had failed to touch Stalin. It was the directness of the letter that had interested him. In his ruthless character, side by side with a despotic demand for total subservience, which was the rule with him, there lay the need to come across exceptions – which was the obverse side of the same rule. At times he evinced something akin to flashes of interest in people who were capable of taking risks, of expressing opinions which ran counter to his own. . . . Knowing himself, he knew the degree of this risk and was all the more capable of setting store by it. Sometimes, that is! Because it was far more frequently the other way round and this was where the risk lay.

This is the normal caprice of oriental despotism. But in Stalin's case it also served, as has been pointed out by many *samizdat* commentators, to make terror more effective by depriving it of the mere obvious rationality of killing suspect categories while leaving others with a feeling of security. As it was, no one felt safe, while everyone felt that with luck he might be spared – psychologically a major component of the terror.

Ehrenburg, as a notorious anti-Nazi, was virtually silenced by the Nazi–Soviet Pact. Until June 1941, the very word 'fascist' disappeared from the Soviet vocabulary. But after the German invasion in 1941 Ehrenburg became the main anti-German propagandist. He had always been anti-German – one of the things which had divided him from the Bolsheviks in the First World War – and now he was given free rein. He had also been hostile to 'fascism' as such, partly but perhaps not centrally for its anti-Semitism. Indeed his main charge had been the literary one of the Nazi book-burning. Goldberg supports this without comment, but there is nevertheless an ambiguity. In her *Memoirs*, Raissa Orlova makes the point that 'They stoked up bonfires for books in our country as well, but . . . they were burned in Russian cities in secret'; and she quotes Ehrenburg himself in a speech in which he cited Babel as having visited a factory for pulping undesirable books into paper: 'hefty wenches sit there and sensually rip off the covers'.

Until the end of the war, Ehrenburg was unleashed for the most violent attacks on Germans as such. Goldberg, acquitting him of urging attacks on German women, implies that these did not take place, whereas it is clear that mass rape and murder was the accompaniment of the advance into East Prussia. At this point, Stalin, who had found the kill-all-Germans propaganda useful during the war, had a censure of Ehrenburg's line published, with a view to establishing a regime of his own in Berlin.

Ehrenburg was not, however, in serious trouble. But he was soon facing the most difficult time of his life. In 1948 the Jewish Anti-Fascist Committee was dissolved. Ehrenburg, as a Jew by birth, had been used as a member of this body when its work had been useful to the Soviet regime. Many of his colleagues on the committee had been prominent in the field of Yiddish culture. Ehrenburg himself was a Russian writer and, as a Jew, an assimilationist. Before the Revolution, Goldberg notes, he had been addicted to the novels of Knut Hamsun, later cursing himself for it, 'not because Hamsun was a reactionary and an anti-Semite of the more primitive kind (most readers rightly attached little significance to his anti-Jewish bias or did not even notice it), but because he was a romantic'. An interesting thing here is not so much that in those days Ehrenburg saw anti-Semitism as something obsolete, like crinolines, but that Goldberg could report it in this way after all the anti-Semitic horrors of later years.

But, when the Nazis had emerged, Ehrenburg took the honourable position that, as he later put it, while anti-Semitism existed, he was Jew. And now, in the late forties, anti-Semitism became one of the elements of Stalinism itself. Over the period 1948–53, over 400 Jewish intellectuals were arrested, and few survived. Most of the Yiddish writers were shot in the 'Crimean affair' in August 1952, after two or three years in labour camp. Ehrenburg meanwhile was sent abroad to defend the regime. He provided a great contribution in the West to the Stalin 'peace campaign' (waged by the World Peace Council, an organization still prominent in Western 'peace' affairs) – this was the period of the 'Stockholm Peace Appeal', signed by millions, including almost all the North Korean army, then on the point of the attack on the south. In addition, he found himself having to lie in a more personal way, claiming to know that nothing had happened to men he knew perfectly well to be in jail awaiting execution. Goldberg plausibly acquits him of a charge that he actually denounced Bergelson and Fefer and the others. But as their colleague on the committee he could hardly have avoided interrogation about their activities, and anodyne answers, however reluctant, were not acceptable to the MGB. The moral ambiguity of his situation was in any case obvious. But at the end of 1952 came the arrest of those accused in the Doctors' Plot, which was designed to bring the anti-Semitic campaign to its climax. By now even Ehrenburg was in danger. He is said to have refused to sign a letter drafted by the party calling for leading Jewish intellectuals to apply for the deportation of the whole Jewish community to Siberia, though his own letter expressing qualms, as given by Goldberg, must either be on a different theme or be wrongly dated: in any case, his 'refusal' was merely a request for instructions, and a promise to sign if 'leading comrades' thought it desirable. However that may be, the idea put forward here that this refusal was what saved the Jews from deportation is quite unreal. The plan seems to have been to hang the 'Zionist' doctors and start the deportation of the Jews in mid-May 1953, and what saved them could not have been any action of Ehrenburg's, however brave and well intentioned. Stalin's death on 5 March was what did it.

At this point Ehrenburg entered his best period. His novel *The Thaw* launched the whole idea of a return to freedom in literature, and not only in literature. Over the next years, he was violently denounced. But by now he was, if not a Grand Old Man, at least a respected senior figure; and his opponents were no longer in a position simply to kill him off. He was denounced, and largely silenced, several times. But, as the political struggle gave openings, he used them to struggle for his views. Finally came his autobiography, *People, Years, Life*, of which Nadezhda Mandelshtam wrote that it was 'the only one of his books to have played a positive part in this country. . . . It may well have been he who first aroused people into reading *samizdat*.'

It is hard to sum up such a career. Yevtushenko says that 'he taught us to survive'. But Ehrenburg made fewer concessions, in a worse period, than the younger man. He survived in part through accident and caprice. He was not a writer of the first rank. But, if we find much of his activity abhorrent, those of us who have never been through the Soviet experience are not in a good position to pass judgement. Indeed, there are murky and disgraceful incidents in his life story. It remains true that whenever he had the power he showed a devotion to literature, including the literature of the West, and defended it as far as he could. Of course literature is not the most important thing there is, but in the circumstances of totalitarianism it is inseparable from a concern with truth for its own sake. Some, like Ehrenburg, are prepared to lie, but in the long run are forced into truth by their literary spirit.

1984

Yevgeny Yevtushenko

At one time Yevgeny Yevtushenko stood forward as the Galahad of liberalism in the struggle against the cold-blooded traditionalists of the Soviet Communist Party apparatus. Vast audiences of the enthusiastic young flocked to his readings, applauded him wildly, and called for poems such as 'Babi Yar' which seemed to embody the hope of a new and freer Russia. In the West too, and especially in America, he was massively welcomed in the same spirit.

But let us first insist that Yevtushenko is a genuine poet, even if not one of the first rank. His poetry has been unnecessarily denigrated. Partly this is the natural result of his massive output of propaganda verses of a lowish order. But, even when he was in his prime, there was a tendency in many circles to underrate his verse for purely aesthetic reasons. Yevtushenko is, or was, an admirer of Kipling, who is notably popular in Russia. His earlier poetry was remarkable for its vigour, directness and rhythmic momentum. These are qualities little appreciated among the traditional avant garde. But this earlier verse was by no means as simple-minded as admirers of extreme subtlety might imply, and its positive virtues are not to be sneered at. The clear 'public' tone made an admirable rallying point for the optimistic Soviet young of the late nineteen-fifties. It is true, though, that when the political situation changed, this tone became a liability. The 'public' poet has few defences against overwhelming political pressure unless (like the 'public' prose-writer Solzhenitsyn) he can rely on profound moral reserves.

In 1956, Yevtushenko was expelled from the Komsomol for a poem that could hardly be thought politically heterodox in any sense. Still, while celebrating the idealism of an 18-year-old Komsomol girl, it expresses a certain worry about the fate of her ideals:

> I am troubled as to what will befall
> Your fair head,
> Tormenting you with anxiety,
> As you reach for the heights.
> I have come to believe in many things
> Just to make you believe in them too.

But the Komsomol, at this time, appeared to be a minor reactionary bastion, and the wave of the future seemed to lie with the independent young.

A number of Yevtushenko's poems were more roughly criticized in 1957 when the first wave of the Thaw was receding. His long 'Zima Station', describing life in his Siberian home town, was attacked in *Komsomolskaya Pravda* (the youth daily) for making the area appear much as it had been in Tsarist times. Another high-spirited poem about the writer listening to an old prospector telling fantastic lies about his adventures was censured in the same issue: The commentator, speaking as an Old Bolshevik and the father of five sons and two daughters, explained that such poems were 'needed by no one'.

A poem starting, 'The frontiers oppress me', went on to say how he felt it 'awkward' not to have been in London, New York and Paris, and ended: 'I want an art – As varied as myself'. It came under attack in *Literaturnaya Gazeta*, the Writers' Union weekly, which commented, 'It would not be so bad if Yevtushenko wanted only to wander through London and Paris. The trouble is that he resents living inside Soviet frontiers'. As to variety in art, the commentator pointed out that this exists only because one 'arouses high ideals' and the other 'low instincts'. But the reaction was only temporary and successive waves of Khrushchevian thaw gave every cause for optimism – and even for the idea that the decisive elements of political leadership themselves favoured the freer atmosphere.

It was the Khrushchev epoch that saw Yevtushenko's rise. At that time, it appeared that Khrushchev himself and his then dominant faction in the leadership were truly determined to destroy the Stalinist tradition. In this they were supported by all that was best in Russia, and in particular by the young writers. After various false starts, this Khrushchevian 'liberalism' came to its climax around the middle of 1962. *One Day in the Life of Ivan Denisovich* was published, on Khrushchev's orders, and many lesser works of truth and promise were appearing.

Khrushchev saw, at least, that a regime founded on palpable lies could hardly hope for much support from men of intelligence. And he was prepared up to a point to interpret Communist aesthetic principles in a less narrow way than his predecessors (or his successors). What he was not prepared to do was to permit any discussion of basic principles.

He was, to some degree, caught in contradiction. And the 'liberals' who supported him were not necessarily either clear or united in their aims. Some saw the attack on Stalinism as the first phase of a far broader 'liberalization' by which full intellectual and civic liberty would eventually be restored to Russia. Others, while basically sharing his view that the final power over thought and literature must remain with the Central Committee, still hoped for relaxations.

It was during this period that Yevtushenko came to identify himself with a definite trend within the Khrushchevian wing of Communism, maintaining a position that might be described as the most liberal compatible with 'working from inside'. His poem 'The Heirs of Stalin' illustrates this point. It was, on its face, strictly within the anti-Stalinist decisions of the 22nd Party Congress of 1961, which was binding upon the whole party. But it nevertheless contained lines to be interpreted only as powerful attacks on Frol Kozlov and the more reactionary Politburo faction he led. Yevtushenko recited it freely for some time before it could actually be printed, but in the end it came out in *Pravda* itself. This was clearly approved by Khrushchev personally. In his developing attack on his rivals, he was naturally delighted to see it pointed out that some of the party Stalinists were 'secretly thinking their discharge is temporary,' while others, still in high places, 'from rostrums, even heap abuse on Stalin but, at night, hanker after the good old days'; and even that Stalinists 'seem stricken with heart attacks these days' – a reference to Kozlov's various coronaries. This poem, while impeccably anti-Stalinist, was yet totally within the orthodox Khrushchevian position.

Up till the last quarter of 1962, this sort of liberalization seemed to have set in as a permanent thing, with the young poets among its most active leaders. Their influence was steadily widening. Yevtushenko himself was cheered by mass audiences in the 10,000 range. His poems were printed in editions of 100,000. But at this point, the traditionalist apparatchiks were able to complain that things were getting out of hand, and Khrushchev himself came to agree with them. On 1 December 1962, he paid his famous visit to the Manezh Gallery and launched a violent attack on non-representational art as 'anti-Soviet', immoral and, in general, the work of pederasts. This was, in effect, a demonstration of how illusory were the hopes of the young writers that they could accommodate themselves and their ideas to even the 'liberalizing' faction of the regime.

Yevtushenko, however, continued his efforts. On 17 December 1962, some 400 creative artists in all fields were summoned to the Kremlin to meet Khrushchev and other party leaders. In the literary world, it had become (the ideological secretary Leonid Ilyichev complained) 'inconvenient and unfashionable to defend correct party positions'. This was now to be reversed. Yevtushenko warmly defended the abstract sculptor Ernst Neizvestny against the charges made against him. When Khrushchev retorted, 'Only the grave corrects a hunchback', Yevtushenko replied, 'I hope we have outlived the time when the grave was used as a means of correction'. He went on to recite the last lines of 'Babi Yar':

> Let the International ring out
> When the last anti-Semite on earth is buried!
> There is no Jewish blood in mine,
> But I am hated by every anti-Semite as a Jew,
> And for this reason
> I am a true Russian.

Khrushchev said flatly, 'Comrade Yevtushenko, that poem has no place here'. There followed the celebrated exchange in which Yevtushenko thanked Khrushchev for his work against Stalinism but said that one problem still remained, that of anti-Semitism. Khrushchev replied with a violent outburst to the effect that no such problem existed in Russia.

It will be noted, that even on this theme, Yevtushenko was still not saying anything that, on the face of it, departed from party orthodoxy. Khrushchev had already attacked Stalin for his persecution of various small nationalities, like the Chechens. And there is nothing in official ideology which in any sense exempts the Jews from decent and equal treatment. Anti-Semitism is simply a traditional prejudice in the post-Stalin apparat, with no more sanction than that of habit. 'Babi Yar' was eventually printed in the USSR in a version inoffensive to the ruling group. Yevtushenko still recited the original when he was abroad, but not when he was at home.

There was now something of a lull in the attack on the liberals. Yevtushenko continued his brave stand. Early in the following year, he published (in the French left-wing *L'Express*) his 'A Precocious Autobiography' with attacks on the dogmatists, including their anti-Semitism, and containing the remark, 'In Russia all tyrants believe poets to be their worst enemies'. In Paris he recited his 'The Dead

Hand,' which had not been published in Russia and which contains such lines as: 'Someone still glares in the Stalin manner'.

On 4 March 1963, he was abruptly summoned home and was among those who had once again to face Khrushchev and Ilyichev. The attack this time was total and thoroughly coordinated. The liberal writers were severely chastized. Most of them remained silent – or rejected the charges, especially the 51-year-old Viktor Nekrasov.

Yevtushenko was among the few who, after a brief defence, gave in. He said he had committed 'an irreparable mistake' and would try to correct his errors in future. *Komsomolskaya Pravda* acquitted him of 'evil intent' but said he must give up his 'political infantilism'. This estimate that, though liable to aberrations, he was yet likely to be useful to the dictatorship was to prove a sensible one.

The writers who had briefly flourished thus went two different ways: Solzhenitsyn and his like into silenced opposition; Yevtushenko and his like, sometimes reluctantly, sometimes in the hope of still influencing matters a little, into well-rewarded collaboration. They could be seen as 'liberal' – in the sense of those who are wholly committed to the one-party system and to the Marxist-Leninist ideology, but who wish it to relax its repressive measures to some extent. They were not, that is, against the suppression of 'anti-Soviet' thought and literature; they merely wished the limits to be defined less narrowly and the necessary repressions to be carried out less brutally. They were like those 'liberal landlords' who, Tolstoy wrote, would do anything for the peasant except get off his back.

The period that immediately followed was, indeed, a milder one for the writers. In poems unpublished in Russia but appearing abroad, such as 'Letter to Yesenin,' and in others such as 'The Long Suffering of Russia', published there only in a censored version, Yevtushenko was again able to put forward a 'liberal' view, in a more restrained and careful fashion. For Khrushchev had again turned on his more Stalinist colleagues, evidently feeling that too severe a crackdown would seriously undermine his own position. The remainder of the Khrushchev period and the first year or so of his successor's was a fairly tolerable period.

All the same, it would be hard to overestimate the shock given to the whole creative community by the campaign of the winter of 1962–63. The hope that things were going to go on improving more or less automatically was brought up so sharply that the mood of the writers changed from one of airy optimism to one of the utmost fear and apprehension. It certainly marks a turning point in Yevtushenko's evolution.

Soon the party's organ, *Pravda*, welcomed Yevtushenko's 'fervent civic-mindedness' – a phrase that in *Pravda*'s usage indicated, of course, complete loyalty to the apparat. On the other hand the novelist Vladimir Maksimov wrote to the Soviet Union of Writers (just before his own dismissal from that body) mentioning Yevtushenko in passing in the most hostile way: 'The Union of Writers, and its Moscow branch in particular, is gradually becoming the domain of petty political marauders, of literary hucksters, of all sorts of Mednikovs, Pilyars and Yevtushenkos'. And there was, for example, a bitter attack on Yevtushenko, circulated in manuscript, by two old friends and colleagues, the liberal writers Vasily Aksyonov and Grigory Pozhenyan. The immediate issue was an article of his on their book 'Gene Green Untouchable', which (they pointed out) went far beyond legitimate criticism, and to which their attempts to reply in print were rejected by the party hacks in control of the journals. They charged him with using his official position as a secretary of the Union of Writers to 'settle personal scores', accused him of 'hypocritical demagogy' and added that 'you bragged that you had provided security for yourself' by dissociation from authors less well regarded by the authorities.

On his trips abroad the darker side of his reputation had already been in evidence. There, he had maligned Olga Ivinskaya, Pasternak's companion and heir who, after Pasternak's death in 1960, was arrested and sentenced to eight years' imprisonment on a faked charge of illegal dealing in foreign currency. She was alleged to have handled some of Pasternak's royalties from the West. His Western Communist publishers instantly made it clear that the whole thing was a frame-up. When in England and elsewhere in the West, Yevtushenko was asked whether he could do anything about her. He simply answered that he had nothing to do with currency offenders. Worse than this, when in Australia, he put about among writers there unpleasant personal gossip about Mrs Ivinskaya.

The significance of this is that, while abroad at any rate, Yevtushenko had already been toeing the Khrushchevian party line, even in its worst characteristics. For it was, of course, Khrushchev who (as Edward Crankshaw put it) hounded Pasternak into his grave and then revenged himself on his helpless relict. Moreover, Yevtushenko did not merely repeat the party's story. He went beyond the call of even this unpleasant duty. No other Soviet writer abroad behaved in this fashion. (Few, even in Russia, associated themselves with the charges – notably the admittedly hard-line Alexei Surkov, though he at least confined himself to the 'currency' matters). Yevtushenko also remarked that *Doctor Zhivago* was 'not worth publishing' in Russia.

It was from this period too (if one looks at it charitably) that he sought to cover his pressure for liberalization at home by the most intransigent adherence to Communist foreign policy in the poems he wrote on world affairs. It would be tedious to quote his verses about the vile imperialists. He went even so far as to refer to Finnish Social Democratic demonstrators against a Soviet-sponsored peace jamboree as 'gum-chewing Fascists'.

Thus, there had been (from what we would regard as a 'liberal' viewpoint) some black as well as white in the earlier, better phase of Yevtushenko's career. Following his 1963 surrender, and particularly since Khrushchev's fall, we find a gloomier picture.

In 1965 came his 'The Bratsk Hydroelectric Station'. This is a poem not without merit, particularly in his descriptions of his own Siberia. But politically it is a more significant. It presents what might be called the liberal-apparatchik view of Stalinism. Like many other projects, the station was largely erected by the labour of starving prisoners. Yevtushenko does not ignore this. But if he does not glorify the Stalin slave-labour system, he prettifies it. The prisoners, admittedly innocent victims, are shown as in no way abandoning their loyalty to the regime. A constant refrain is: 'We are not slaves'! This notion – that, in spite of everything, everyone had a long-term trust and knew that the party was really right – can be compared with *One Day in the Life of Ivan Denisovich*. But then, Solzhenitsyn was actually in the camps himself and was concerned to say what they were truly like.

Andrei Sinyavsky in a much-circulated article made this point at some length. When Sinyavsky himself, with Yuli Daniel, was brought to trial in February 1966, in the most famous and brutal blow struck by the Brezhnev regime against literature, Yevtushenko was among the few well-known writers not to sign the moderately phrased 'Letter of the 63' protesting the action. Even the veteran waverer Ilya Ehrenburg found it possible to sign.

Yevtushenko was now deeply involved in what may be thought of as a Faustian situation. But it may also be true that his bargain with the ideological devil was not merely a cynical one. With all his compromises, and worse, he still apparently hoped that in the long run things would improve. After the invasion of Czechoslovakia, he telegraphed a protest to the Soviet leadership. It is true that prudence then prevailed and he refused to confirm that he had done so or make any further trouble after the first anguish had passed. But at least, in the heat of the moment, the signs that he did favour Socialism with a human face was something that an age of prudence could never retract.

Meanwhile, another poet, Yuri Galanskov, was dying in a labour camp. He had been consigned there for 'anti-Soviet propaganda' in 1968 at the celebrated Ginzburg-Galanskov trial, the conduct of which outraged the norms of even Soviet law. It was denounced by Bertrand Russell and other Western writers, and by the Communist Parties of Western Europe. Yevtushenko was not one of the many Soviet writers who also signed letters of protest at the time, though he is reported to be one of those who said they would have to resign from the Writers' Union if all such signatories were expelled from it. Galanskov was ill with a stomach complaint, and his physical condition soon deteriorated owing to the failure, outraging both law and humanity, to make the necessary medical and dietary arrangements. His relatives approached Yevtushenko in the hope that he might use his influence to help the prisoner. It is their belief that he did not do so, at any rate with any vigour, since at the time he was concerned with preparing a trip to Allende's Chile.

For his most notable activity was now these visits to foreign countries, which took him all over the world – even to Spain and Portugal in their 'Fascist' phase. On these jaunts, he continued to denigrate (and worse) real liberals in the USSR. In addition to his public statements about Sinyavsky and Daniel, he made, less publicly, much nastier remarks about them. On his various tours abroad in 1966 and in 1968, he frequently attacked them – for example, in Dakar, New York and Mexico City. On one trip to the United States he was asked by students what he thought of their imprisonment. In accordance with the line he had evidently chosen (and elsewhere repeated), he said he felt they had been guilty but had been punished too harshly. But then he asked the audience, 'How would you react if one of your writers published a book in Europe under an assumed name'? When they laughed, he was baffled. It seems, in fact, that his understanding of the West was very superficial. In Mexico, in March 1968, he first claimed he knew nothing of the Ginzburg-Galanskov trial (though his own first wife had been censured for protesting), and later attacked the defendants as traitors and black marketeers. Representatives of all the progressive and revolutionary organizations in the University of Mexico denounced him publicly.

At the same time, these trips could be of benefit to himself and to the Soviet regime only if he maintained a certain air of liberalism. The Ideological Department of the Central Committee (where he has

friends) operated with reasonable sophistication and clearly understood the point. While his major public statements were violent
attacks on Western actions and policies, he permitted himself to say
things implying certain imperfections in the Soviet Union. Though,
as we shall see, not very telling ones.

I have only once met Yevtushenko. That was at the launching
of Apollo 16. As a genuine rocket buff, a member of the British
Interplanetary Society since the 1940s, I was delighted to be able to
get a press card and a splendid view of that remarkable spectacle.
Afterward, I went along to what I understood to be one of the press
conferences on the launching. I did not at first identify the vaguely
familiar figure led by with a few mumbled words of introduction. I
had not known he was there, and if I had, it would not have occurred
to me that his comments would have been particularly instructive to
the press corps. However, he was soon on the platform, wearing his
Paris-painter-of-the-nineties cap stuck at a becoming angle, inviting
questions. I stayed for the first, which was a general one. Yevtushenko, whose interest in rocket launchings, as opposed to press conferences, had not been great enough to get him to any Soviet launching,
spoke largely to the theme of his, as he put it, 'bosom friend' Yuri
Gagarin. He claimed that Gagarin, and American spacemen too, had
told him of their feelings as they looked down on the earth, so single
and so small, from out there in space, thinking how sad it was that
it should be divided by frontiers that people could not easily cross.
I suppose that anyone finding himself in such a position, particularly
if he regards himself as the spokesman of his Government, must
produce this sort of benign-sounding platitude. But all the same, one
could not but reflect that there is nothing on the American side to
prevent an American poet, or any other citizen, from going anywhere
he wishes, including Russia, or from watching a Soviet rocket launch;
that the West would equally welcome the free movement of Soviet
citizens across their frontiers into their own countries. What prevents
this, in each direction, is the action of the Soviet Government alone.
The fact that Yevtushenko was allowed to visit Cape Kennedy, while
the vast majority of Soviet citizens were not, was one of those exceptions that proved the rule through and through. He had earned what
was not a right but a privilege, and he was hard at work continuing
to earn it. When one adds that Yevtushenko was one of a very few
Soviet private citizens with a passport of his own, and not merely
the single-trip affair issued on departures and withdrawn on return,
the point is illuminated with special force.

Western readers will not need a full review of the scenes at his later visits to the United States. Even on his famous 1972 trip, while he was able to give readings in company with prominent American poets like Richard Wilbur, Stanley Kunitz and James Dickey, numbers of his fellow readers (including Eugene McCarthy) are reported to have been disgusted by the crude and false propaganda tone of the verse he produced on these occasions: Yevtushenko later accused McCarthy of hypocrisy and wishing to please both left- and right-wingers. When one woman, an American journalist, asked him why he was allowed to travel and other Russian writers weren't, he was shaken enough to refer to her as a 'hyena' – a Stalinist term of abuse not much employed since the time it used to be applied to T. S. Eliot. On the other hand, he received a certain amount of adulation, including an honorary degree from the New School for Social Research. While in America, too, the bombing by Jewish extremists of Sol Hurok's office in New York roused him to a poem in which he compared it with Nazi genocide; though the bombing was deplorable, the comparison seems far from exact. But more interesting still, the poem was telephoned home from New York and printed at once in *Izvestia*. In it, a handful of terrorists were held up as a major American phenomenon. For once, the Soviet press (which rarely reported Yevtushenko's foreign tours) rubbed the story in with such comments as one reprinted from the American Communist *Daily World*, which linked the bombing with 'Zionist forces which are attempting in conjunction with the CIA to depict the Soviet people as monsters against whom war is not only necessary, but urgently necessary'.

Even his harangues about Vietnam, where he had spent a few days en route from Moscow, did not strike an acceptable note, even among opponents of the war. Apart from embellishing them with a singularly improbable tale about having seen the body of a North Vietnamese youth clutching a copy of Ernest Hemingway's *For Whom the Bell Tolls* (or, on another occasion, *The Old Man and The Sea*), he seems to have given the impression of overestimating the power of demagogy. William Jay Smith recalled that another Soviet poet had told him in Moscow: 'It is all too easy to write about killings in another country'. Yevtushenko replied to this sort of criticism in the introduction to the American edition of his *Stolen Apples*: 'Somehow they find it morally questionable to speak of the corruption of the Western world when in the Soviet Union the price of cognac is rising, the meat supply uncertain, and the shops, in general, unjust'. These were not, in fact, the main objections generally felt in the United States to Soviet internal conditions.

If, as he frequently did, Yevtushenko wished to refer to Kent State, for example, it was commonly felt that he might balance it with such acts as the rather larger-scale shooting down of Soviet crowds in those years in such incidents as those at Dnepropetrovsk (1972), Chimkent (1967) and the like – where the dead are believed to have run into the hundreds, and where rioters were later executed.

One of his 'Western' poems was on 'The Victory in Vietnam,' published appropriately in *Pravda*. It celebrates:

> . . . a world of friends
> In the West as in the East.
> with victory, Picasso,
> with victory, Jane Fonda,
> with victory, my Petka,
> with victory, Doctor Spock.

Rotten luck on Doctor Spock, but, even including him, the circle of friends seems rather a limited one. Friendship between East and West under the aegis of the organ of the Central Committee of the Communist Party of the Soviet Union might just possibly have ranged a bit wider in those days of detente.

Yevtushenko's poems on public themes are in any case fairly poor, even in that notoriously poverty-stricken genre. In translation, they retain almost no flavour except that of political harangue. Perhaps large Western audiences could more easily digest this simple stuff, while retaining the illusion that they were involved in something cultural. The whole question of the presumed 'mass audience for poetry' arises here. One can only say that similar audiences would probably reject an evening of simple patriotic American songs. And that a number of poets concerned rather with poetry regarded the whole thing as suspect: Allen Tate's remark, after dismissing Yevtushenko as 'a ham actor, not a poet', was that 'this kind of circus is a demeaning and vulgarizing of poetry. It will just lead people astray who think it is the real thing.'

Yevtushenko's reputation, nevertheless, presented quite extraordinary contradictions. There were still those who thought of him as in some sense a daring opponent of establishmentarianism, while at the same time he was rejected by Soviet liberals. This paradox has a simple explanation: ignorance. Ignorance, that is, on the part of the Western audience. Naturally, ignorance of this type, maintained in the face of a vast amount of relevant information, is not an organic blindness, but a compulsive one, of the type associated with certain psychological states. Albert Camus once remarked of pro-Soviet Frenchmen that it was not so much that they really liked the Russians as that they 'heartily detested part of the French'. Though the phenomenon was already rarer in Western Europe, it seems clear that in the United States there were still people who have only to know that a man or regime was opposed to their own country, or to a selection of its policies. This instantly established his credentials. This sort of global double standard – exactly what Solzhenitsyn complained of in his Nobel speech – is probably the most dangerous, one might almost say the most criminally negligent, element in the world today.

More generally, Yevtushenko appealed to people who could not quite swallow unvarnished Soviet orthodoxy. Above all, his reputation in America was founded on 'Babi Yar' and his stand against anti-Semitism. In fact (as we have noted), Yevtushenko yielded to pressure on this poem, eliminated two lines and added two others to include Russian and Ukrainian victims of the massacre – that is, to play down the theme of anti-Semitism. The new text appeared in the score of Shostakovich's 13th Symphony. In the West, he recited the original, evidently with official permission. In the USSR, it did not exist in print. But even here, he took the line (eg, in an interview in *Playboy*, December 1972) that what anti-Semitism there was in Russia survived among uneducated people, while 'official' anti-Semitism did not exist.

All the same, the case of Yevtushenko was not to be seen in black and white, as a simple moral melodrama. He was not just the shining liberal knight who sold out and became a mere cynical agent of the oppressor. His original liberalism was of a limited nature, and it was not he, but his Western fans, who made higher claims. And several other arguments can legitimately be advanced in his favour. Some of his intellectual opponents have at least partly been motivated by the usual jealousies of the literary world. He later showed once again that he personally would much prefer a less oppressive style of rule, particularly in the literary fields. He could urge that his collaboration gave him at least some slight opportunity to inject milder advice into the ears of the ideological apparatchiks. And, as pointed out above, his ostentatious support of the Soviet political line when abroad might be the price he paid for the opportunity to influence the apparat when back in the USSR.

But even if one recognizes that the role of the man of good will seeking to influence a despotic regime from within is a difficult one and, generally speaking, involves an element of moral compromise, we still can make some judgements as to how such a role should be played. Tvardovsky was a genuine believer in 'liberalization' from within the system. He was an old party member and even, in the sixties, a candidate member of the party's Central Committee. Yet, with all the ambiguities which inevitably haunted him, his attachment to the party in no way affected an unprejudiced concern with Russian literature, however nonpartisan, and a devotion to truth. He disagreed with the total liberals, but on no occasion did he harm them or slander them. He supported Pasternak, and after him Solzhenitsyn. And during his long tenure on *Novy Mir*, he secured for that magazine the maximum coverage of literature conceivable under the system, without ever feeling it necessary to stoop to betrayals. When he was removed in 1969, it was quite openly done to destroy the liberal tinge he was still, in the most adverse circumstances, giving to *Novy Mir*.

It is not really for those of us who do not have to face such conditions to judge the conduct of a Soviet writer. Nevertheless, the almost unanimous judgements passed on Yevtushenko by his colleagues could not be publicly expressed by them, and this can only be done for them by the public judgement of the West. Moreover, our interests and our feelings are legitimately engaged, even apart from the overriding unity of *Weltliteratur*. For Yevtushenko came to our countries, loosed off political verses attacking their external and internal policies, represented himself misleadingly as representative of Soviet literature and attacked his colleagues who were already in difficulties.

One of his later books of verses, *When A Man is Forty*, describes his feelings on reaching what for a professional 'young' poet must be a definite climacteric. It contains the lines:

> Up until then life's a party:
> The hangover comes when you're forty.

When we consider the whole Yevtushenko phenomenon, we seem to find a curious amalgam of politics, publicity and poetry, with some psychological trace elements thrown in for good measure. And indeed, in the 1980s he once again urges a greater adherence to historical and other truth, if only, as he himself put it, because the blatancy of Soviet falsification puts Soviet intellectuals at a disadvantage in arguing with Westerners. This stance, whatever the moral ambiguities, may yet be of service to his country, to politics and to literature in dismantling at least the more extravagant falsehoods hitherto propounded. Yevtushenko is sometimes described contemptuously by

Soviet liberals as 'a politician'. But if he is to be regarded primarily as a politician we might yet accept that in Soviet circumstances his record, with all its shifts and compromises, may merit, on balance, a positive assessment.

1974/1982

Yesenin-Volpin

A. S. Yesenin-Volpin's *A Leaf of Spring* is a phenomenal book. The poets of the USSR, from Pasternak down, have shown themselves incorrigibly assured in their rejection of the barren orthodoxies of officialdom. The teenage verse-writers of the Literary Institute, even, have been censured again and again for 'decadent' tastes. But Volpin, the natural son of Sergei Yesenin, is not only a poet, but also a leading logician. He combines the emotional sensitivity which rejects the constrictions with the analytic mind which penetrates the cant. The result is, in the prose section of this book, as if Bertrand Russell had collaborated in writing *Les Illuminations*.

One of the most interesting things about Volpin is that he shows how impossible it is for even the most efficient system of thought-control to prevent the spontaneous arising of the old questions and aspirations. He says of his own views, 'I do not claim to be the most intelligent person in Russia. Much that is written here is not new. But every student in Russia who has arrived at philosophical scepticism by his own thinking can consider himself a new Columbus'. And he adds that he will be very pleased if all that he says is uninteresting to foreigners because 'it is familiar to everyone'. Much of it *is* reasonably familiar: it is its spontaneous rebirth from a barren soil that is so striking – that, and the sharpness given it by the unfavourable circumstances themselves, stropping a keen mind yet keener.

Volpin, who had already been in prison in Stalin's time, wrote his philosophical essay in a hurry, expecting the rearrest which came shortly afterwards. He sent it abroad together with a number of his poems, covered by a message asking for publication regardless of his own fate. The publishers have produced it in a Russian-and-English edition, which is a good thing, as some of the poems are too 'poeti-

cally' translated ('lofty' for 'tall', 'an alien land' for 'abroad', etc.).
Volpin's verse is in many ways admirable, if scarcely up to the
standard of his famous father's. Many of the poems given here were
written in the Lubyanka prison, in the psychiatric wards of Leningrad
prison or in exile in Karaganda.

Their themes are the personal life, truth and freedom – 'The
irrational goal of liberty'. In the essay he devastatingly criticizes
official Marxism for confusing morality and truth on the one hand
with expedience and advantage on the other. He adds:

> I cannot resist being sarcastic about the quibbling definition of 'freedom'
> as 'realized necessity'. This definition implies that, if I find myself in
> prison I am not free until I have realized that I cannot walk out; but as
> soon as I have become aware of this, I shall immediately discover 'free-
> dom'. Need I explain that such a terminology is very convenient for the
> 'liberators of mankind'? . . . Since I am speaking of freedom, I should like
> to remark that we value freedom conceived as the possibility of choice:
> certainly not because we like to choose (the necessity of a choice is
> sometimes simply horrible and almost always unpleasant!), but because
> we desire to choose without compulsion.

He is also clear on the inapplicability of historical materialism to
Soviet reality: 'a powerful state authority can change the economic
system from an agrarian to an industrial one. How then can the state
authority remain the "superstructure over the economic basis"?' He
sees, too, that 'a purely political tendency towards power and authority is prevalent in the Soviet Union'. These are simple but far-
reaching criticisms.

He is not concerned with erecting a counter-system to Marxism,
feeling rather that 'I reject an orderly system; but what do I propose
in its place? Nothing, for the present; in fact I want nothing but
freedom of opinion on this question.' And we find in this cool sceptic
a common ground with Pasternak, for his reason for rejecting system-
atic philosophy is that all systems are closed, finite, whereas 'existence
and life, by their very nature, are infinite'. The inexhaustibility of
reality, the point where philosophers and mystics, poets and logicians
meet, is the final issue between all that is good in Russia and the
closed minds of the ruling caste. Volpin predicts of official ideology:
'These self-deceits are well known. I shall merely say that, if they
themselves believe in their theory, they will perish in their blindness.'

In a verse fragment he is more vehement, as he faces not the hopeful future, but the torments of his present:

> You will not force me to believe in good,
> Hangmen, hangmen, hangmen!

1961

Tvardovsky and *Novy Mir*

One's first feeling when faced with this volume of excerpts from *Novy Mir*[1] is of the richness and variety of Soviet work – and of *published* Soviet work at that. Michael Glenny, after a model introductory essay, gives us poems by Pasternak, Akhmatova, Tsvetaeva; fiction by Pilnyak, Platonov, Tarsis, Solzhenitsyn, Bulgakov; belles-lettres and reminiscences by Biely, Anikst, Pasternak, Kapitsa, Gladkov.

After the first dazzlement, however, a closer look at the contents and at the circumstances of their original publication gives us a rather different sort of insight into Soviet literary conditions. Almost all the contributors suffered in one way or another from the actions of the state – except Andrei Biely, who had the good fortune to die in 1934. The first name is Boris Pilnyak, executed in the late 1930s; the last – Boris Pasternak – 'hounded to death' (as Edward Crankshaw puts it) in the Fifties. Between them come Akhmatova and Tsvetaeva, Platonov and Tarsis, Kapitsa and Solzhenitsyn. Over the whole period, some of the literary contributions were in fact themselves the centres of political storms – in particular Pilnyak's 'A Tale of the Unextinguished Moon' and Solzhenitsyn's *One Day in the Life of Ivan Denisovich* (of which about twenty-six pages are included in this collection).

However, this is a selection covering more than forty years from the best magazine in Russia, and it could not easily be multiplied, even if the whole country's published literary production for the period were taken into account. Above all, it is notable that, with all its riches, there is not a single item from any issue between 1939 and 1956. And this is absolutely right: there is nothing in the magazine over that period, even though it was still the best of its kind in Russia,

[1] *Novy Mir, 1925–1967*, edited by Michael Glenny, Cape (London).

that matches the material Mr Glenny has printed. (In fact, there are only two items here even between 1933 and 1961: a story by Tarsis in 1938 and a poem by Pasternak in 1956). This is, of course, a mark of the dark night of Stalinism that occupied the interim. Nor is there anything, it may be remarked, from the later years of Brezhnevite reaction. Thus, the editorial periods covered are in effect those of Yakov Polonsky, up to his removal in 1934, and of Alexander Tvardovsky, during that long and lonely struggle for literature that ended in his dismissal in 1969.

In addition to the great creative names, we find such phenomena as the essay in which the critic Alexander Anikst provides a remarkable example of a traditional Russian genre going back at least to the 1840s: the use of a literary piece, and one concerned with foreign (American) works at that, to convey extremely strong implied criticism of Russian reality. There is also Professor Kapitsa's address to the Royal Society in 1966 on his recollections of Lord Rutherford, printed in *Novy Mir* the same year. This is not only fascinating as a memoir of the eminent British scientist but also for Kapitsa's frank statement of how, on one of his regular visits from Cambridge to his relations in Russia in 1934, he was virtually kidnapped and forced to stay. Kapitsa's role in the USSR was always benign. He was one of that odd handful of men for whom even Stalin had some respect, and he was just able to save the great Landau from death by making use of this. Kapitsa was, indeed, under house arrest from 1946 to 1955, but was allowed to continue his research. Though his name did not figure among those liberal activists, he was one of the group of similarly quiet, and similarly prestigious figures who wrote a devastating letter to the Soviet leadership strongly condemning any attempts to rehabilitate Stalin.

We have, too, Valentin Berezhkov's account of his experiences as a diplomat in the Soviet embassy in Berlin, where he tells of going with his ambassador to receive the German declaration of war. The ambassador is quoted as making a brave and patriotic retort. But he is nowhere named. The reason is that to have named him would have caused certain difficulties, since he was V. G. Dekanozov, executed as a member of the 'Beria gang' in 1953, and when named only describable, even now, as a vile agent of the enemy.

Tvardovsky's sponsorship of such pieces, both literary and non-literary, met with continuous and ever-increasing opposition. (Solzhenitsyn tells us, for instance, that army libraries in Russia were forbidden to subscribe to *Novy Mir* under Tvardovsky's editorship). Still, in the period of his editorship from 1953 to 1954, and, more important, from 1958 to 1969. *Novy Mir* was incomparably the best periodical in Russia both for the quality of the writing and the comparative freedom of expression Tvardovsky sponsored. He printed Bulgakov's *Black Snow* and, after years of difficulty, even Pasternak's 'People and Situations'. It was solely owing to Tvardovsky's sponsorship (and the accidents of the party struggle that led Khrushchev to assent) that *One Day in the Life of Ivan Denisovich* saw the light. That issue of *Novy Mir* in November 1962 sold out within minutes of reaching the stands and probably did as much as anything to make literate Russia immune to any successful spiritual (as against merely administrative and political) re-Stalinisation.

Within the limits of what was possible, he and his paper were, in fact, the bearers of everything independent and genuine in Russian literature – that is to say, of the great humanist tradition that is the alternative to, and opposite of, Leninism-Stalinism. Tvardovsky's character as a Soviet 'liberal' within the Communist Party is crucial to an understanding of the whole Soviet situation. He was even a candidate member of the party's Central Committee under Khrushchev, though removed in 1966. Yet his attachment to the party in no way contradicted a total love of Russian literature, however non-partisan, and a similar and parallel devotion to truth and to some freedom of expression. In some of the East European countries, such an attitude came to be held by a fair number of Communists, even among leaders such as Imre Nagy; and they were actually able, in Budapest and Prague, to take temporary control of the party. It must be said at once that in Russia, unfortunately enough, Tvardovsky was an exception. Of the 300-odd Central Committee men, he was the only one (even in Khrushchev's time) to take such a position.

All the same, if we are to retain any optimism at all, we might do worse than to regard him as a lone precursor of a possibly peaceful evolution of the Soviet system into something tolerable to its own people and to the world at large.

His case, in fact, raises the whole question of the nature of Soviet 'liberalism' – indeed, so-called liberalism and liberalisation in any highly authoritarian society. In those circumstances, the completely non-collaborationist rebel, like Solzhenitsyn, deserves straightforward moral admiration. But it would be inappropriately patronising – especially for a member of a culture not faced with these problems – to condemn those who try to work within the established system with a view to improving it, to gaining or extracting benefits from it. The difficulty, as ever, is in considering what sorts of compromises, what acts of abasement, what cooperation in harming the innocent, the collaborationist feels justified in accepting. On these criteria we may judge between Tvardovsky and others sometimes spoken of in the West as Soviet liberals. Tvardovsky disagreed with the total liberals, but I know of no occasion on which he either slandered them or harmed them. He wrote in what he regarded as a loyal Communist spirit, but he never stooped to falsification or to justifying or even palliating the evil deeds of the dictatorship.

When Khrushchev asked Tvardovsky how Pasternak compared with him as a poet, he put his hand to his knee and said, 'That's where I come up to on Pasternak'. Nevertheless, his own verse is vigorous and honest. His *Tyorkin in the Other World* (published in 1963) was a striking fantasy, undisguisedly attacking the Stalinist terror; and before his death in 1971 other anti-Stalinist work, unpublished in Russia, had reached the West. When he was removed from the editorship in 1969, it was done quite openly as a move to suppress the liberal tinge he was still, even in the most adverse circumstances, trying to give to the paper.

When Tvardovsky died in 1971, he received no public tributes, and Solzhenitsyn was one of the few writers to attend the funeral, afterwards celebrating him in his moving 'In Memoriam'. He has indeed also given us a merciless examination of the moral contradictions inherent in Tvardovsky's position: but to the man himself he extends sympathy and charity. As Solzhenitsyn put it on another occasion, through his hero Vorotyntsev in *August 1914*, 'Party differences, lieutenant, are a ripple on the water', going on to explain that the important difference is 'the difference between decency and non-decency'. The decencies of modern Russia, as well as her talents, are outstandingly demonstrated in this collection.

1971

Orwell: *1984*

One does not establish a dictatorship in order to safeguard a revolution; one makes the revolution in order to establish the dictatorship. The object of persecution is persecution. The object of torture is torture. The object of power is power.

There have been regimes from the earliest times which have kept themselves in power by what was regarded as an excessive and illegitimate use of violence. But our first use of 'Terror' with a capital 'T' is in the history of the French Revolution, when opponents of the regime, or anyone speaking against it, went to the guillotine or the *noyades* in numbers which then appeared enormous, and which were, at any rate, enough to cow the population.

With the French Revolution, and even with the very first phase of Lenin's regime, terror was usually seen as what may be thought of as a war measure, or an immediate postwar measure, to crush dangerous and still powerful political opponents. Orwell gives us something else: terror as a permanent policy in a stable environment.

Above all, he melds this permanent and total terror with permanent and total falsification. The key phrase about the *Nineteen Eighty-Four* regime is: 'Power is in tearing human minds to pieces and putting them together again in new shapes of your own choosing.' The terror which pervades the book is not just extreme terror in a traditional sense. It is terror definable in a single mix of torture-execution-*doublethink*-Newspeak, and its parts cannot be treated separately.

Orwell began work on *Nineteen Eighty-Four* early in August 1946, and finished it in early November 1948. He died on 21 January, 1950. His views on a number of matters had changed over the years, and in dealing with his intention in *Nineteen Eighty-Four*, it is only permissible for us to refer as I shall do here to what he was thinking in this final and mature period of his life.

Nineteen Eighty-Four is fiction, not prophecy. Orwell did not regard anything as inevitable – and indeed censured intellectuals for thinking that things are bound to go the way they happen to be going at a given moment. He certainly regarded a future of the *Nineteen Eighty-Four* type as at least unpleasantly possible, but no more than that.

There are two constituent elements in the sort of regime Orwell predicates. He was much impressed by, though also had his reservations about, James Burnham's thesis (in *The Managerial Revolution*) that a managerialist oligarchic society was emerging everywhere, with the world about to be divided among three exemplars of this new type of order. They would be, as Orwell put it in 1947, 'collectivist not democratic, and would be ruled over by a caste of managers, scientists, bureaucrats who would destroy old-style capitalism and keep the working class permanently in subjection. In other words, something like "Communism" would prevail everywhere.'

While Burnham expected a world of managerialist powers, the only one he granted to be already in full existence was the USSR. He saw it as immensely powerful, established so firmly that it could never be shaken. But Orwell did not, in real life, accept the totalitarian permanence he offers us in fiction. He wrote in 1946:

It is too early to say just in what way the Russian regime will destroy itself. If I had to make a prophecy, I should say that a continuation of the Russian policies of the last fifteen years – and internal and external policy, of course, are merely two facets of the same thing – can only lead to a war conducted with atomic bombs which will make Hitler's invasion look like a tea-party. But at any rate the Russian regime will either democratise itself, or it will perish. The huge, invincible, everlasting slave empire of which Burnham appears to dream will not be established, or, if established, will not endure. . . .

It is important to note that Burnham and Orwell differ on one major point. Burnham seems to have held that all of the world's major political and social orders were inevitably tending toward this managerial oligarchy. Orwell, even at the time when he was most inclined to accept Burnham's thesis on the whole, had his reservations: 'It is even possible that if the world falls apart into three unconquerable superstates, the liberal tradition will be strong enough within the Anglo-American section of the world to make life tolerable and even offer some hope of progress.'

Orwell could scarcely have written convincingly in a Russian or Chinese setting. Nor would that have much interested an Anglo-American readership. So his setting is inevitably England. But the Oceania of *Nineteen Eighty-Four* is neither Burnham's model derived from Western actuality, nor the possibly semi-liberal managerialist state of Orwell's practical hopes. It is made perfectly clear that the *Nineteen Eighty-Four* system has not arisen through capitalism – the Party hates capitalists and is explicitly shown to have overthrown capitalist rule and 'expropriated' the capitalists. Nor is it the product of the Labour party's policies – the old Labour party is referred to in the text as something extinct, and Orwell issued a denial that he was in any way targeting Attlee's (highly anti-communist) Labour Government, which he in fact supported, if not uncritically. But Ingsoc (like communism) 'grew out of the earlier Socialist movement and inherited its phraseology'; and, while rejecting all that Orwell understands by socialism, 'chooses to do it in the name of Socialism.'

The foundation of *Nineteen Eighty-Four* is, in fact, Stalin's Russia. In his *George Orwell*, Raymond Williams (writing from a left-wing viewpoint) criticizes him for this. Williams rightly argues that he could have gone beyond 'a single political tendency' and sought models all over; and in effect censures him for *not* seeing a potential totalitarianism in the Western system.

Had Orwell indeed thought that the *Nineteen Eighty-Four* regime could have arisen from the corruption of conservatives, capitalists, Labourites, or whatever, he had a particularly good opportunity of developing it – with a neo-capitalist-conservative totalitarianism in Oceania to balance 'neo-Bolshevism' in Eurasia. He did nothing of the kind, and those who argue that every political culture, with its imperfect politicians, insensitive bureaucrats, occasional abuses of power, sporadic euphemisms and falsifications, is seen by Orwell as equally liable to breed totalitarianism, are simply not reading the book (or, come to that, Orwell's other explicatory writings of the same period).

He did not do so, because he did not in fact see the West as seriously tending in that direction. Much as he detested Conservatives and Catholics, press lords and movie moguls, he did not envisage them as precursors of the terror state. And he saw Western culture, on which they were the warts, as nevertheless the hope of the world. Sometimes that hope might appear strong, sometimes feeble. But at worst he felt (in 1946) that 'our own society is still, broadly speaking, liberal.' The Soviet Union, on the other hand, was his model of a frightful local present and a possible frightful world future.

There are, of course, a number of ways in which Oceania is not a precise homologue of the USSR, though mainly in its exaggeration and extrapolation in the natural direction of logical caricature. But it is remarkable how much is derived directly from, and only from, the Soviet record. Even Big Brother's style is modeled on Stalin's! Goldstein is, of course, a pure Trotsky figure.

The 'unperson' is entirely based on Soviet practice. The most usual procedure in Moscow has been the omission of important figures from history. But sometimes more Orwellian methods have been employed. Many readers will know of the occasion when, after the fall of Beria, subscribers to the *Large Soviet Encyclopedia* were sent a set of fresh pages on the Bering Sea and an obscure eighteenth-century courtier call Bergholz, with instructions to remove certain unspecified but numbered pages with a razor blade and paste these in instead. When Malenkov lost the premiership, but not all his power, the next edition of the *Encyclopedic Dictionary* differed from its predecessor solely in shortening his entry, making up space with a minor fortress, an engineer who had invented a six-wheeled bogie, and a hitherto neglected strawberry called *malengr*. Dozens of similar examples might be cited. For American observers, perhaps the most remarkable rewrite came in the volume of the *Small Soviet Encyclopedia* which was rolling off the press in 1941. In some copies, evidently the earlier part of the print, Franklin Roosevelt appears as an agent of American business and instigator of imperialist war; in others, he has become a representative of the aspirations of the people and opponent of fascist aggression.

The unperson disappears not only from the written, but even from the visual, record. The most famous case is the classic picture of Lenin addressing a crowd, in which two other faces were previously visible by the rostrum: Trotsky and Kamenev. In the picture as it has appeared in Russia for the last fifty years these have been eliminated. There are pictures of delegates to party congresses, in which, for later versions, previously existing faces have been blurred into other people's greatcoats. There is, too, a celebrated photograph of Stalin in exile with a handful of other revolutionaries; in the earlier version Kamenev is on his left, in the later he has become part of a tree.

The tradition continues. There are two instances of otherwise identical photographs of groups of Soviet cosmonauts appearing in different versions; in each case the later one showing no sign of one of those present in the earlier. In one, the figure is now merged with a doorpost; in the other, with the wall of an aeroplane. Their offence and fate is unknown.

Winston Smith's memory of the presence of Jones, Aaronson, and Rutherford in New York, when it is alleged at their trial that they had flown to Eurasia to conspire with the enemy, is matched by the moderate leader Abramovich's presence at the Hague when he was allegedly conspiring in Moscow – and even more closely by the Communist veteran Pyatakov's mythical flight to Oslo to conspire with Trotsky.

Above all, Orwell takes the central point – that the accused in the Moscow Trials were required not merely to confess to their imaginary criminal acts, but to *repent*, to admit that Stalin was right and that they themselves were degenerate scum. As to the mental state of the victims, the Czechoslovak communist Evzen Loebl, one of the three accused not executed after the 1952 Slansky Trial in Prague, describes the effect on him of the long interrogation process, even when, after confession, he had been allowed adequate food and rest: 'I was quite a normal person – only I was no longer a person.'

As has been pointed out by Soviet dissidents, the Gestapo tortured people to find out their resistance or other secrets, and had no further aim, except that of general terror. The Nazis, though responsible for the most frightful mass slaughter, imposed a terror with characteristics different from those of the Soviet Union or *Nineteen Eighty-Four*. It is true that the Hitler regime was in power a comparatively short time, had not seriously attacked a number of fairly autonomous groupings like the churches and the Officers' Corps, had not gone so far into totalism as had been possible in Russia. And it is quite plausible that a victorious Nazism might have developed that same insistence on brainwashing and full control of the victim's, or citizen's, mind as was implicit in Stalinism. But at any rate, it was not the model here for Orwell.

Even as to *facecrime*, an authoritative instruction issued in Moscow about this time runs:

> One must not content oneself with merely paying attention to *what* is being said for that may well be in complete harmony with the Party programme. One must pay attention also to the *manner* – to the sincerity, for example, with which a school-mistress recites a poem the authorities regard as doubtful, or the pleasure revealed by a critic who goes into detail about a play he professes to condemn. (*Oktyabr*, No. 2, 1949)

Again, in the realm of literature proper, when Orwell writes of how it was necessary to 'produce garbled versions – definitive texts they were called' of poems which had become politically objectionable, but which it was not wished to suppress entirely, he is describing a purely Soviet phenomenon. Modern work by unpersons, of course, simply disappeared. But such things as traditional folk epics posed more of a problem. In 1940 the Kalmyk national epic *Dzhangar* was found to be 'imbued with religious and reactionary content' and ordered to be 'carefully purged,' while its heroes were also transferred to a new epic, *Yorel*, in which they assist Stalin to 'build the land of eternal youth.' The Kirgiz epic *Manas* was ordered 'expurgation' in 1952, but when the new 'composite version' was ready in 1956 – after Stalin's death – while it was accepted that it was now free of mysticism, nationalism, and so on, idealization of the feudal past still seeped through, and further action was recommended.

The 'Spies' are a not very farfetched caricature of the Komsomol and its still younger equivalent, the Pioneers. S. Pavlov, the First Secretary of the Young Communist League in the Khrushchev interlude, told the November 1962 Plenum of the Party Central Committee that under Stalin 'the very first task of all Komsomol work was the necessity to seek out and recognize the enemy, who then had to be removed forcibly, by methods of economic pressure, organizational-political isolation, and methods of physical destruction.' More specifically, Orwell would certainly have known of the case of Pavlik Morozov, a fourteen-year-old Pioneer who denounced his father for 'hoarding' grain, and was himself killed by villagers. He became, and remains, a Soviet hero – the Palace of Culture of the Red Pioneers in Moscow was named after him, and even in the Khrushchev period *Komsomolskaya Pravda*, official organ of the Party youth, told of 'the sacred and dear' Pavlik Morozov Museum in his own village: 'In this timbered house was held the court at which Pavlik unmasked his father.' Nor was he a lone figure. In his speech marking the twentieth anniversary of the secret police, Mikoyan went out of his way to praise two other children who had turned in their relations, and these were representative of tens of thousands enrolled to report on the peasantry.

The public hangings of *Nineteen Eighty-Four* seem to have been founded on that of junior German war criminals in Kiev: Orwell had objected strongly to the British left-wing press 'gloating' over it. In fact this was almost a lone episode, though we may perhaps see a proleptic point in the fact that Stalin seems to have planned a public execution of the unfortunate doctors of the 'doctors' plot' in 1953 – from which they were saved by his death.

The sudden switch of alliances in the middle of a party orator's speech is modeled on the circumstances of the Nazi-Soviet pact, when some editions of communist newspapers of the same day accused the Germans of war-mongering in the afternoon, and celebrated them as friends in the evening.

Doublethink is virtually a translation of the Russian *dvoeverye*. Of dozens of examples which might be given, the most obvious is Soviet elections. *Vybor* (election) in Russian as in English means 'choice.' The ballot forms contain elaborate instructions on crossing out all but one name. But there never is more than one name . . . Or again, 'concentration camp' was changed in Stalin's time, as the camps got more deadly, to 'corrective labour camp': 'joycamp' takes the process further still.

When it comes to the *Nineteen Eighty-Four* fetishism of the Party as such, as early as 1929, Pyatakov (to be a major victim of one of Stalin's confession trials) was saying that he 'would be ready to believe that black was white, and white was black, if the Party required it. In order to become one with his great Party, he would fuse with it, abandon his own personality, so that there was no particle left inside him which was not as one with the Party.'

As to the general atmosphere, the writer Isaak Babel had said, 'Today a man can only talk freely with his wife – at night, with the blankets pulled over his head' – precautions which were inadequate to save Babel himself from arrest and death.

We should note, however, that the scale of arrests and terror in *Nineteen Eighty-Four* is in one sense a reflection not of the height of the *Yezhovshchina* – the super-terror of 1937–38 – but rather of the level maintained under successful Stalinism, around 1950, when all the machinery of repression was working smoothly, and a comparatively limited number of arrests was adequate to keep the pressure up on the population.

Orwell had never been to a totalitarian country. It is true that his time in Catalonia had given him a direct and priceless experience of Communist lies and terror during the struggle for power, but the final product he could only gather through his ability to use the eyes of others. A Balkan Communist once said to the present writer that Orwell's intuitive genius was demonstrated, as against earlier anti-utopian writers, by his not making his totalitarian state a machinery of soulless efficiency, but on the contrary, just like the real USSR, a place where you can't get razor blades and the lifts do not work. In this as in other matters, Orwell knew by some instinct or by sufficient sense and experience what the true picture was and what the fake, among the many reports emerging from Moscow – a rare gift.

Above all, Orwell had the imagination to understand that there are people who would find it perfectly satisfactory to see the future in terms of 'a boot stamping on a human face – forever.' The parochial notion that everyone is much the same, that we all dislike war or terror, is absent from his view of history – as well it might be in the twentieth century. He saw that Stalin, like Tamerlane or Jenghiz Khan, was not in the least put out by the idea of the killing of millions. He knew that there have been cultures where torture was commonplace. That is to say, he knew that there are people, now as in earlier ages, who are not the product of the moral principles to which he himself gave assent.

Even today, the greatest hurdle to understanding the Soviet Union or similar regimes is the unthinking and inexplicit assumption that the basic motivations of the Soviet leaders differ little from our own. It was an advantage to Orwell that he knew nothing of one sort of 'political science' – a supposed discipline which to this day, by concentrating on forms and structures, removes the essence of a given polity from active consideration. It is a notable fact that Orwell, like Koestler, was a novelist and journalist, and that in general, the record of such writers is far better than that of many 'serious' students. Perhaps the reason is that to understand the Stalin regime took an effort not only of the intellect, but also of the imagination.

Thus in spite of its clearly established Stalinist background, it is sometimes said that *Nineteen Eighty-Four* is intended to satirize not the Stalinist possibility in particular, but 'tendencies to totalitarianism' in all societies. In the sense that its intention is to satirize tendencies to Stalinism, or to the excusing of Stalinism, in all societies, this is true. But, as we have shown, it is not true in the sense that Orwell was writing about some supposed tendency for all societies to become totalitarian, or was making some general attack on Stalinist and non-Stalinist attitudes alike.

Orwell's stature is such that people try to recruit him for their own beliefs. 'What would Orwell think of' some more recent phenomenon is a common distraction. On the whole this matters little. But when it is perverted by writers of forewords or afterwords to Orwell's books, as in the latest Signet edition of *Nineteen Eighty-Four*, it is a particularly presumptuous – but also misleading – attempt to preempt Orwell's attitudes, providing examples calling for special attention.

Walter Cronkite, in a vapid introduction, suggests (quite contrary to the economic lessons of *Nineteen Eighty-Four*) that 'greater efficiency, ease and security may come at a substantial price in freedom' whereas, of course, Orwell saw that totalitarianism destroys efficiency, ease and security together with liberty, and *because* of the destruction of liberty. Cronkite even gives Khomeini as a typification of Big Brother. But no, the mere existence of an age-old style of tyranny and terror was not Orwell's target, but rather a specific and modern phenomenon of which he had taken the measure.

Again, Eric Fromm, in his Afterword, gives as a supposed instance of doublethink the claim that nations may 'prepare for war in order to preserve peace.' Now, this proposition may be fallacious, but it is in no way self-contradictory. More important in our context, Orwell several times made it clear that he believed it to be true. And more generally, to apply Orwell's highly specific totalitarian terror-falsification concepts to assorted Western notions is to dilute, indeed to stultify, Orwell's point. Fromm is entitled to his views: he is not entitled to give them a spurious prestige by bringing in Orwell to validate them. Above all, this sort of thing distorts Orwell's view of the totalist terror state as something distinct and different from our own imperfect societies – indeed, something to be resisted at all costs.

Orwell hated the distortion of truth, the mental cheapening to be found in the Western press and film. (It is true that he was also able to condemn his much loathed movie moguls for active pro-Stalinist propaganda, as in the Hollywood film *Mission to Moscow* based on Joseph Davies's book of that title.) But for him a partisan exaggeration or oversimplification was not just a lesser offense, but a lesser category of offence, than the complete substitution of fiction for fact and the total suppression of rival accounts. *Nineteen Eighty-Four* distinguishes flatly between the two. The newspapers and history books of the past were 'coloured and biased,' yet, 'falsification of the kind that is practiced today would have been impossible.'

Of course all views, even when rational in themselves, are accompanied by a penumbra of angled and simplified phrases to some degree distorting or caricaturing reality in favour of the given opinion. Orwell, though himself offending as often as the rest of us, was in principle against such phraseology and concerned to make people avoid it in the interests of clean thinking. However, when he writes in 1946, 'The connection between totalitarian habits of thought and the corruption of language is an important subject and has not been sufficiently studied,' he goes on to give examples of this not from Catholics or Conservatives, with the idea that such linguistic practice makes Catholicism or Conservativism more totalitarian each time it is performed; his examples are solely from admirers of the Soviet Union, writing abjectly and above all *badly* on their own favourite subject. What he is clearly seeking to show is less that any sort of misuse of language produces totalitarianism than that totalitarian habits of thought need a jargoneering and confusing dialect to maintain themselves.

Why did *Nineteen Eighty-Four*, with all its faults, have the feeling of reality? Because in some fundamental sense everyone knew (even if in some cases it was only a repressed consciousness) of the actualities of Stalinism. Because, on the other side of the equation, Orwell carried conviction through his clear and confident understanding of Stalinist phenomena.

When Orwell wrote, his main concern, as he makes clear time and again, was less to attack the Stalin regime as such than to combat a whole herd of intellectual quislings at home; to expose the delusions of intellectuals. He remarks, in his 1947 Introduction to the Ukrainian edition of *Animal Farm*, 'I would not have condemned Stalin and his associates merely for their barbaric and undemocratic methods. . . . But on the other hand it was of the utmost importance that people in Western Europe should see the Soviet regime for what it really was,' his aim being 'the destruction of the Soviet myth' in Western minds.

One of the motives of Western pro-Stalinists, Orwell suggests, was hatred of their own country; another, the wish for a society in which the intellectual had at last got his hands on the whip.

It is precisely Orwell's view that there is no moral symmetry between the West and the Communist world, and that, on the contrary, the West needs to defend itself against a fearful political threat, but in particular against its own misrepresentations and misunderstanding of this threat. What he found most contemptible, though also most characteristic, was the fact that opposition to the Marxist-Leninist regimes was always represented as 'insane or activated by the worst motives' and never discussed on its merits as a reasoned opinion based on facts.

Arthur Koestler wrote of 'the thousands of painters and writers and doctors and lawyers and debutantes chanting a diluted version of the Stalinist line.' After a generation of hard work by those who have sought out and presented the real facts of the USSR in Stalin's time, delusions about it have at last almost wholly dissipated. But human nature, the will to be deceived, does not change, and it will be surprising if there are not many Western intellectuals who in twenty or thirty years will in turn – one trusts not too late – have to abandon delusions about similar regimes, whose legitimization is, as ever, merely their similar hostility to the West, and their ability to project similar misapprehension about their real acts and aspirations. If the meaning of the book is distorted to deal with other targets, however deserving, Orwell's intent is lost.

1984

Snow on Their Boots

To Soviet writers, more than almost any others, has fallen the task
of preserving and forwarding the non-totalitarian values: and it is
both intellectually and morally important that the Western consciousness be properly apprised of this. In the gloom of the Brezhnev era,
literature – even published literature – still lives in Russia: but it is
fighting for its life. All the more reason that a distorted picture of it
should not be offered to the outside world. Those who present it,
then, have an important responsibility: they do not always fulfill it
satisfactorily. For example we have *Stories from Modern Russia*, edited
by C. P. Snow and Pamela Hansford Johnson, a collection of modern
Soviet work. It is poor, unrepresentative, and in the main very dull.
The dullness is quite unnecessary. Any Soviet reader concerned with
the reputation of his country's literature – its reputation as literature,
that is, not as political piety – must shudder at the thought of this stuff
being put before American and British audiences as representative of
what is published in modern-day Russia.

Even politically it does the Russians a bad service. For it is bound
to give the impression that the regime grants even less freedom of
expression to its writers than it actually does. The only person one
can think of it satisfying is the hard line Aleksei Surkov, whom the
editors evidently admire. (They write, 'the front line soldiers in their
dug-outs sang the war poems of Surkov'. Perhaps some of them
did, but the astonishing phenomenon of the War was the immense
circulation in manuscript of poems by poets: Boris Pasternak, for
example).

The phrase 'cold war' occurs frequently in the introduction. It
means drawing attention to any facts, or expressing any opinions,
unpalatable to the Soviet leadership. The Snows assure us that it is
wicked to look at Soviet literature with any political considerations

in mind, since we would not do so with literature of other cultures. This really is fantastic impudence! Soviet literature, as we are told day in and day out by Russian politicians, cultural bureaucrats and orthodox writers, is (or should be) 'a weapon for Communism'.

In a country where a good deal remains unpublished for political reasons, it is impossible to look at what *is* published without some consideration of what makes it acceptable. Again, the fact that when the cultural bureaucrats relax a little, a literature of moderately outspoken revolt immediately starts getting published is something to which one cannot simply blind oneself. But of course, the Snows do not mean what they say. They would have us accept Russian literature as indicating the hearty adherence of Soviet writers to the Soviet Establishment. A political message is all right, you see, as long as it is on your side.

The Snows represent attention to unorthodox literature as a search for a mood opposed to 'Communism'. That is not the point; it is not the social system that the humanist writers object to; it is the bureaucracy and the lack of freedom of expression. The Hungarian writers who led the original revolt against Matyas Rakosi were mostly Communists, too.

For the editors, Soviet literature is produced by writers 'devoted to' their country's political system, and in spite of disputes among themselves, in general accord with the Party and with each other. Though the older ones have lived through difficult history and had bad times, 'they were always respected by their colleagues, even in the middle of bitter disagreement'. And that is all the Snows have to say about the troubles of literary men in a country where large numbers perished in labour camps or before firing squads, or committed suicide; where, as this book came out, Olga Ivinskaya, the literary executor of the country's greatest writer, himself lately dead in disgrace, was in jail for attempting to secure the publication abroad of his surviving works.

Not that we should transfer to most of the writers in this collection any blame for the editors' attitudes. Most of them, if less than their colleagues who are not represented in the book, have shown signs of wanting more liberty. The Snows (who find it possible to maintain that Russian writers can reproach English ones with 'being too willing to distort the truth for the sake of the drama') are free agents: more shame to them. The writers, for obvious reasons, are not.

The veteran Konstantin Paustovsky was always a moderate and modest author. It is unpleasant to find Snow representing him, among the others, as a devoted adherent of the *apparat*. Paustovsky, who appeared at Pasternak's funeral with Olga Ivinskaya on his arm, spoke up bravely when he could. In 1956 he strongly attacked the bureaucrats who, as he put it, had murdered Vsevolod Meierhold and Isaac Babel and still ruled the country, ignoring culture and spending their time cracking anti-Semitic jokes. He later wrote what was long described as 'Paustovsky's unfortunate article', which put the theme of intellectual liberty in less provocative, but evidently still provocative, terms.

The introduction is worse than the selection. The editors have sought stuff to suit their theme, but fortunately they have sometimes misunderstood the material. Vladimir Tendryakov is represented not by his most celebrated and most moving story, 'Three, Seven, Ace', but by the much less striking 'Potholes'. Even here he describes a situation which does not fit properly into the official picture. But, when he concludes that a character is a 'bureaucrat turned murderer', the Snows hasten to point out that the Government also attacks bureaucracy, and that Tendryakov thus associates himself enthusi-astically with official policy.

Naturally, in a published piece, Soviet writers do not say overtly, 'and that means you too, Comrade Minister'. But there is a big distinction between attacks on bureaucracy of the type officially approved and those which are just barely got away with, as can be seen by comparing, say, Vsevolod Kochetov's unreadable hack novels and Vladimir Dudintsev's much censured *Not By Bread Alone*. The official attacks are part formality, part demagogy. The literary attacks are (and are heartily denounced as) implicit assaults on the whole bureaucratic set-up.

It is not that Tendryakov is the most critical of the writers, nor does he express any hostility to communism as such. But it is evident to both factions in the dispute that his writing by its mere humanism induces political 'confusion'. *Pravda* does not often intervene directly against individual writers, but it found it necessary to produce an article on 'Three, Seven, Ace' under the heading, 'Who is being accused'?

There are numbers of other writers who are quite as skilled and far fresher than most of the Snows' favourites. One thinks of N. I. Dubov, F. A. Voronin, Yury Nagibin, Victor Nekrassov and Yury Kazakov (greatly praised by Paustovsky, incidentally) whose absence is an undoubted blemish on any view whatever. But not for the Snows, except marginally, the literature of the Thaw. Burintern soli-darity forbids.

The editors rightly remark that the War was a terrific Russian experience and that Russian losses were incomparably greater than our own. Yet the census figures published in 1959 show a population deficit of males even higher in the age groups that were adult in the thirties than among the young men who were in their twenties in the War. The purges, even physically, were thus at least as humanly destructive as the War itself. Psychologically, they were much worse.

As a character says in *Doctor Zhivago*, the War with all its horrors came as a blessing compared with the 'reign of the lie' which preceded it (and which of course succeeded it, too). A Soviet critic wrote of the purges, during the 1956–57 Thaw, 'Many are aware of this theme much more strongly than any other theme that has blossomed in the poetry and prose created by the reality of forty years of Soviet life'. Nothing about that here; nor, even on the War, the truly moving stories like Nekrasov's 'The Second Night': bad for morale.

This sort of thing is simply an insensitive insult not just to common humanity but also to Soviet literature; an attitude it would be charitable to call obtuse. Snow has consciously aligned himself not only with the British establishment, which is bad enough, but with the worst foreign one he could turn up. One is reminded of the controversy between Lord Acton and Bishop Creighton, when the Anglican was inclined to excuse Innocent III's persecutions on administrative grounds, while the Catholic condemned them absolutely for reasons of inhumanity. Each of these solidarities – the bureaucratic and the humanist – in fact transcend mere political and religious allegiance. On any barricade I can think of, there is many a communist I should prefer to have on my side than Snow.

1961

A General View

The view of modern Russian literature commonly held in the West is bound to be an incomplete one. We all know that the great periods of Russian literature before the Revolution, with Pushkin and Lermontov, Tolstoy and Dostoevsky, Turgenev and Chekhov, have not been equalled in Soviet times. We are all aware of the contemptible cruelty with which the cultural bureaucracy wages its feud against independence of mind. We are inclined to underestimate the vigorous writing which, though spurned, attacked and occasionally silenced for years at a time, has nevertheless been a persistent and important current in Russian life. As Walter Laqueur and his contributors to *Soviet Literature Yesterday and Today* show, Soviet culture may have been hobbled, bridled and blinkered by the apparatchik, but it remains a fine animal, with enormous capabilities.

Even Khrushchev, in a key speech to the writers in July 1961, put horribly forthrightly the view that 'The development of literature . . . proceeds plan-wise as directed by the party', condemning writers who had, in 1956, 'got out of step'. This view is short-sighted even on its own showing. Literature that is in any conceivable sense truly helpful to society has never been produced under the guidance of political leaders. Not even literature presenting their own politics in a creditable light could ever emerge that way. Moreover, none of this nonsense is a necessary concomitant of Soviet-type society as such. And two essays in this collection, 'The origins of literary control', by Ernest J. Simmons, and 'Pilnyak and Zamyatin', by Max Hayward (who fittingly quotes Gorky's bold rebuke to the persecutors which doubtless postponed Pilnyak's arrest and death), remind us how different things were in the twenties. The extreme political pretensions are among the stigmata of Stalinism, of the control of party and state by the omnicompetent bureaucrat. It is significant that

Khrushchev, in the speech quoted above, had to censure *party* branches among the intelligentsia. One of the most depressing things
about the official attitude is that literature, like every other field,
becomes a 'front', on which a political 'struggle' is always taking
place. We get such *niaiseries* as the following (on the Dostoevsky
jubilee), quoted here by D. L. Fangar in his essay 'Dostoevsky today':

> Soviet literary scholarship made a significant contribution to the cause of
> a genuinely scientific study of Dostoevsky's work, and at the same time
> it has successfully won the battle against reaction in this area of culture.
> If before the jubilee, the reactionary press in the West felt itself master
> of the situation, set the tone, and obliged the Soviet press to take a
> defensive position, *after* the jubilee Soviet literary scholarship became
> dominant, carrying on an active, aggressive struggle.

And yet, at the same time, excellent criticism is being written,
sound scholarship is being pursued, and – even more surprising – a
certain amount of fresh and interesting fiction and poetry is being
published. All this does not spring from nothing. Independent traditions were maintained until quite recent times by other of the older
writers than Pasternak. Zoshchenko, who was rightly popular in this
country for his short stories, was considerably more than a shock
humourist. In his longer work, a tragic levity carried the true and
deep feelings of traditional masculine humanism before the often
puzzled censors. Hugh McLean writes of Zoshchenko's 'unfinished'
novel *Before Sunrise*. The book is only unfinished in the sense that a
mere two instalments appeared before it came in for public denunciation. And that is another reason for the queer appearance Soviet
writing has long presented. Missing work, much of it in the files of
the KGB, is probably at least as important as what we have been
allowed to see.

The decline in published Soviet humour has, naturally enough,
been notable. But, as Maurice Friedberg points out in 'A note on
Soviet satire', the one genre in which it flourishes is the newspaper
feuilleton. A Soviet critic explains this as being due to the fact that
these squibs about real events are taken to be merely particular:
presented as short stories, they would be regarded as generalizations
slandering Soviet reality. The *feuilletons* are often extremely lively.
But again the important point is that they show continued potentialities: as with the rest of Soviet writing, the fact that the great moods
of literature are not published does not mean that they are extinct.

Two considerations have influenced Soviet politicians in their occasional comparatively liberal interpretation of a narrow view. In the

first place, the insistence on a rigid orthodoxy led to works recognizable even to the politicians themselves as particularly worthless. The more important point is that the Soviet literary world has been the one element in Russia which it was impossible completely to assimilate to the political culture. The literary standards, even of the most communist-minded of the genuine writers, were persistent, and evaded party discipline. Frequent attacks took place on the solidarity of a 'public opinion' associated with literary circles in Moscow. It is true that the party finds it possible to promote and extol hacks like Surkov, but it is beyond its power to get him accepted by the literary world.

Khrushchev's remarks were crude. But we need not see in them only a doctrinaire notion of how to produce a Soviet literature. He clearly realized something else: that the humanist tradition in Russian literature, the search for candour and for charity which has been found in writers of all opinions since it emerged in the works of the great novelists of the nineteenth century, is a rival to the party's view. When Khrushchev said in 1957 that his finger would not tremble on the trigger if it became necessary to handle the writers the hard way, he was in a sense facing up to a real threat. But if Stalin himself was unable to eradicate it, it is one which is ineradicable. Herbert E. Bowman writes here (of Pasternak), 'no sharper judgment of political realities is made than by the observer who insists on remaining human'. That is what the Soviet writers, communist and non-communist, have mostly done. The preservation of such a tradition is no small thing, and may in the long run do much to save Russia, and the world, from a barren cul-de-sac. Meanwhile Soviet literature, even with many of its best branches lopped and pruned, is worth watching for its own sake – more so than any other contemporary foreign writing.

1958

Solzhenitsyn and the World

August 1914 is only part of a larger work and thus perhaps not very susceptible to a ready judgement; so it may be more important at this point to consider what Solzhenitsyn feels himself to be doing.

He has been on record as to these intentions in his Nobel Prize speech. First of all he says of literature that it is 'the living memory of a nation' preserved from one generation to another. 'It nurses and preserves the nation's lost history in a form which is not susceptible to distortion and slander.' And it is true that, with all the extravagant falsification of history which has marked the Soviet period, past literature has not been rewritten to any significant extent. *War and Peace* has remained untouched.

More broadly, a nation's literature constitutes, particularly in an autocratic state, an alternative set of principles. And it seems quite clear that, if any single factor can be given the credit for preventing the total and irrevocable atomization and Stalinization of Russia, it is the voices of the Turgenev and Chekhov, of Dostoevsky and Tolstoy, which were never totally suppressed.

So much for Solzhenitsyn's aims as regards his own countrymen. But he recognizes a task of yet broader scope. In the modern age (he argues in the Nobel speech), 'World literature can transmit the concentrated experience of one land to another in such a way that we shall stop seeing double . . . that the different scales of value shall coincide.' In fact, he sees his work and all great literature as being essentially a powerful weapon against ignorance, both at home and in the other countries and cultures of the world.

He is frank, even blunt, about the sort of ignorance, the sort of double standard, he means to combat in the West; as when he writes:

What, according to one scale, appears from afar off as enviable flourishing freedom, according to another scale, near at hand, is perceived as vexatious constraint, calling for the overturning of buses. What, in one area, could only be dreamed of as unattainable prosperity, in another area gives rise to indignation and is considered extreme exploitation demanding an immediate strike.

Again, it is quite clear what he is talking about when he writes:

There are different scales for punishment and for crime. According to one scale, a month's imprisonment, or banishment to the country, or to a so-called 'punishment cell', where they feed you with white bread rolls and milk, shocks the imagination and fills the columns of the newspapers with anger. According to another scale, people find acceptable and forgivable prison terms of 25 years, dungeons where there is ice on the wall but where they strip you to your underwear, lunatic asylums for the sane, and the shooting on the frontier of countless people who won't see reason and who keep running away, one doesn't know where or why.

Any serious observer of the Western press, particularly the 'liberal' press, must have noted that it affects to base its judgement of foreign countries not on openly politicized criteria but on objective standards of humaneness, but that in fact this becomes a competition in atrocity propaganda. It is not the extent of human suffering in a given state which counts so much as what the publicity machines of its opponents can make of it. In *The First Circle* Solzhenitsyn already gave us an example in a comparison of Russian and Greek prisons. The remarks quoted above generalize all this; and he also complains, for example, of 'the venal prejudice of the majority' of the members of the United Nations, which guard the liberty of some peoples and not of others.

He sees a comparable form of dangerous and unethical ignorance among the Western 'young': 'Young people, at an age when the only experience they have is sexual, at an age when they have no years of personal suffering and personal comprehension to draw on, young people are enthusiastically repeating the discredited platitudes of our Russian nineteenth century, and they think they have come up with something novel.' But he also notes their admirers among the old: 'They try to ingratiate themselves with the young – anything so as not to look "conservative". And this is yet another Russian phenomenon of nineteenth century origin: Dostoevsky called it "being in bondage to advanced notions".' And the writer too may be infected: 'If his young compatriots blithely proclaim depravity's superiority to modest toil, if they succumb to drugs or seize hostages, then the stench of it mingles with the writer's breath.'

In particular, he refers to the cult of revolutionary violence. His objection to it is not simply to the 'superficiality' (as he puts it) of the ideas of some of the Western young who feel all they need to do is to throw out their current rulers, 'and the next lot – that's us! – We'll be just and understanding once we've laid aside our bombs and guns. But of course they won't!' More importantly, he notes that, while, at the beginning, violence 'acts openly and is even proud of itself', once established, it 'cannot survive in isolation: it is inevitably bound up with the lie . . . anyone who has once proclaimed that violence is his method is inevitably forced to choose the lie as his principle.'

In the course of a controversy in the *Times Literary Supplement* over Solzhenitsyn's novels some correspondents urged that in judging them political considerations should be put out of one's mind. But, of course, in his earlier work the political issues are introduced far less by Solzhenitsyn, or by his Western and other admirers, than by the Soviet authorities themselves – and, indeed, by the mere nature of the Soviet system. If, for example, the description in *The First Circle* of a 'scientific prison' in Stalin's time was banned from publication, then it is those who banned it who have made the issue an immediate political, rather than a merely historical, one.

It is in a similar sense that his complaints on the persecution of Christianity are political. His 'Lenten Letter' condemns the Patriarch for speaking in favour of bringing up children as orthodox Christians in the Russian community abroad, while failing to insist on the same thing in Russia itself. In it he makes such comments as 'we have to hand over our defenceless children not into neutral hands but into the domain of atheist propaganda of the most primitive and dishonest kind.' He actually categorizes the basis of the moral upbringing given to Soviet children as 'the abyss between the propagandist's notebook and the criminal code'. And he even adds, 'Half a century of the past has already been lost, and I am not talking about trying to save the present. But how are we to save the *future* of our country?'

Of course this is political. But it is so because the CPSU has made it so. Similarly, Solzhenitsyn's complaints of Western self-delusion imply criticism of certain political positions. But, as always, his view is that if truth were substituted for glib formulae, if minor local grievances were seen against the actual condition of the rest of humankind and the actual workings of other social systems, then all would be well. The province of literature is not to argue, but to convey these realities, to bridge the chasm of falsehood and ignorance: in fact, to carry the truth. This is, indeed, a literary aim often spoken of, but it will be seen that Solzhenitsyn gives it a special scope.

In all this, of course, Solzhenitsyn invites the comparison often made with Tolstoy. But Solzhenitsyn's view of history is of course different, and consciously so. Indeed, his General Blagoveshchensky is shown as coming to grief through an acceptance of Tolstoy's notion about Kutuzov, that a historical mystique is itself more powerful than the wills of individuals, so that the true leader, in war as in peace, need only relax and let events take their course, that he need only fit into the grain of a historical pattern. Against this (and contrary, too, to the mystical strain in *Doctor Zhivago*), Solzhenitsyn strongly asserts the view of history being to a considerable extent the province of accident, and of the wills of individuals applied at crucial points. As against Tolstoy, indeed, Solzhenitsyn can set the experience of the past half-century. Where Tolstoy's Man of Will (Napoleon) is defeated, and (at least it could be plausibly argued) is defeated precisely through conflicting with the natural trends, Solzhenitsyn's (Lenin and Stalin) were able to impose their wills against those trends.

There is one other notable difference from *War and Peace*. Solzhenitsyn's War is far larger, his Peace minuscule. And this is reflected, if not in an absence of, at least in a far lesser role for, women. The bulk of Solzhenitsyn's work, indeed, has this characteristic. *One Day in the Life of Ivan Denisovich* is set in a totally womanless environment. This is not the case in *The Cancer Ward* or *The First Circle*, let alone in *Matryona's Home*, but in the first two at least, although the women's role is touching, sensitive and generally necessary, it is still a largely subordinate one, especially compared with such figures as Tolstoy's Natasha. And so it has actually been in history, or in history's main events – particularly its central concentrations of war and revolution, which are Solzhenitsyn's focus. For, even more than in *War and Peace*, the hero of *August 1914* is in a sense history itself, or more specifically is Russia, the Russia of this century expressed in and including the individuals of the narrative.

As against Tolstoy's and Pasternak's, the Solzhenitsyn attitude to history is one which is, on the whole, shared by most historians. There are, indeed, many people, even if few historians, who have a taste for the idea of history as a single vast process which can be subsumed under some grand formula. They tend to feel that a view of history in which accident plays as important a role as Solzhenitsyn implies is somehow a narrower and meaner outlook. But, of course, Solzhenitsyn sees – perhaps more clearly for want of theoretical spectacles – the great sweeps of feeling, the tides and the deeps of national existence, as much as anyone.

And, in fact, anyone who has studied this century's Russian history must be struck time and again by the extravagantly decisive role played by the merest accident. The only generalized view I have ever heard applied to it with even superficial plausibility is that Russia is for some reason doomed always to have the worst luck possible in any given circumstances. (As Nadezhda Mandelshtam puts it, 'In Russia every path always leads to disaster.') The tsarevich's haemophilia; the accidents of Lenin's character; his survival till after the 10th Congress; his early death; the survival of Stalin after 1945 . . . at almost every point the worse of the two possibilities prevails.

August 1914 seems above all intended to demonstrate the potentialities and the virtues – and the weaknesses – of a people seen on the eve of its descent into a wilderness. We find in it – and this seems essential to Solzhenitsyn's position, as to the position of all humanism in Russia – both the new Western liberal element and the old traditional Christian element of Russia facing their crisis before a truly successful amalgam had been attained. Both elements, as Solzhenitsyn has frequently demonstrated elsewhere, were to be crushed by the communist regime, whose harsh and shallow ethos was a compound of a different kind, formed from the archaic brutality of Russia and the narrow theoretical-terrorist tradition of the West.

More broadly, what may be seen in the whole of Solzhenitsyn's work, concentrated out of the experience of millions of his compatriots, is an entirely new historical phenomenon – a liberalism of the catacombs. For this is the first time that, over a long historical period, modern humanist ideas which had already emerged in a national literature and an intelligentsia, have been crushed and repudiated. The difference in tone between Solzhenitsyn's Russian attitudes and our own is not so much one of essence, as a matter of this experience which he and his have faced and we and ours have not. On the one hand, he is harder, more hammered and tempered, than the writers of the West; on the other, his liberalism has been purged of illusion – the comfortable fat has been sweated off it.

Judgements on *August 1914* in the West have been varied. In the end this seems to boil down to a matter of the predilections of critics. The taste for the great set-piece historical novel has rather gone out in many Western circles. Most objections to it are in effect that it is not 'psychological' in the sense that its highly individual individuals are all the same seen as part of a great sweep of public events; its 'intellectuals' are not shown as being outside, apart from, superior to and beneficially influencing those events.

It may be argued that the modern Western literary sensibility has narrowed the traditional scope of literature – in which in the old days history, philosophy, biography, were as highly regarded as (often more highly regarded than) the novel, which is now for some reason rated as specifically 'creative' in a sense which reduces the others to the second level. From this, it to some extent appeared to follow that a novel which is itself part history is of a lower or less interesting type. This is illogical; but literary tastes and fashions are not matters of logic. In my view we are likely to find, in the long run, that Solzhenitsyn's work will mark a change from the extremes of subjectivity and of obliquity into which much of our literature has been directed at the expense of the larger scope of the strong mind and the deep heart.

1973

Vasily Grossman

Grossman's *Life and Fate* is one of a handful of works in our time which should be seen above all, and apart from any other qualities, as testimony. What is attested is the nature, in the profoundest sense, of National Socialism and Communism, locked in decisive battle around Stalingrad as the events of the book take place. Grossman's standing and qualifications in the task of presenting this factual and moral record are unique.

Grossman, born in the then great Jewish centre of Berdichev in the Ukraine, was only in his middle teens at the end of the many-sided Civil War, in which (as he tells us in his *In the Town of Berdichev*) he saw the place change hands at least fourteen times. In 1933 he started his career as a writer, orthodox as to both form and content. From 1941 he was a war correspondent for the Soviet Army paper *Krasnaya Zvezda*, and was present at Stalingrad and later battles. He was one of the first to see the Nazi death camps, in which his own mother perished; and he then published a terrible documentary *The Hell of Treblinka*, one of the first writings on the Holocaust. He was (with Ilya Ehrenburg) joint editor of the Soviet section of the *Black Book* on Nazi atrocities – which was never published in the Soviet Union.

He was in trouble in the 1946 literary repression, but his huge novel of the War – *For a Just Cause* – was treated as a Soviet *War and Peace*. In 1953, however, he came under violent attack, and there is little doubt that he would have been a victim of the new anti-Semitic purge which had already claimed dozens of lives of Jewish writers, had Stalin not died just in time to save him. In the 'thaw' of the immediate post-Stalin years he was well regarded. It was then that he wrote *Life and Fate*, a sequel to *For a Just Cause*, covering a later period of the war, in particular the Battle of Stalingrad. But everything has changed. *For a Just Cause* was thoroughly orthodox; *Life and Fate*, remaining totally anti-Nazi, represents the Soviet system itself as in the same mould and spirit.

The mere adventures of the manuscript are themselves highly illuminating. It was finished in 1960, submitted for publication and rejected as anti-Soviet. All known copies were confiscated by the KGB – even used carbons and typewriter ribbons. Grossman himself, when he died in 1964 in his late fifties, deeply depressed, in poverty and pain, seems to have believed that no copy existed. He had therefore hurriedly completed his shorter *Forever Flowing*, which lacks the vast architectonic of *Life and Fate*, but which is often deeply effective: in particular, its chapter on the slaughter of the peasantry in 1930–3 is perhaps the most full and moving short portrayal of that period ever to appear.

But, unknown to Grossman himself, an almost complete manuscript of *Life and Fate* somehow survived on microfilm, and was later brought out to the West by that remarkable writer Vladimir Voinovich. The briefest skim leaves one astonished that Grossman should have thought it publishable in the USSR, even at the height of the Khrushchev thaw.

Like its orthodox predecessor it is a huge book – more than 150 'chief characters' are listed at the end. A central thread links many of them to the relations and connections of the Shaposhnikov family, and in particular the Jewish physicist Viktor Shtrum. The story ranges through the grinding battleground of Stalingrad, the intrigues in a scientific academy, a prisoner-of-war camp in Germany, the Lubyanka prison, a Soviet labour camp and the Nazi death camps.

Some of his most moving passages, combining power and pathos, are on Jewish families from before the time they are taken from their homes to their actual death in the gas chambers. Grossman rightly insists that the Jewish experience is unique; that the Holocaust, the attempt to destroy an entire people, in camps whose sole rationale and purpose was death, was an unparalleled crime. But he does not stop there.

The Nazis were crude and so easier to understand, and the researchers – including Grossman himself – have stood in the site of Treblinka and made its horrors manifest, while, as he puts it, 'Komi, Salekhand, Norilsk, Kotlas, Magadan, Vorkuta, Kolyma', and so on, are uninvestigated except at long distance.

In an interview in the *New Republic* Primo Levi has given some comparisons between what he knew at first hand about the Nazi death camps, and what he had read about Stalin's labour camps, making much the same basic distinction as Grossman. However, he believes that the 'death of the prisoners was not – even in the darkest years of Stalinism – expressly sought'. True, even the sentence 'without right of correspondence' did not *expressly* mean death; but it was in fact a code word for it. In camps prisoners were often told by officials that they were there to die. Again, the banning in 1938 of fur clothing and felt boots, allowing only wadded jackets and canvas shoes in the coldest climate in the northern hemisphere, was not *expressly* a death order; but it was so in reality and in common sense. (There were indeed death camps proper in the USSR. There seem to have been some, in Novaya Zemlya and elsewhere, from which no one ever returned; and there were execution camps like Serpantinka – but on a far smaller scale than the German, with only tens of thousands killed.)

Levi also believes that Soviet camp guards were less brutal than Nazi ones, because the latter were trained to regard their prisoners as rubbish. There is something in this. But the Soviet establishment under the class enemy principle were almost equally able to regard their prisoners as scum. Grossman himself, than whom no one can have greater standing in the matter, makes the point flatly (in *Forever Flowing*):

> They had sold themselves on the idea that the so-called 'kulaks' were pariahs, untouchables, vermin. The 'kulak' child was loathsome, the young 'kulak' girl was lower than a louse. They looked on the so-called 'kulaks' as cattle, swine, loathsome, repulsive: they had no souls; they stank; they all had venereal diseases; they were enemies of the people and exploited the labour of others. . . . And there was no pity for them. They were not human beings; one had a hard time making out what they were – vermin, evidently.

And again (a character thinks):

> What I said to myself at the time was 'they are not human beings, they are kulaks'. . . . Who thought up this word 'kulaks' anyway? Was it really a term? What torture was meted out to them! In order to massacre them it was necessary to proclaim that kulaks are not human beings. Just as the Germans proclaimed that Jews are not human beings. Thus did Lenin and Stalin proclaim, kulaks are not human beings.

Another difference Levi might have added was that children, or at any rate infants, were not killed in Soviet camps. There are none of the dreadful stories of mothers and babies thrust into gas ovens. But Grossman will not allow too much to be made of this. In *Forever Flowing*, he goes back to the mass infanticide by hunger in the terror-famine of 1933, when, as he puts it, 'The decree required that the peasants of the Ukraine, the Don and the Kuban be put to death by starvation, put to death along with their little children.' He describes this vividly: 'And the peasant children! Have you ever seen the newspaper photographs of the children in the German camps? They were just like that. . . . And by spring they no longer had faces at all. Instead, they had birdlike heads with beaks, or frog heads – thin, wide lips – and some of them resembled fish, mouths open. Not human faces.' He compares this directly with the Jewish children in the gas chambers and comments, 'these were Soviet children and those who were putting them to death were Soviet people.' One of the *Life and Fate* characters is an old party propagandist who, in the early thirties, had written 'that kulaks were burying their grain and refusing to eat, that whole villages – little children, old people and all – were dying simply to spite the state.' (Estimates are that about 2½ to 3 million children died of hunger.)

Because the slaughter of the Jews was unimaginably, uniquely frightful, this does not mean (Grossman implies) that anyone is entitled to dismiss other massacres even if not so total – of the Armenians under the Sultan, the Ukrainians under Stalin. Grossman's complete empathy about 1933 in the Ukraine does not weaken, but rather strengthens, his even more powerful damnation of the Jewish Holocaust.

One gets the impression that even the Holocaust is to some extent fading from the public consciousness; for example, regarding the recent excitement about Mengele, that many Westerners felt it was all a long time ago, and we can hardly remember. Such charity fades quickly when one reads what Mengele (and not only Mengele) did – for example, in the now republished 'In the German Mills of Death' by the Ukrainian nationalist Petro Mirchuk. Ukrainian? Yes, for in addition to the 3 million Jews killed in Auschwitz there were some hundreds of thousands of Ukrainians, Poles, Russians and others, who were hanged, shot, beaten, starved, but who yet realized (as Mirchuk, like Grossman, makes clear) that their chances were far better than those of the Jews.

Grossman's concern, as a novelist of 'realism', is to re-create the events and the tone of the various Soviet (as well as the German) phenomena. The Soviet labour camps, the cells of the Lubyanka, the petty bureaucracy, the mean persecution of all disagreement, the air of suspicion and checking of all officers, scientists and others, with the disgrace and disappearance of innocents whether secretly dissident or thoroughly orthodox, differ from their Nazi equivalents. The savour, the traditions and customs of the two regimes are at variance in many ways. Hitler's are, personally, different from Stalin's. Stalin's anti-Semitism was not based on race-theory. Nor did he ever undertake the extirpation of any complete group, not even the kulaks, of whom about a third survived – and the deported nations of 1943–5 lost only about 40 per cent of their members, while the rest were meant to disappear as cultures, not races.

But the two systems do not differ, Grossman insists, in their essence. Here again, Viktor 'thought to himself "To me, a distinction based on social origin seems legitimate and moral. But the Germans obviously consider a distinction based on nationality to be equally moral." ' He powerfully condemns the Germans, but goes on to say 'but then we have the same principle' – that is, it does not matter to either if a man is 'good, bad, gifted, stupid, stolid, cheerful, kind, sensitive, greedy', and only his 'category' counts. The orthodox communist prisoner Mostkovskoy, being questioned by the intelligent Obersturmbannführer Liss, has no defence against the latter's insistence that the quarrel between them, however vicious and bitter, is really a family one, that their differences are over inessentials. In an ever more pointed way, one of the Nazi gas chamber operators, Roze, is a mild character who 'had never doubted that the Party had set itself one aim only: the wellbeing of the small and weak'. For, Grossman insists, about the Nazis too, 'the sun has been extinguished by the smoke of the gas-ovens. And even these crimes, crimes never before seen in the Universe . . . have been committed in the name of good.'

Grossman's essential argument is that the human being must be treated as an individual, not as a pawn in some struggle of transcendent theories: even Tolstoy seems to him to err in this direction. He appeals, in a magnificent apostrophe, to Chekhov as the exemplar of humanity as against Lenin and all other inhuman manipulators. His central point is that 'the extreme violence of totalitarian social systems proved able to paralyse the human spirit throughout whole continents'.

'The human spirit' . . . But it is not only overt violence which is its enemy. The lie is the other side of the coin of terror. A sphere in which the Communist Party and its ideology are operating to the disadvantage of both liberty and truth is the Academy where Shtrum works. He once makes a mild joke about Stalin to a close colleague; instantly realizing that what he is doing is 'banging a flask of nitroglycerin with a hammer'. Shtrum's worst moral problem, however, is when he is asked, or rather told, to sign a denunciation for the West of a scientific colleague just arrested. The squalor and anxiety of party-sponsored intrigues, made worse yet by incipient anti-Semitism, are perhaps less easy for Westerners to envisage than straightforward slaughter and terror. Grossman, as well as his documentation of war and of the camps, gives us the concomitant strain on the moral and intellectual faculties of living under an unendingly mean and intrusive regime of mediocrity, and of what Pasternak called 'the inhuman reign of the lie'. This was the state which 'had dismissed the genuine heroes of long-past events and appointed new ones. The state had thee power to replay events, to traansform figures of granite and bronze, to alter speeches long since delivered, to change the faces in a news photograph.' Against this, the suppressed longing for truth eats away at the minds of his characters, as it still does among the Soviet intelligentsia.

Robert Chandler's introduction serves as a useful commentary, and his arguments are almost invariably well taken (not always, as with Solzhenitsyn's 'idealization of nineteenth century Russia'; and the great physicist Landau was surely arrested in the 1930s and not in the anti-Semitic purge of the 1950s). He quotes a Russian friend of Simon Markish's who admires Grossman's morality, but does not want to read 'another Tolstoy'; and Chandler himself no.es that *Life and Fate* is in form an old-fashioned set-piece, with its large panorama of characters, it interweaving of various levels within the USSR, and interlocking of Soviet events with those in Germany and under German occupation.

That Grossman has been 'untouched by the influence of modernism' will worry few. His lack of 'sparkle' is a sounder criticism. And my own usual preference is for a less heavy type of fiction. (Incidentally, one has only to read *Life and Fate* to see how Solzhenitsyn, sometimes represented as in much the same line, is in fact at a different level of flexibility, lightness and penetration.) Yet, in the present case, the heaviness is more aptly described as weightiness – the hammering effectively pounds the point in.

Grossman writes in the tradition of the social-realist novel. Of course, in the Soviet Union where this is the orthodox form, 'realism' has usually been a synonym for falsification. It was even laid down officially at the 19th Party Congress that the 'typical' was not what happened most often in reality, but what 'typified' the social and political scene: so that in a socialist country one splendid skyscraper in a city of slums was typical, while in a capitalist country one slum house in a city of skyscrapers was typical.

By a splendid irony, Grossman uses the method undistorted by such pieties, so that this is the first true social-realist novel ever to come out of the Soviet Union. It is a thick stew, but when you have eaten it sticks to your ribs. Moreover, this huge book reads better second time through. So perhaps Grossman's method is the most appropriate to his theme. For any of the many in the West who claim to wish to understand the Soviet Union, this is, in any case, one of a handful of key texts.

It is clear what Grossman wants. A brave officer of 'kulak' stock, Yershov, is 'certain that he was not only fighting the Germans but fighting for a free Russia: certain that victory over Hitler would be a victory over the death camps where his father, his mother and his sisters had perished' – Soviet camps, that is to say. And, on the issue of truth, another character suggests what should happen when the war is over:

'Yes, comrades,' said Madyarov suddenly, 'can you imagine what it's like to have freedom of the press? One quiet morning after the war you open your newspaper, and instead of exultant editorials, instead of a letter addressed by some workers to the great Stalin, instead of articles about a brigade of steel-workers who have done an extra day's work in honour of the elections to the Supreme Soviet, instead of stories about workers in the United States who are beginning the New Year in a state of despondency, poverty and growing unemployment, guess what you find . . . ! Information! Can you imagine a newspaper like that? A newspaper that provides information!

'You begin reading: there's an article about the bad harvest in the region of Kursk, the inspector's report on conditions inside Butyrka Prison, a discussion about whether the White Sea canal is really necessary or not, an account of how a worker called Golopuzov has spoken out against the imposition of a new State loan.

'In short, you learn everything that's happened in the country: good and bad harvests; outbursts of civic enthusiasm and armed robberies; the opening of a new mine and an accident in another mine; a disagreement between Molotov and Malenkov; reports on the strike that has flared up in protest against a factory director who insulted a seventy-year-old chemical engineer. You read Churchill's and Blum's actual speeches instead of summaries of what they "alleged"; you read an account of a debate in the House of Commons; you learn how many people committed suicide in Moscow yesterday and how many were injured in traffic accidents. You learn why there's no buckwheat in Moscow instead of being told that the first strawberries have just been flown in from Tashkent. You find out the quantity of a *kolkhoz*-worker's daily ration of bread from the newspapers, not from the cleaning-lady whose niece from the country has just come to Moscow to buy some bread. Yes, and at the same time you continue to be a true Soviet citizen.

'You go into a bookshop and buy a book. You read historians, economists, philosophers and political correspondents from America, England and France. You can work out for yourself where these writers are mistaken – you're allowed out onto the street without your nanny.'

Forty years after the war, it still had not happened.

1986

PART III HISTORY AND PSEUDO-HISTORY

Lenin According to Volsky

Following its publication of the memoirs of Victor Serge and Ivanov-Razumnik, the Oxford University Press continues to fulfil the duty of a university press in this field in model fashion, with Volsky's (Valentinov's) *Encounters with Lenin*, an extraordinary record of the Bolshevik leader during a key period at the beginning of the century. This modest and revealing account, which has hitherto only been available in a (non-Soviet) Russian edition, is the true material of history.

Current Soviet treatment of Lenin is very much a personality cult of the kind for so long reprobated in connection with Stalin. Any criticism at all of him has met with cries of (literally) 'Sacrilege!'. But even outside Russia there have been few real attempts to give us a live Lenin. Partly this is due to his own reticence, on which Volsky is most illuminating. But preconception of various types – often giving the impression of a certain fear of picking up so white-hot an object in any but the longest of tongs – has also certainly played a part. Volsky's benign but bouncy attitude, tending neither to reverence nor to revulsion, makes his testimony particularly valuable. Even after his disputes with Lenin he shows no sign whatever of the *odium theologicum*.

Stalin (his own secretary remarked) owed much of his success to having the gift of silence: 'In this respect he was unique in a country where everybody talks far too much.' Lenin's strength was different, but equally un-Russian: another early colleague, Potresov, wrote of him that he was that 'rare phenomenon, particularly in Russia, a man of iron will and indomitable energy'. For in both cases it is worth remembering that if they won power it was against very poor fields. But it was part of the nature of the case that no Menshevik Noske was available, only Martov.

The split between Menshevik and Bolshevik had, in fact, just developed when Volsky came to Geneva in 1904. Like many of the younger revolutionaries he was at once attracted to Lenin and Leninism. He explains why. They had taken to Marxism as against the older Populism because it had a more modern and more Western look. Having become Marxists, they found that the real Marxists foresaw decades of capitalist development in Russia before the socialist dawn could come. So when they turned to the one 'Marxist' who could combine the new evangel from the West with traditional Russian revolutionary hopes of a short cut to victory, they had found the right blend.

Volsky's most interesting point, outside his more personal information, is on the immense influence of Chernyshevsky on Lenin, and the extent to which he acknowledged it. In effect, the whole of Leninism is Marxist in theory only, and Chernyshevskyite in all practical matters. The idea of elites organizing as conspiratorial groups, seizing power, ruling by terror and raising backward countries to socialism through sheer will-power is totally un-Marxist, but is all in Chernyshevsky, and in other primitive revolutionaries of the mid-nineteenth century.

Lenin astonished Volsky by his huge enthusiasm for Chernyshevsky's ill-written and cheaply apocalyptic *What is to be Done?* At the same time, he accepted as dogma the Marxian theoretical background. It was, he told Volsky, not 'subject to revision'. This was just the time when modern economics and the theory of marginal utility were penetrating even Russia, and when the first elements of modern linguistic and positivist thought were appearing in philosophy. Lenin was particularly incensed at Machism, and wrote his *Materialism and Empiriocriticism* against Mach and Avenarius – without, however, as Volsky tells us, having devoted more than two and a half days to reading their subtle and voluminous works.

It was not his dogmatism so much as his dishonesty in controversy which finally repelled Volsky. Believing in the unquestionable rightness of his doctrines, Lenin did not want them discussed seriously and honestly. His line (the phrase is Plekhanov's, but Lenin much admired it) was: 'First let's stick the convict's badge on, and then we'll examine his case.'

Lenin remarked that he would never again sit at table or shake hands with such an 'enemy', when he and Volsky finally broke with each other. After this bitter split there was no contact between them for eighteen years. Then Lenin, by now unchallenged ruler of Russia, replied in friendly fashion to a letter from Volsky and promised to see him when he felt better. For it was just in these last two years of his life that a new Lenin began to emerge, who saw the intolerable faults of the system he had created and who started to sketch out, against the will of a large section of the party, a scheme of moderation.

It was to Volsky too that (at a later period than that covered by these memoirs) the most striking postscript on all this was addressed. While in exile in Paris, he chanced to meet Pyatakov, then just restored to favour in the Soviet Union after his repudiation of the left-wing deviation. After some hot words, Pyatakov suddenly burst into a harangue. The true Lenin, he said, had not been the Lenin of the last years, whose views and policies were the product of tiredness and sickness. The real Lenin had been the man who had created a party on the principle that limitless coercion and discipline were all that are needed to impose on Russia a social order for which no Marxist had thought she was ready, a party in which the individual could abandon his own personality.

And (though Pyatakov himself became a victim) these were the principles that prevailed, while Lenin's maturer conclusions were forgotten. Could he, in his dying days, have remembered Volsky's arguments? Did he perhaps ask himself prophetically, as he looked at the unprepossessing features of those who, unlike Volsky, had remained faithful:

> And what rough beast, its hour come around at last,
> Slouches towards the Kremlin to be boss?

1968

Lenin According to Solzhenitsyn

The work on which Solzhenitsyn is now engaged, the great *roman fleuve* which started with *August 1914*, I take to be his masterpiece. What he has done in *Lenin in Zurich* is to bring together a chapter omitted from that volume, with sections from the as yet uncompleted *October 1916* and *March 1917*. He argues that meanwhile Lenin's experiences over the period form in themselves a coherent whole.

And so they do. When the whole series is completed it will be good to see this material taking its place in the wider sweep. Meanwhile, we have here a work of great interest and great power in which one totally committed giant has undertaken to master and portray another. It raises all sorts of questions in the realms of fiction, of history, of politics.

Does Solzhenitsyn give a picture of Lenin and his plans and activities which has the authentic ring? Yes: the personality has been grasped with subtle skill – and, as Solzhenitsyn points out in a note at the end, anyone who feels sceptical, anyone who is 'surprised by V. I. Lenin's choice of words, his way of thinking and acting', can be referred to his works and his correspondence, in which Solzhenitsyn has fruitfully immersed himself. He vividly conveys the circumstances of the political scheming, the skill and obstinate attention to detail and to long-term advantage which marked every moment of Lenin's manoeuvres, from the dangers of the escape from Galicia to the moment of boarding the Sealed Train nearly two and a half years later.

The difficulties of handling a historical figure in fiction are notorious. And in some ways Lenin appears to be one of the most refractory characters for this sort of treatment. When I wrote a short book on him, I conscientiously read through the bulk of his writings and his correspondence. A feeling of gloom and horror, but especially of gloom, was the result: far more intense, strange as it may seem, than when dealing with the admittedly dreadful personality of Stalin. In a curious way, Stalin appeared the more human of the two. His faults of character, frightful though they were, were those of a really bloody human being. Lenin, on the contrary, seemed an alien being centred on a single cold obsessive drive. Nor would he necessarily have felt this an unfair appreciation. Chernyshevsky, he said, had not only showed that every right-thinking and truly honest man must be a revolutionary, but had also described 'what a revolutionary must be like'. What Chernyshevsky had written was 'A man with an ardent love of goodness cannot but be a sombre monster.'

The period of which Solzhenitsyn is writing is of course that immediately following Lenin's sole brush with sentiment – his connection with Inessa Armand, of which so much has been written, mainly on whether or not they were, technically speaking, lovers. In itself, that is scarcely the major point – which is, rather, that a thread of colour now appears in the greyness of Lenin's material. The writer has also made effectively restrained use of Lenin's occasional descents into periods of nervous depression.

For it would not be true to say that Lenin really lived up to the image of a pure and hard political pragmatist, that he was totally lacking in emotionalism. His description of his first quarrel with Plekhanov is astonishing proof to the contrary. He had had (he said) an 'infatuation' with him and been 'brutally spurned'. He had been 'in love with him'. 'An enamoured youth receives from the object of his love a bitter lesson: to regard all persons "without sentiment"; to keep a stone in one's sling.' In fact, of course, Lenin had behaved at least as badly as Plekhanov in this row; for when it came to the point his obsessional conviction of the rightness of his own views proved more powerful than any feeling he had for the older man. But in any case the emotionalism is extravagant and expresses itself thenceforward with the stones of hatred, mistrust, the total subordination of everything to his political ego.

All the same, to delve objectively but interestingly into this generally rocky psyche is a task which few novelists would care to face, and none has previously done so with any degree of success. Solzhenitsyn is not, of course, a refuser of challenges. He has wrung out of this harsh material a work of art which yet conveys, in sensuous as well as intellectual terms, in colour as well as in diagram, in the heart as well as in the phenomena, some of the reality of Lenin and of the great vortex centred on him.

He has made full use of the supporting characters – from the

pathetic Krupskaya and the ineffectual Zinoviev, through the ener-
getically 'charming' Hanecki and the erratically intelligent Radek, to
the huge, fantastic Parvus – a truly splendid re-creation of that
hippopotamoid hedonist with the irrepressible revolutionary intellect
and powers of clandestine action, whose career twines into all the
underground activities of early twentieth-century Europe in a way
respectable historians find hard to untangle, and preferable to ignore.
Solzhenitsyn, quite legitimately in every sense, uses him as a foil –
and more than a foil – to Lenin, in a magnificent central scene of
their physical meeting of minds and temperaments, when Parvus
comes to Switzerland to plan the overthrow of Russia.

One must stress the general authenticity of all this, though the
occasional nuance might be taken as unproven. But, of course, authenticity does not mean literary success. From apparently unpromising
materials Solzhenitsyn has once again shown that history may be
vividly subsumed into literature. The only question that is harder to
answer, if one has any special interest in or knowledge of the subject,
is whether the lay reader would be both instructed and held. My
feeling is that he would.

When I saw Solzhenitsyn in Zurich soon after his arrival in the
West, he told me he was working on those chapters of his great cycle
of novels about the First World War and the Revolution which dealt
with Lenin's stay in the same city, I remarked how strange it was
that things had come full circle, that after the passage of sixty years
the great symbol of the Russian spirit's rejection of all that Lenin set
in motion should be back in the same spot. He answered that when,
several years before, he had started working on this theme it had
never occurred to him that he would ever be in Zurich in his life. As
so often with great symbolic manifestations, the whole thing was
mainly accident after all – just as the subjectivist Marxist schemes
which Lenin had nourished had little except verbal relation to what
was actually to occur in Russia. The richness, the variety, the unpre-
dictability, of the real world is available to Solzhenitsyn as it is not
to the schematists of revolution. It has taken a giant human being
to come to grips with this giant alien, and to demonstrate without
unfairness or tendentiousness that humanity is superior. Solzhenitsyn
can understand and include Lenin: Leninism cannot understand or
include Solzhenitsyn.

1976

Intervention

Richard Ullman's scholarly and readable *Intervention and the War* deals with events more fogged up with myth than almost any others in modern history. It is maintained, even to this day, that the Russians have every right to remain implacably hostile and irreconcilably suspicious of the West because of the attempt made to strangle the infant regime at birth. One hears this even from people who would impatiently reject, say, the notion that Algeria was entitled to permanent resentment against France. (And this is to say nothing of such perennial falsehoods — fully dealt with by Ullman — as the alleged shooting by the British of the twenty-six commissars.)

As Ullman says, Allied policy towards Russia at the time largely originated in London, and most of the British figures involved, Curzon, Balfour, Lockhart, Buchanan, come out rather well from this American study. They were often wrong; but on their information, within the political possibilities, they acted quite rationally and dispassionately. Even Knox is shown to be nothing like the fanatic he has been supposed. In particular it was widely understood that no further Russian effort against the Germans was possible. This was occasionally forgotten in moments of crisis such as followed the defeat of the Fifth Army, when any phantom of a Second Front was grasped at eagerly. But in general, as Cecil said in answer to a parliamentary question, government policy was simply to keep Russia, if not anti-German, at least non-German.

The British forces at Murmansk landed with the agreement of the local soviet, and most of their fighting was done in support of the Finnish communists against the 'White' Finns. Dunsterforce was invited to Baku by the local soviet and, though it is now much denounced by the Russian authorities, the 'bitter fighting' it put in was at no time against the Bolsheviks. Elsewhere, on various occasions, the British detachments were in armed conflict with the Bolsheviks. Yet our total losses in the entire intervention ran only to a few hundred, so the myth of a vast military effort is clearly absurd.

It is curious, reading the documents Ullman quotes, to find how much of the context we have been inclined to forget – and in particular that Britain was then engaged in a fight to the death on the battlefields of France and Flanders, with the outcome in the gravest doubt until the summer of 1918. The result was that natural suspicion about the hostility to the 'Bolshevik fanatics' played a very minor part in the motivations even of men we now thing of as reactionary. The government was 'wholly absorbed in the events of the last year of a terrible war' and was willing to work with or against the Bolsheviks, depending on the expediencies of the struggle with Germany. 'Progressive' opinion here only swung against Lenin's regime when the Constituent Assembly was dissolved in January 1918, and 'reactionary' opinion only when the tsar was shot in July. Yet even these emotional pulls remained wholly subsidiary to the German issue.

The period of 1919–20 (after that covered by this volume) saw a hardening of lines and an international civil war. The British battalions at Archangel, the Socialist Revolutionary governments beyond the Caspian, were matched by the Red Army in Poland and the Communist governments in Munich and Budapest. Why one should be thought more reprehensible than the other is a mystery. Both were, of course, failures and can thus be condemned in the light of hindsight. The British failure was due basically to the absence of complete conviction about the absolute irreconcilability of the Bolsheviks. The documents make clear that this irreconcilability was determined from the start. There is no reason at all to believe that but for the intervention the Soviet regime would have moderated its attitude to the democracies.

1961

Preobrazhensky and After: Slave Socialism

When Preobrazhensky went to the execution cellars, it was not simply as part of Stalin's settlement of the dispute between the party's economists and its apparatchiks, which was ending, as Professor Swianiewicz points out,[1] with the almost total liquidation of the economists. For Preobrazhensky was something more than a theoretician. As a former Secretary of the Central Committee he was denounced in the 1937 trial as a major terrorist, spy and saboteur; yet he never appeared in dock, then or later. (This alone might even then have persuaded apologists that something was amiss with Soviet justice.) The presumption is that he refused to confess. His book on the economics of industrialization in Soviet circumstances has similar uncompromising boldness.[2] For it was he who asserted flatly that the money to finance industry would have to be squeezed out of the peasantry.

The great dispute of the time, 1926–7, appeared to be between him and Bukharin, and he has generally been presented as the father of the 'hard line' in the countryside eventually pursued, with such horrible results, by Stalin. In fact, Preobrazhensky's *method* of getting the funds from the peasantry was to be fiscal, and compatible with a general increase in peasant welfare (as it had been in Meiji Japan) – an approach not unassimilable to that of the Bukharinist 'right'.

This first English edition is welcome. For the book is a classic of the older, higher style of Marxist polemic, and the last serious Soviet

[1] S. Swianiewicz, *Forced Labour and Economic Development* (Oxford University Press).
[2] E. Preobrazhensky, *The New Economics* trans. Brian Pearce (Oxford University Press).

attempt to deal with a genuine problem relevant today in many undeveloped or partially developed countries. The Stalinist approach involved an abandonment of all 'principles of social morality, except the abolition of incomes from capital', as Professor Swianiewicz puts it. This narrow formulation, not yet extinct even in the West, was combined with the semantic trick of using the word 'socialism' to mean simply industrialization. It ignored rather nastier possibilities like private ownership of the state, first by a single entrepreneur, and then by a limited number of shareholders. And Marx himself had, of course, thought many things worse than capitalism – slavery, for example: Stalin revived this institution.

Professor Swianiewicz's careful and well-documented estimate of just under 7 million in the forced-labour camps in 1941 is rather lower than investigation on the same lines has led to in the past; but he gives good reasons for the discrepancy. It is the merit of this remarkable book that, while concerned with social ethics, the author concentrates solidly and effectively on the *economic* origins and consequences of the Soviet slave labour system – its effects on productivity, on consumer demand, on inflation. Though less optimistic about free development in China and the communist East, he sees a probable petering out of the system in the Soviet Union itself, for social-economic reasons. But he does not discount the hostile ideological gradient presented by the *apparat*. For the Soviet planning method 'was an outcome of the irrational forces which have been released and are not easily to be mastered'.

When Pyatakov was shot, Walter Duranty (then a leading presenter of Russia to Western liberal opinion) was convinced of his guilt by one solid argument: Stalin could not have deprived himself of the services of the 'genius of Soviet industrialization' except for unforgivable crimes. The alternative, and true, explanation was that rationality of the sort implied did not lie behind Stalin's decisions. Once a party indulges in the belief that there are 'no fortresses it cannot storm', then thought and prudence become defeatism and treason. Once it is committed to a vicious policy, it falls into the desperate solidarity of accomplices in crime. Impossible plans, faked results and random victimization are the outcome.

Nevertheless, some economic gains may perhaps be achieved in this way, even if not those predicted or claimed. Professor Swianiewicz, with admirable balance, enquires into the real nature of such results. The collectivization terror, with all its negative and destructive features in ruining the country's agriculture, gave certain advantages; for (Swianiewicz argues) the forced-labour pool resulting from it was composed of surplus labour. The Yezhov terror was totally destructive, and the labour camps were filled from an already over-strained labour market. It is the first phase that has its attractions for the Afro-Asian intellectual. Yet it was the inhumanities and irrationalities then already dominant that led irresistibly to the second. Terror is not simply a mechanism to be used and discarded at will. It builds up its own institutions, cadres and habits of mind and these are economically as well as morally disastrous.

1965

Mensheviks

Boris Nicolaevsky, one of the last of the Old Mensheviks, died in 1966. He had lived long enough to see it clearly established that the Mensheviks were right and the Bolsheviks were wrong in their views about methods of reaching socialism – if by socialism is meant anything resembling a social, political and economic democracy. I saw him a couple of years earlier, still physically and mentally in his prime, and it was extraordinary to recall that his first arrest had been sixty years previously, in 1904. It is, of course, one of the great pro-Bolshevik myths about the Mensheviks that they were not only more moderate as to policy but less active in their revolutionary work. Nicolaevsky was arrested eight times under the tsar; exiled to Siberia three times; escaped twice from Siberia and once from prison – a record equalled by few Bolsheviks.

The Menshevik dispute with Lenin was essentially not on the revolutionary fight or militancy, but on his principles of organization – the servile, centralized group from which totalitarianism emerged. Indeed, in the seizure of power itself, it was men whose underground life had been Menshevik – like Antonov-Ovseyenko, and indeed Trotsky – who provided much of the revolutionary impetus, while Lenin's closest disciples like Zinoviev, Kamenev and Nicolaevsky's brother-in-law Rykov wavered and waffled. These ex-Mensheviks had swallowed their clearly understood and well-founded objections to Leninism in the revolutionary enthusiasm of the moment, and were henceforth unable to break loose. They all perished in the purges, though some Menshevik renegades who came over *after* the Revolution, like Vyshinsky, survived. Nicolaevsky, remaining a good Menshevik, was director of the Marx-Engels Institute in Moscow in the first years of the Soviet regime, until his arrest in 1921 and deportation the following year, and he retained and extended his knowledge of and good sense about the regime for the rest of his life.

The celebrated (and long anonymous) 'Letter of an Old Bolshevik' is the core of a group of his essays printed as *Power and the Soviet Elite*. It was clear when it was first published in 1936-7 that it represented authentic opinion and information from the higher levels of the party, and that this had to be given in disguised form to protect the sources. In an interview printed here, he reveals that it was largely based on conversations with Bukharin early in 1936, supplemented by information from other party sources later in the year. As George Kennan says in the preface – one of his most striking and brilliant essays – the 'Letter' is 'the most authoritative and important single piece of source material we have on the background of the Purges' (though this should be amended to give the memoirs of the NKVD defector Orlov, at least as regards 1936-7, equal status). Yet there is a tendency to describe it as 'fiction'. Such criticism shows a misunderstanding of the nature of 'documentation' in dealing with the affairs of a secretive and totalitarian regime. As Academician Maisky pointed out, personal memoirs are even now required to supplement our information, since official documents are not always reliable (an extremely mild way of putting it). That is, the recollections of inexpert participants are valuable decades after the events. Yet the 'Letter' is criticized as a source of Bukharin's views because the clear-minded Nicolaevsky wrote it six months after they talked . . .

Boris Nicolaevsky established the school of interpreting the political scene in Stalin and post-Stalin Russia in terms of a struggle of groups and factions. This has now, I take it, become generally accepted. Though he is sometimes unconvincing or skimpy in detail, the essays from the later part of his book are useful and often penetrating exercizes in the genre. Mr Kennan argues from them that in the long run no system can be devised to protect men in power from terror if they will not extend the same protection to the humblest of their subjects. He gives it as his personal conviction that the present elders will not find the answer to this problem within the framework of their party alone. Sooner or later, he feels, a neo-Menshevism, after generations in the wilderness, must prevail.

Academician Maisky, another ex-Menshevik of the Vyshinsky vintage, also survived, though only just; an account of just what happened to him in 1952-4 would greatly illuminate those years for us. Only very slight interest attaches to his memoirs, and that mainly for the sharp and rather malicious portraits of his fellow members of the Non-Intervention Committee. He has no difficulty in showing

that the fascist powers behaved brutally, and the democracies pusil-
lanimously. But, in defending Moscow as impeccable, he has been
overtaken by Soviet disclosures (eg Ehrenburg's) on the extent of
Russian involvement in Spain: in fact it was a field day for Yezhov's
mobile squads and Dolores Ibarruri's terror-oriented faction in the
Spanish C.P. Maisky's version of the Barcelona insurrection of April
1937 as a 'Fascist inspired putsch', in particular, is little more than
the regurgitation of a hoary Stalinist lie.

1965

Roy Medvedev: Ideology and Truth

The publication of Roy A. Medvedev's splendid *Let History Judge*[1] is an event of real importance. This is the first time a Soviet writer has tackled the whole question of Stalinism, attempting to analyse the entire dreadful phenomenon and place it historically. Whatever weaknesses we may note in the book, we must still feel it is a splendid effort. That Medvedev, brought up in the strictest party orthodoxy, and still by no means wholly free of that heritage, can yet rise to the level of a huge critical effort, is a matter for unstinted praise – far more, in this sense, than should be given to a scholar writing in full liberty in the West. On the other hand, it would be insultingly patronizing to pass over blemishes uncritically, simply out of respect for the moral and other exertion put into the writing. Medvedev's book deserves the compliment of being discussed seriously.

The existence of Roy Medvedev's manuscript (which was finished in its present form in 1968) had been known for some years; it was referred to, for instance, by Andrei Sakharov in his *Progress, Coexistence and Intellectual Freedom* – Sakharov noted that Medvedev would regard him as deplorably unorthodox from a Marxist point of view. And in fact a major point to be made about Medvedev's Leninist position is that it is by no means typical of the Soviet liberal intelligentsia. Some are opposed in the abstract to the system they seem to believe exists in the West, with its totally unrestrained exploitation, absence of free education, of social services, and so on. But there are people who are better informed: the celebrated Programme of the Democratic Opposition specifically condemns attacks on 'capitalism'. Even Sakharov is clear that revolution (even without bloodshed or eventual

[1] Roy A. Medvedev, *Let History Judge: The Origins and Consequences of Stalinism*, Trans. Colleen Taylor.

Stalinism) would not be economically beneficial to the American working class. Once it is realized that 'capitalism' is in one usage a Soviet code-word for any non-communist system – or even on occasion for an aberrant communist system such as that of Yugoslavia – part of the confusion abates.

In any case, intellectual opposition in the USSR is not essentially concerned with Lenin and Leninism. What it looks for is the establishment of a legal and civic order, of intellectual and political freedom, in the Soviet Union. Some of those who seek this may really believe that a return to Lenin would produce it; others at least find that to claim Lenin to be on their side is a useful pragmatic defence against a hostile Party. In fact, when it is said that disaffected Russian writers are 'really' devoted to 'communism', though wishing for a slightly different form of it than the one presently available, this is in almost every case merely a verbal matter: a pre-empting of the *word* 'communism' to mean almost exactly the opposite of what it has hitherto meant in Russia.

Roy Medvedev is in this sense an exception, one of the few who remain unequivocally devoted to Lenin and to what he regards as Leninist principles and the Leninist style of communism. Medvedev even hoped originally to get his book published legally in the USSR. By 1968 this was wishful thinking, but if Khrushchev had survived and evolved just a little further it is not inconceivable that the book might have appeared: it is *almost* within the range of party feeling, or Khrushchevite feeling. Even so, of course, some excisions might have been demanded – in particular, Medvedev's hostile references to some of the Stalinists shot during the purges and since rehabilitated.

For, on Medvedev's showing, practically all Lenin's comrades and successors come out badly: Stalin, Trotsky, Zinoviev, Bukharin, even Kirov. Both the oppositionists shot in the purges and the 'moderate' Stalinists who followed them to the execution cellars are heavily criticized. Although their fates are recognized as the products of a cruel and baseless frame-up, Medvedev has the courage to point out that men like Postyshev and Krylenko, now rehabilitated and held up by the 'anti-Stalinist' wing of the party as true Leninists, were in fact among the most odious accomplices of Stalin during earlier phases of the terror.

But (this is of course not a new point), if Lenin was the only good and sound Bolshevik, how could he have entrusted the state to a cadre of leaders whose actions were almost invariably either mistaken or criminal? Medvedev in effect argues that Lenin was always right, while the system he created invariably produced wrong. However highly one might regard Lenin, this surely must be accounted a major, incapacitating defect in the claim that he was a faultless political leader. Either the Stalin regime and the present situation in Russia are the legitimate consequences of Lenin's actions – in which case he should be judged accordingly; or they are illegitimate, unforeseen – in which case Lenin must still be considered to have submitted the country to the sufferings of terror, famine and civil war in the name of a theory which proved catastrophically defective in mastering and predicting the course of events.

Two rather contradictory strands run through Medvedev's particular presentation of Lenin. First, he holds him up as a supporter of freedom of the press – on the strength of a few promises made shortly after the seizure of power to the effect that press censorship would be a temporary measure for a few crucial weeks. Of course, Lenin broke all these promises at once, and there is no reason to believe he ever intended to keep them: after all, he simultaneously promised to honour the decisions of the Constituent Assembly, then about to be elected, even if the vote should go against the Bolsheviks; but he did not.

Secondly, Medvedev believes at the same time that Lenin was justified in his use of terror, practising 'necessary' cruelty only, as with the execution of the imperial family. Even apart from the fact that a tsarist restoration (especially of Nicholas or his son) was already a dead issue in the Civil War, the young Grand Duchesses had in any case no claim to the succession or to its transmission; nor did the doctor, the nurse or the dog. Lenin in fact habitually urged terror on his sometimes reluctant subordinates; and, far from being 'necessary', it 'made . . . victory in the Civil War more difficult', as Adam B. Ulam has observed.

On the whole Lenin period Medvedev shows much less of the fair-mindedness which in the main marks his treatment of later Soviet times. In the Civil War, for instance, all non-communists are called 'White Guards'; the peasants who oppose grain requisitioning in 1918 are all 'kulaks'; the Kronstadt rebellion is 'counter-revolutionary'. While he sees that the great public trial of Social Revolutionaries in 1922 was 'not irreproachable', Medvedev exculpates Lenin and blames it on Stalin. In fact, Stalin had practically nothing to do with the trial. Lenin was very much the moving spirit – and when the Bolshevik negotiators promised the Second International that there would be no executions Lenin was furious.

Medvedev's account of the earlier years of the Bolshevik Party and of the Soviet regime contains some interesting and previously unknown material (for example, on the quarrels in the Bolshevik Committee in Petrograd in 1917), but in general it is an exercise largely concerned to show the continual errors of Stalin. Even Stalin's *failure* in the post-revolutionary period to get involved in open opposition to Lenin is held against him as a mark of insincerity!

It would be unfair to call this a mirror image of similar exposures in Stalin's time of the party records of Trotsky and Zinoviev. But all the same there is a disquieting resemblance, an uncomfortable reminder of the narrow and sectarian habits of the party mind even at its best. This holds true even in the section on the Stalin and the post-Stalin periods, when Medvedev does not suppress facts, but where his party-mindedness sometimes leads him into contradiction.

Thus, while criticising Stalin's leadership of the collectivization of agriculture in the 1930s (and showing his usual post-Lenin frankness on the horrors of the 1933 famine), Medvedev yet describes it as 'the major revolution, the great economic and political crisis that determined the victory of socialism'. It is interesting to contrast this with Andrei Sakharov's view of collectivization as having caused 'a profound and hard-to-correct destruction of the economy and way of life in the countryside', and the 'almost serf-like enslavement of the peasantry'. Medvedev also follows an orthodox Soviet line on the Nazi-Soviet pact, though he does condemn the way in which Russian propaganda, and communists outside Russia, overtly took the German side. He is full of praise for Brecht, on the strength of a poem which he wrote (but did not publish) when his friend Tretyakov was shot. But Brecht fully supported Stalinism in every other way and even in this poem proposed a ratio false to fact and insulting to the majority of victims: 'Among fifty who are condemned one can be innocent.' More revealingly still, Medvedev is led into condemning Stalin for having introduced a foul and horrible system of rule in the Soviet Union while at the same time hailing the extension of Stalinism to eastern Europe as 'a great victory of the world socialist revolution', and bemoaning Stalin's failure to assure similar victories in France and Italy.

There is a certain tendency among Western observers to applaud Medvedev's views above those of other Soviet liberals, just because they are 'Leninist'. Why? He should be praised, rather, for having liberated part of his mind from dogma, not for having failed to liberate the other part. The editors of *Let History Judge* rightly remark that 'The level of analysis [and of honesty, one might add] in Medvedev's book is especially remarkable when one considers the background from which it emerges: the official school of thought on Soviet history.' Just the same, there are other Soviet liberals – the majority of them in fact – who have freed themselves more decisively from this background.

Yet Medvedev's major virtue – of seeing that in the long run a party or an opinion cannot be defended on the basis of total falsehood – shines through as do the thought and labour he has put into illustrating his central point. He rightly argues that no regime with the remotest claim to intellectual legitimacy can go on treating the Stalinist experience as negligible, or nonexistent. Even in Khrushchev's time nothing like a full revelation, or repudiation, of the past was made. His successors were in the absurd position of possessing no official story, true or false, of some of the major events of the 1930s. This Medvedev has sought to correct.

He is not (as he himself concedes) a historian. Striking though much of his new material is, it is cited mainly in episodic form as illustration of various general points. To the student, the most useful parts of the book are the accounts of particular incidents during various stages of the terror. Medvedev adds to our knowledge of the atrocious tortures practised and gives a number of fresh instances of the lunacy of some of the accusations. And, with many important figures, he provides information as to their fate which had hitherto not emerged from the literature of that frightful period. His sources are, first of all, various books published and speeches made in Russia which had mostly been available anyway in the West, so that much of the most striking material is not in fact new to us; secondly, various manuscripts or oral information given him by members of the families of victims of the great purge – some of these of the utmost interest and importance (though a disadvantage of the episodic approach is that there is less possibility of using these admittedly rather indirect sources to reinforce or refute one another); and, thirdly, a certain amount of Western literature which had rather haphazardly penetrated Soviet circles: he cites, for example, Victor Alexandrov's *L'Affaire Toukhachevski*, which is mere guesswork.

Among the most interesting parts of the book is the section where Medvedev has assembled, from public but not widely known Soviet economic sources of fairly recent date, the (presumably) real figures on the fulfilment of the various five-year plans. (Much of this, indeed, has already been published in the West – eg by Professor Tibor Szamuely – though not widely remarked.) When one remembers that the terrific, but falsified, alleged successes of the Soviet economic system were one of the major propaganda themes in the West, one hopes that many readers and students will carefully study these figures.

Finally, while he sometimes appears to treat Stalin and Stalinism as a frantic aberration, Medvedev yet perceives that 'although his rise to power was not inevitable, it did reflect certain tendencies that existed in our country and our party before the period of terror and then flourished because of Stalin.' More generally, he gives a broad and vivid picture of Stalin as something between a Caligulan villain and a locus of disastrous imponderables. (He has no use for the rather more ambiguous attitudes of Isaac Deutscher, whom his American editor feels obliged to defend against him.) Still, it is difficult to accept, for instance, his contention that Stalin's 'primary motive' was revenge, since he often treated his most servile followers just as badly as those who had opposed or offended him, and the bulk of those who perished were known to him barely if at all. And, when Medvedev tells us – as a major point – that in many matters 'Stalin talked one way and behaved another', one can only comment 'So did Lenin.'

I have not conveyed the richness of this book's detail which, whatever its defects of organization and of argument, renders it a truly astonishing contribution. The peculiarity of Medvedev's opinions, the tension between his honesty and his Leninism, should not lead us to dismiss the usefulness of much of his factual material, nor should it diminish our respect for his efforts and his sincerity. Medvedev's achievement is in fact remarkable; all the repressive mechanisms of the ideology implanted in his mind have not been enough to overcome a deeper drive for the truth.

1971

The Russian Dead

More people died in a few months in Leningrad than, probably, in any other city ever. Not the Mongols at Herat, let alone the atom bomb at Hiroshima, seem truly comparable. A million dead – almost entirely from hunger – may be an underestimate. More died, it is true, at Auschwitz and Kolyma: what is particularly shaking about Leningrad's case is that it was in the main, by all established standards, a legitimate act of war.

The facts have been given before in English, in Leon Gouré's book, and in a translation of Dmitri Pavlov's Soviet work on the siege. But they stuck to the coolest documentation and statistics. In his *The Siege of Leningrad*, Harrison Salisbury, who saw the city in the immediate aftermath, has given us the horrible story in a form which is neither shrill nor laboured, yet real and urgent. He has not strained after horror and effect: he has not needed to. He has found the right tone. He has read and used, critically and sensibly, all the great body of Soviet work in any way relevant to his theme. He covers the background of Leningrad's purgatory in the great Stalinist terror, the bungling of the preparations of Russia's defence, the crumbling of the defences facing von Leeb, and then the long agony of the siege itself. He gives everything, the suffering and the wavering, the self-sacrifice and the cannibalism. He ranges from the events in the military and political leaderships to the efforts of the dystrophy-crippled ordinary citizen. All in all, this is a large, humane, rational and passionate book.

On the face of it Hitler's attack on Russia had no chance of success. He was attacking an adversary with larger forces, a superiority in aeroplanes and armour, and a vast territory for retreat, manoeuvre and defence. The army group which poured through the Baltic area up to the gates of Leningrad at a speed which astonished even veterans such as Guderian – 300 miles in eighteen days – was on paper very little stronger than the troops facing it. The extent of the gamble has seldom been appreciated. Hitler could hardly have won that war unless he himself had played all his cards just right, and political and military miscalculation on the Russian side had been on an unbelievable scale. But Stalin did miscalculate, and almost enough to justify Hitler's most sanguine hopes.

One of the curiosities of the reception of Salisbury's book was its treatment in the US press by British reviewers. A. J. P. Taylor in the *New York Review of Books* and (less forthrightly) C. P. Snow in the *New York Times* took objection to Salisbury's putting much of the blame for the catastrophe on Stalin. Taylor makes the true but irrelevant observation that it was Hitler, not Stalin, who caused the death of the victims. It was the German machine-gunners who killed the victims of the Somme and Passchendaele, but that has never been thought an adequate defence of Haig, any more than final victory was. The foulness of the Nazis should not be made an excuse for the foulness, or the blunders, of Stalinism.

Stalin's military faults were not of the idiotic type. That is no reason for giving him a full military rehabilitation. His main errors, some of them literally criminal, are clear. First and most important, the totally unjustified purge of nearly all the experienced officers had left the army not only almost headless, but also almost brainless. The Voroshilov-Mekhlis clique had reverted to First World War tactical methods, and the morale of the whole officer corps had been reduced to a timid spiritlessness. Second, he had refused to face – had actively prevented attention to – the obvious possibility of a German attack in 1941. In 1893 von Schlieffen had written, 'The Russians can no longer be taken by surprise'. On 22 June 1941 Halder was able to report, 'Tactical surprise of the enemy has apparently been achieved along the entire line'. And thirdly, Stalin intervened disastrously on several occasions, above all in refusing to allow a retreat from Kiev in 1941, which resulted in the biggest losses sustained by either side in any battle of the war. (And the similar disaster at Kharkhov the following year was procured in precisely the same way.) Mr Salisbury deals justly with the similar though lesser errors committed in the Leningrad situation.

Taylor justifies the execution in 1941 of the generals who were just obeying mistaken orders, on the grounds that it was only by such draconian expedients that the war was finally won. This is not so. The execution of the Commander of the Western Front, Pavlov, and his deputies, and of the various aviation commanders, in the early months of the war shook the Soviet Command severely, and victory only began to be won when Stalin ceased this superficially impressive, but actually fatal practice (he never shot the worst ones anyway, for they were all his own old stooges). Soviet military memoirs – an excellent selection of which, by Professor Seweryn Bialer (*Stalin and his Generals*), is available in English – are quite decisive on all the above points.

Both Taylor and Snow quote, and partly in defence of Stalin's ruthlessness, the comparative losses of Britain, the USA and the Soviet Union in the war. (Taylor makes the contrast supererogatorily striking by using, in each case, figures for casualties in Europe only). They give the figure of 25 million Soviet dead. This figure, five million higher than that commonly given in recent years in the speeches of Soviet leaders, requires comment on several counts. As the Soviet historian of the siege, Dmitri Pavlov, remarks, the story is 'so grim that there is no need for historians or writers dealing with these events to deepen the shadows'.

The figure of 25 million was originally arrived at by Warren Eason in a famous article in *Foreign Affairs* (July 1959). Eason, in one of the first analyses of the 1959 Census, concluded that there was a population deficit since the figures published for 1939, of c.45 million. The deficit among those up to ten years old at the end of the War was c.20 million: this included both the birth deficit and actual infant mortality. The deficit among those older was 25 million – c.21 million male and 4 million female.

Now first, Eason's base figure was faked: the 1939 Census (replacing the Census of 1937 which was suppressed, with the arrest and execution of the Census Board) was at least 5 million too high, according to a Soviet census-taker's calculations long since registered in the literature (*Perepis Naseleniya v. SSR*, P. Galin. Munich 1951, p.34). And to this mere exaggeration by the census takers, we must add that the NKVD reported separately on those under its control. Indeed, a very high proportion of those shot in 1937–38 were misleadingly sentenced to '10 years without the right of correspondence' so were, technically speaking, still alive. By this and other methods the NKVD is believed to have contributed up to a further spurious 3 million odd to the 'Census'. Eason's conclusions must be lowered accordingly. On the other hand, though fertility greatly decreased, his under-10 figure must include several million excess infant and child deaths. This may roughly balance out, and 25 million may not be far off the true figure, or even below it.

But Eason includes all premature death in this – when it comes to the war, not merely the casualties proper, but those dying on home territory from cold, disease and other indirect products of the war not included in the Western casualties with which Taylor and Snow compare them. And, far more important, he specifically includes deaths in Soviet labour camps in the period between 1939 and 1959, and we must add those executed or dying in the mass ethnic deportations of 1941–49. The total can hardly have amounted to less than c.7 million. So, even if we accept Eason's 25 million, the war dead would be c.18 million (or if we increase Eason's to 27 million, then the official 20 million would be about right).

Official Communist figures for the period are indeed sometimes unreliable. The published total of war dead in Yugoslavia was, Djilas tells us, 'a most exaggerated figure put about by Yugoslav propaganda', being in fact 1.2–1.3 million rather than the official 1.7 million. The French Communist Party constantly claimed that over 70,000 of its members has been shot under the Nazis, while the total execution of the French resistance, Communist and non-Communist, were established at the Nuremberg Trial to have been 29,660.

On the other hand Stalin, contemplating an aggressive foreign policy, would have no incentive to represent his military losses as more crippling than the reality: indeed it might be argued that the tendency could have been the other way.

The official figure for those killed in the armed forces given in Stalin's speech of 6 February 1946 was just over 7 million. If we accept it in principle, increase it to as much as 8–9 million for later premature deaths due to wounds, and add 3½ million for the Soviet prisoners of war dead in Nazi POW camps, we have c.12 million soldiers dead and so c.6–8 million civilians: c.1 million in Leningrad and c.5–7 millions others.

There are some points to be made about both the military and the civilian casualties. First, the dead Soviet prisoners of war at least cannot be pleaded in favour of the regime. Solzhenitsyn points out, as have other Soviet liberals such as Peter Yakir, that Stalin had much of the responsibility for their deaths, by treating them as deserters, rebuffing the German approaches for a POW agreement and refusing the offices of the Red Cross (and, it may be added, arresting their relatives as spies, and sending almost all the million odd survivors to Soviet camps after the war, when many of them died). These things are not forgotten in Russia, though they may be by comfortable Westerners.

Again, a large part of the civilian casualties must be attributed to the Western territories annexed by the USSR under the Nazi-Soviet

Pact, and Soviet citizens solely on that count. In particular, the contribution to the Jewish Holocaust from the post–1939 Soviet Union was very high: again we only have estimates, but it seems to have been at least 2 million. These, as we know, were never made anything of in the Soviet Union. Efforts to draw attention to the special Jewish fate were always suppressed, as with the attempt to mention Jews on the projected Babi Yar monument. Casualties of those only Soviet citizens by force, and particularly of those whose deaths you will not mourn, cannot be reasonably accounted part of your losses.

Politically speaking, these are valid reservations; but of course, however taken, they do not affect the devastating death-toll inflicted on the Soviet population by the war. However we take the figures our debt to the Soviet peoples and the Soviet Army is incalculable. But even at this level it cannot be extended to much of a debt to the Russian ruling clique, (which had itself, in any case, inflicted higher losses on its subjects). Russian losses were at lowest 20 or 30 times as great as our own. But when we turn to the ruling bodies the proportions are strikingly reversed. The Soviet Central Committee suffered the loss of *one* of its members, surrounded at Kiev (plus another who seems to have gone over to the Germans). The House of Commons, four times as large, has 20 MPs on its War Memorial.

1970

Vlasovites

Lieutenant-General Vlasov, whose treason did not prosper, has received a fairly hostile verdict from history. This is no more than he expected, nor is it unfair. All the same, his movement was a highly significant one and he himself by no means a despicable figure. (Curiously enough even in Russia, Ilya Ehrenburg, in his memoirs published in the Khrushchev period, was able to give a comparatively favourable account of him). Vlasov, the son of a peasant, was one of the few fairly senior officers to survive the great purge with his loyalty unquestioned. In the manoeuvres of 1940 his 99th division showed itself the best. After the Battle of Moscow in 1941, his was one of the eight photographs of military men featured in *Pravda* as responsible for the victory. But in 1942 his Second Shock Army was destroyed on the Volkhov and he was captured while attempting to hide out in the woods.

During the summer he agreed to become leader and spokesman of a group of senior Soviet officers prepared to collaborate with the Germans in attempting to overthrow Stalin.

The disasters suffered by the Red Army in 1941–2 were greater, the casualties heavier, the German penetration deeper by far, than those suffered by the tsar's army in the First World War. The resentments against the regime were also sharper. But Stalin had his ubiquitous and tightly organized machinery to detect and suppress the merest hint of this disaffection as Nicholas II had not (indeed, dissolution of the rudimentary internal security organization of the Russian army in 1914, on the grounds that it was an insult to the soldiers' loyalty, may perhaps have been decisive three years later). Hence, Vlasov felt, no internal resistance to Stalin was possible. He understood the stigma attached to working with the enemy, but took the view that there was no other conceivable hope of bringing down the Stalinist dictatorship except by working with whoever happened to be fighting it.

For the first time in Russian history a large number of her citizens fought for the enemy. The German invaders were at first welcome, and in a few months 800,000 Soviet auxiliaries were serving the Wehrmacht. Had the Nazis not been foolish as well as foul, it seems very possible that they could have used this anti-Stalinist mood in Russia to win the war. Hitler was betrayed by a rigid loyalty to his horrible principles. Had he merely pretended to support the Russian democrats as Stalin pretended to support the democrats of eastern Europe, he too might have been in a winning position to betray them later.

Wars, particularly wars with revolutionary implications, inevitably produce over and above the stated loyalties of the main struggle cross-currents not so easy to be judged either morally or politically.

The First World War had produced a number of figures and movements which tried to use one side against the other for their own political ends, such as Casement, Pilsudski (and, in another sense, Lenin). In the Second World War Asia saw various attempts by nationalist or democratic forces to use the Japanese – in Indonesia and in Burma, for example. Some of these were later reconciled and assimilated to the post-war order: for example, the (admittedly much resented) incorporation of the 'Indian National Army' into the real Indian army.

In a general sense, the coalition against the Axis can truly be seen in black and white. But there is much detail that will not fit into this overall picture. Democracy against totalitarianism? But Finland (and even Hungary) were notably more democratic than one of our first allies, the then Greek military dictatorship – let alone Chiang Kai-shek's China, or Stalin's Russia.

Those who had experienced Stalin were unable to believe that Hitler could be as bad. They were reinforced in this delusion by the extraordinary amount of latitude and individual responsibility the German officers seemed to enjoy in comparison with the tight political control over every act and word already long established on the Soviet side. As late as August 1944 von Cholitz's surrender of Paris to avoid the city's destruction made a deep impression on the Vlasov officers. There were still some German generals (he commented) who would take such responsibility on military and humanitarian grounds contrary to party orders.

All this was true, but it was a superficial point. Hitler had not yet had the time and opportunity to tighten things up to the required level. Vlasov was misled in imagining that, at any serious level, Hitler's political decisions were to be influenced or amended by the comparatively liberal moods of the Wehrmacht officers he himself was in contact with. In everything essential the decisions were made by Hitler; these were based on a vicious fanaticism and will, and there was no way of amending them.

In his *Against Stalin and Hitler* Captain Strik-Strikfeldt gives us not a formal history but a firsthand memoir of the Vlasov movement from the point of view of these Germans, many of whom (including von Stauffenberg himself) were to perish in the military conspiracy against Hitler in 1944.

Vlasov despised Nazism. His programme was democratic and in his Prague Declaration he avoided even token obeisance to anti-Semitism. Indeed, one of his leading colleagues was a Jew, though the fact was naturally concealed from the Nazis. His German sponsors were also disaffected from Nazism, and had no use for the schemes of total victory and of the treatment of Slavs as sub-men.

Vlasov wished to use the Nazis in the hope that Hitler or Hitler's successor would be forced to moderate his policy in eastern Europe and accept an independent democratic Russia. But the whole idea was misconceived. While the Nazis were victorious, they saw no need of Vlasov and his Russian help. When they were obviously losing, Vlasov's appeal to Russia lost all its plausibility.

By the time Vlasov was able to put two divisions into action, the Red Army was on the Oder; they gave a good account of themselves, and, curiously enough, attracted a number of deserters from the other side, even at this hopelessly late stage. Later, Vlasov's troops played a major role in liberating Prague from the SS.

His aim now was simply to keep all non-Soviet forces in existence with the expectation that Stalin, like Hitler, would overplay his hand and attack the West. But Stalin's methods were not so crude. Those eastern European democrats and nationalists and socialists who hoped to use him, as Vlasov had hoped to use Hitler, to establish free regimes, were to face similar disillusion, but not yet.

Vlasov and his leading colleagues were, of course, executed in 1945. The rank-and-file Vlasovites were all sent to labour camps. But, ironically enough, they only got the ten-year sentence then customary. When the Soviet prisoners of war who had been in German camps and refused to join Vlasov were in their turn sentenced for 'desertion' by the NKVD, they mostly got twenty-five years. This anomaly naturally led, as Solzhenitsyn pointed out, to much ill-feeling in the camps. Survival, under either of the two maniacs who fought over Europe in those days, was a chancy business.

1973

Genocidal Operations

Alexander Nekrich is a historian. He was also a central figure in a major Soviet scandal, and thus himself a living lesson in the great issues of truth and falsification. Thinking minds of every type eventually got into trouble in the Soviet Union. Dr Nekrich's confrontation with the authorities is particularly interesting and illustrative, since, as a professional historian, he had the impertinence to turn his hand to modern themes. Now, the single area which the Soviet rulers least like to have researched and written about is, of course, the record of their own regime.

In Moscow in 1965 Nekrich published his book, *June 22 1941*, an account of the start of the German invasion. From his investigation it was clear that Stalin and his closest subordinates had made enormous political and military miscalculations, had refused to listen to evidence showing this, and – when the invasion actually took place – had fallen into something like panic. The book was condemned, removed from libraries and destroyed. Nekrich was expelled from the party, and a large-scale row shook the Institute of History, which at one point was totally dissolved.

It was, of course, due only to what remained of the Khrushchevian 'thaw' that Nekrich was able to accomplish his research and publish *June 22 1941* at all. But even then there were vast areas of Soviet history which could not be referred to. The extent to which falsehood and suppression prevail and major truths are denied or ignored in the USSR is astonishing to the Western mind. But there is more to it than that. Those who cover up the crimes and follies of Stalinism are telling us a great deal not only about the past, but also about themselves and how they look at the world today, for they thus ostentatiously identify themselves with the frightful period that produced them. Until they publicly purge themselves and their party of this guilt and let truth be told, they remain not only Stalin's heirs but also his accomplices.

The revulsion of Soviet historians – the unanimous revulsion of all genuine Soviet historians – against the reimposition of total falsification produced tactical problems for the party *apparat*. In the end, although in disgrace, Nekrich retained his salary as the equivalent of a full professor and was allowed a quota of one article a year in an academic magazine of limited circulation.

Nevertheless, he managed to write *The Punished Peoples* while he was still in the Soviet Union, and the manuscript was sent out before the author himself came West in 1976. The book deals with one of the most extraordinary of the Stalinist monstrosities: the deportation *en masse*, with enormous casualties, of eight whole peoples, men, women and children, numbering over a million and a half souls during the period 1941–44.

For a Soviet historian, it is better to be in the West. It is true that here he does not have access to a great deal of documentary material; but, even apart from crucial documents permanently under lock and key, the historian there who has once given a true account of something is thereafter barred from even the minimum materials necessary to his profession. On the other hand, Westerners who have written on modern Soviet history have the disadvantage of never having had access to such material (although there is material in the West that is practically unknown even to serious Soviet students). But, above all, Western historians inevitably lack the background of years of professional conversations, firsthand experience, and so on, of their Soviet counterparts. In the future, Nekrich will be in a position to enjoy the advantages of his new milieu, while retaining the benefits of his old one.

Meanwhile, if his book has (for us) a fault, it is the feeling it gives of being written for a Soviet audience. Thus the author goes to some length to try to demonstrate that the deported peoples did not deserve their fate because they were innocent of anti-Soviet feeling. Admittedly, he is not rigid about this, conceding that the Kalmyks and the Chechens, for instance, were generally less well disposed to the Stalin regime than were the Tatars. But to be anti-Soviet after years of repression is not in the least reprehensible. The extent of the disaffection is not easy to determine; but at any rate the official documents of different periods, alternately showing deep devotion and mass treason, are not in themselves to be trusted.

Surprisingly little has appeared in the West about the whole ghastly episode. Solzhenitsyn has a chapter in it in the last volume of the

Gulag Archipelago, and there have been a few other short descriptions. But the only books prior to Nekrich's, as far as I know, are my own. Nekrich pays most generous tribute to my work; however, while in the USSR, he was in a position to use only the first (*The Soviet Deportation of Nationalities*, published in 1960). He did not have access to the later and more complete *The Nation Killers* (1970). There is a discussion in it, for example, of the confidential police documents, made public by General Grigorenko, about the Crimean Tatar death-rate, leading to rather different conclusions from Nekrich's – conclusions also reached, later still, by the underground *Chronicle of Current Events* (no. 31).

There is certainly room for more than one book on this astonishingly neglected subject, and Nekrich adds a great amount of detail to our previous knowledge. He was himself in the Crimea in May 1944 when the Tatars were deported, and he quotes many conversations with locals in addition to his documentary material.

The facts Nekrich has to tell are as significant as the falsehoods he exposes. In 1941, the 400,000-odd Volga Germans were deported to Central Asia, charged with harbouring Nazi agents. Their 'autonomous republic' was suppressed, and their name and heritage disappeared from the official record. In 1943, they were followed by the 130,000 Kalmyks, an ancient Mongol and Buddhist race of the steppe, and the 75,000 Turkic Karachai of the Caucasus. In 1944, more Caucasian nations followed – the 40,000 Turkic Balkars, and the peoples who had inhabited the area from prehistoric times, the 400,000 Chechens and the 90,000 Ingushi; after them went the formerly great Islamic nation of the 240,000 Crimean Tartars. All of them were charged with collaboration with the Germans. They disappeared into the category of un-nations, and their lands were taken by Russians. At the end of the year the Muslim inhabitants of the Turkish frontier, the groups known as Meskhetian, were similarly deported, to the number of 200,000, without any specific reason being given. After the war, all the Greeks of the Black Sea region were also taken.

Such are the bare bones of the story, which at first could only be deduced from a couple of public decrees and some unexplained changes in the maps and textbooks. In each area, the flesh and blood of human suffering, of which Nekrich gives some shattering examples, began when thousands of police troops, supposedly present for manoeuvres, invaded the villages and gave the inhabitants a few hours to assemble for deportation. The deportees were allowed less than 30 pounds of baggage, the rest of their property being forfeit.

They were loaded aboard fleets of Lend-Lease Studebakers and taken to the railhead. There they were packed into cattle trucks under appalling conditions – some trains arrived after the five-to-six-week journey carrying no survivors at all. And this diversion of troops, concentration of trucks and movement of trains took place at a time when every effort was needed at the front; Nekrich tells us that the mere diversion of rolling stock amounted to 40,200 freight cars. When the refugees reached the deportation areas, they found desolation, an absence of even rudimentary housing, starvation rations. They died by the hundreds of thousands, men, women and children.

After 1956, these peoples were gradually rehabilitated, and now all but the Crimean Tartars, the Volga Germans and the Meskhetians have been allowed to return to their homelands. But even the favoured returnees do not seem grateful: the Chechens regularly blow up the statue of the nineteenth century Russian general who subdued them. And Nekrich tells a horrifying tale of a Russian anti-Ingush race riot in 1958, in Grozny, which lasted four days. In 1973, the Ingushi in turn demonstrated massively against continued repression. As for the three unreturned nations, their mass movement has attracted world attention. The plight of the Crimeans in particular is, objectively speaking, one of the most crying colonialist scandals in the world today.

This was only one episode in Stalin's holocaust; perhaps no more than half a million died in it. But Stalinism as a whole still gets remarkably little attention here compared with Hitlerism, which is odd when you consider that the former still lives.

1978

The Other Middle East

When we say 'the Middle East' we are usually thinking of a physical area bounded on the south by the Sahara and the waters of the Indian Ocean; a cultural area where Islamic and Arab civilization is the dominant factor. In one direction only we find neither a cultural nor a physical frontier but simply a political barrier: the boundary of the USSR. Yet this is nothing but the line reached by tsarist colonial expansion at the beginning of this century. Beyond it there is another huge area which is equally the Middle East, part of the great Islamic cultural belt.

The Russian Empire expanded to the Pacific by the end of the seventeenth century, across the more or less vacant expanse of Siberia. South of this stretch were not empty lands, but areas of old Mohammedan states and cultures. Samarkand and Bokhara were Islamic centres as well known as Kairouan or Baghdad. The north Caucasus was not finally conquered by the Russians until the 1860s, and the emirates of Turkestan not until a generation later.

Moscow managed to divide the Middle East by an Iron Curtain just as it divided Europe. Yet the setting up of miles of barbed wire and the intrusion of divisions of Russian frontier troops have no more de-Islamized and de-Turkized central Asia than they have converted Poland into a non-European community.

In the southern, or free, part of the Middle East the Russians strongly advocate the unity of the various Arab-speaking peoples. In their own area they strongly suppress pan-Turkism, the equivalent. In their propaganda they conduct violent attacks on alliances between the United Kingdom and independent states of Arabia. Criticism of their own rule over the colonial territories of Turkestan and the Caucasus is treated as vicious incitement.

Colonel Hostler's *Turkism and the Soviets* is an encyclopaedic assembly, from all the available sources, of material on the Turkic elements in the Soviet Union, a most thorough and unpretentious job on a neglected subject (though not entirely without slips – for instance, the Pomaks are not Turkish-speaking). As he shows, the Russians have taken every possible step to destroy Islamic and Turkic sentiments. First, they have split up the nationalities of Turkestan politically and attempted to exaggerate the diversity and to deny the common features of their languages and cultures; and they have provided them with false histories. Turkestan as a unit – indeed, even as a word – survives in the USSR only in the 'Turkestan Military district', under a Russian general.

These Russian measures have not been successful, and a high-pressure campaign against pan-Turk sentiment and Islamic custom continues. Nor has the culture in practice been assimilated to the Russian, as planned. The Uzbek cotton-grower has not, as he was supposed to, 'accepted the ideals of the Leningrad worker'.

The national sentiments of these people were made fairly clear when the German advance reached the northern Caucasus where some of them live. The punitive measures that followed the German withdrawal involved most of the nations of the area. Three Turkic and three non-Turkic races shared in Serov's mass deportations.

When Russia attacks our 'imperialisms' in the Middle East, too often the Soviet's own record is allowed to go by default. This is an area where independent states existed until the last century, and where they were again set up in 1918–20, only to be destroyed again by Moscow's army. Yet the mere existence, even, of this large Russian intrusion into the Islamic sphere is often forgotten. But it is important not merely as a debating point. For the whole of the vast area of the Soviet Middle East retains a potential dynamism against communist rule, just as – indeed, much more than – Arab nationalism does against the more flexible West. When and if the Soviet regime breaks up or evolves, this area will come back into the world. Even in its present unbreakable quarantine, it plays an important part. It is kept alive by the existence of the great Islamic culture to the south of it; and at that same time that culture, with all its temporary emphasis against the West, never entirely forgets the far greater hostages it has had torn from it, and looks forward to one day receiving back.

1957

In Defence of Kremlinology

Quis? Quid? Ubi? Quibus auxiliis? Cur? Quomodo? Quando?
(mediaeval legal hexameter)

There have been many attacks on the practice of Kremlinology. I took particular note of these arguments when they found expression in connection with my own *Power and Policy in the USSR*. This was essentially a large-scale exercise in the genre, and it naturally attracted (and I naturally read with particular interest) reviews by numbers of scholars for whose opinion I have great respect, and several of whom stated their reservations about the whole approach in cogent terms.

I did, indeed, detect a certain competitiveness of approach, a certain possessiveness even, which seemed to lead to exaggeration. Sir William Hayter, for example, wrote of Kremlinology that I 'would probably argue that it is the only valid branch of, or indeed coextensive with, sovietology'. But of course I would do no such thing. In fact, I have myself written on several other sides of Soviet life. But it does not seem reasonable to blame me when, in a book about the struggle for power, I treat economic and other matters only, or mainly, for their relevance to it. Sir William seems to be in the position of a man who criticizes a book on the climbing of Mount Everest because it ignores the – to him – more important question of the geology of the Himalayas. In fact I had written (and I imagine this would be the opinion of most Kremlinologists):

> Writings on the subject of questions of power in the USSR are often criticised roughly on the grounds that they ignore the existence of large-scale social forces. It should be said at once that although this book is not in principle concerned with the forces it does not for a moment deny or denigrate them. The Soviet leaders do not live in a vacuum, and

however much the totalitarian apparatus is designed to enable a few at the centre to manipulate the mass social tendencies, this does not mean that those tendencies do not exist nor, particularly when there is dissension at the centre, that they can fail to be taken into account. But this study is concerned with those large-scale movements only in so far as they are given political expression. And, in Soviet circumstances, they are not given any direct political expression: they figure simply as influences, competing with other and often more powerful influences, on the moves made in the only area where political change is possible – the central group of politicians.

In fact, the student of the struggle for power does not, as Sir William implies, deny the importance of sociological and economic developments within Russia. On the other hand, Sir William does appear to deny the significance of the political. But we are confronted in the Soviet Union not by a faceless society and economy but by an organization of actual rulers operating in accordance with definite standards of behaviour and preconceived doctrines. Any approach which ignores this tends to reduce the USSR to an abstraction of social forces not very different from our own. I suggest that the 'value' of the study of the struggle for power is that it shows how the political machine and the men composing it conduct themselves.

The temperamental reservations felt by many people against the study are not limited to the vague feeling that power on the one hand and personality on the other are nebulous subjects compared with the decent, impersonal, readily abstractifiable phenomena of general sociology and the homely and comfortable equations of the economists. They are also, I think, directed against the type of research worker who becomes involved in this unrespectable field. He is seen, perhaps, as a sensationalist – or, if not that, perhaps as a man who prefers an area in which speculation must remain the norm, just because this provides an opportunity for the construction of crackpot theories. And it is true that in its time Kremlinology has attracted such people. Yet there is another and different temperament which, I think, finds such subjects particularly fascinating. That is, the type of mind which is drawn to areas where the information is not adequate and a great effort has to be made to force the deductions from recalcitrant material.

That this temperamental distinction within the subject is not confined to Kremlinology may be illustrated in another field. The Vinland problem – the attempt to deduce the location of the brief Norse settlements and their other place-names in North America around the year 1000 from the available documents and the facts of geography –

has recognizably drawn two quite different types of enthusiast. One is concerned to prove, with immense and laboured detail, that favourite spots answer to each point; these usually work in a large amount of local evidence which could equally well prove anything. On the other hand, there are those who may reach virtual certainty on one or two points, high probability on others and complete bafflement on still others: men who are truly concerned not merely to establish the truth but to consider the impossibility of establishing it; and to balance the claims of two alternatives, when the evidence does not answer. These letters seem to me to be admirable, perhaps the most admirable type of intellectual exercise in existence – just as Namier seems to me to be worth a hundred Toynbees.

Such a man, in the Vinland case, was J. R. Swanton, whose comment is extraordinarily apt to Kremlinology too:

> The fact of the matter is that the data are just strong enough to tempt one to theorise and just weak enough to open the door for an immense amount of speculation, especially if one has an undisciplined imagination and a plentiful supply of local pride or wishful thinking. . . . it is one of those investigations which enable men who pride themselves on their acumen to prove it by leaving the problems ostentatiously alone or by registering scepticism, the cheapest way there is to acquire a reputation for scientific ability.[1]

The temperamental objection to such an attitude comes out again, I think, in Sir William Hayter, when he writes: 'A classic specimen of the kind of thing I have in mind occurs when Mr Conquest describes the twentieth party congress at great length without ever mentioning what were, to my mind, its most important results, the revision of the doctrines about the inevitability of major wars and the possible achievement of socialism by parliamentary means.' Now, in the first place, I was not especially concerned to decide in a general way what were the 'most important' results of the congress, but merely to deal with it as it affected the study I was engaged upon – just as it would be unfair to a writer of the history of the British Cabinet in the 1830s to say of him that he seemed to think the only important thing about the development of the railway engine was that one of them had killed Huskisson. But I feel, still, that Sir William shows very strongly the dangers of too great a revulsion from Kremlinology. Of the two points he takes as being the most important one, the theorising about the attainment of power by parliamentary means, strikes me as very

[1] John R. Swanton, 'The Wineland voyages', Smithsonian Miscellaneous Collections, vol. 107, no. 12.

minor and largely concerned with verbal propaganda. Suslov, Mikoyan and the others who put it forward combined it with strong attacks on reformism and gave as their example of a parliamentary evolution what had already happened in Prague and elsewhere in eastern Europe! (I have, as a matter of fact, dealt with this elsewhere.) The non-inevitability of war was, indeed, an important theme. And it may be taken as registering the acceptance by Moscow of the undesirability of a nuclear clash. But even on this one may perhaps doubt it was more than the transformation into theory of what had already happened in practice.

But, in any case, not to grant equal status as a major political event to the attack on Stalin seems to be greatly overdoing things, on any view. After all, it launched a series of vast political changes throughout the communist world, which are still going on. (And is it irrelevant to note that the *Observer*, in which Sir William's review appeared, had at the time devoted an entire issue to the Secret Speech?)

A taste for what one might call anti-politics leads to the neglect of matters not only important in themselves but often actually decisive in the fields which anti-political man is trying to cultivate as autonomous enclosures. As I said in *Power and Policy*:

> There seems to be a definite feeling among sociologists that the actual events of politics and war are in some way superficial. They believe that deep social tides are more basic to all change in human circumstances and that battles and *coups d'état* are somehow rather petty subjects. And it is true that to concentrate attention on them in such a way as to imply a denial of the existence of deeper movements would be absolutely wrong. Just the same, it is a little unreal to deal only with the deeper movements and ignore the visible political and military climaxes. It is rather as if a man interested in racehorses should study only their form and their general condition, without concerning himself with the actual races.

This view of history is dubious enough at the best of times. 'The best of times' was probably in the nineteenth century, when economic forces were exceedingly powerful and political ones comparatively weak – and, in any case, often disoriented by the current theory that political intervention in economic matters was bad doctrine. Even then, Engels had been able to point out that 'Force is itself an economic power'. It is the great discovery of the twentieth century that political and political-military technique and organization can be developed to such a degree of power and efficiency that they are able for the first time in history (if we except some special cases like

Inca Peru, as Plekhanov noted) to take the economic forces head on and thwart and divert them. Sociologically, the totalitarian state is a lever by which one man, or a small group, can exert the same weight as whole social classes.

Ironically, it was in the USSR that this discovery was given practical form. Stalin's collectivization and industrialization were the imposition of policy decisions against the wish of the whole people and the tendencies of the economy. Their dynamic – and it was one which defeated the supposedly unconquerable forces arising naturally in the economy and society – was a theory in the minds of a few policymakers, will-power in the skull of a paranoid Georgian. For once, an Idealist Conception of History was correct.

Our own epoch has been the scene of a number of attempts prematurely to erect into rigorous disciplines various studies which are not yet prepared for this. The prestige of the true sciences has been so great that there has been a rush to make some of it rub off on investigations which cannot yet meaningfully absorb it. In part this has been abetted by the creation of academic institutions to which the erection of 'scientific' theory gives added *raison d'être*. Thus we have seen the pretensions of 'literary criticism' blown up past bullfrog-bursting point. There is the now crumbling structure of Freudian psychology. And, to my mind, a great deal of what passes for scientific sociology is of a similar nature. (One of the distinctions between a scientific journal and one aping science is that in the former the interest always lies in the anomalous, that which appears *not* to fit existing conceptions, while in the latter, as in a theological journal, everything proves the theorist right all the time.) But even bona-fide science has produced many an erroneous theory. Its past it littered with astrologies and phrenologies. The tide seems to be running against the last batch.

But one of the saddest by-products of a dubious sociological attitude has, in any case, been the persistence of historicism – of the notion that there are forces assessable by economic or sociological means which are determinative of history. That is, in effect, the formal denial that politics are anything but an epiphenomenon of other processes. Or, even if the 'superstructure' is permitted to react upon the base, it reacts according to rules ultimately determined outside itself. This view is one which typifies the over-tidy mind, the simplifier who has, moreover, already oversimplified for himself even the 'base'. It arouses not only rejection, but also resentment, because it is in political action too often an excuse for inhumanity, the theorist being prepared to accept the real and visible sacrifice of generations and nations in the name of the (one would have thought) less tangible future predicted by his patent method. I cannot believe that this is an accidental correlation, that it is mere chance that the idolater of the abstractions of System and History is also the worshipper of Power and the shrugger-off of the suffering of the mass of individuals.

What, in any case, is the nature of the Soviet polity? Professor Leonard Schapiro has written:

> How little as yet (one cannot safely make predictions about any political system) public opinion of any kind can hope to operate on politicians who, over a period of forty years, have mastered the art of keeping all power safely in their own hands – even though they may fight to the death inside their own narrow circle.

And he adds that the amateur is inclined

> to project on to the Soviet system political principles with which he is familiar in his own experience. They very seldom apply. For example, in democracies politicians quarrel over policies and if need be resign in the hope of making a comeback. In the Politbureau and the Presidium it is the other way round: politicians quarrel over power, using policies as a means of struggle.

And I suppose it would be agreed, except by superficial and optimistic journalists and their readers, that the 'liberalization' which took place in Russia after Stalin's death did not register any advance in the positive political power of the ruled. The *pays légal* was still limited to a few hundred or a few thousand apparatchiks. The autocracy shifted from repressionist to concessionist tactics as other autocracies have in the past, but it remained an autocracy. And the ruling class consisted as ever of the cadres who got their training under Stalin. The characteristics of this class – philistine, hypocritical, short-sighted, bigoted, ruthless, totally indoctrinated with their own right to rule – do not change overnight. Though some may be better than others, they are a special breed. And it is in the internal struggle that we can really see what they amount to.

The apparatocracy may, like previous ruling classes, crumble in the face of crises it is ill equipped to deal with. But it is extremely tenacious, and meanwhile the politics of Russia consists of the moves and manoeuvres of its members. If the contestants were called Michael the Drunkard or Basil the Macedonian we would have no difficulty in making the emotional effort of understanding that their ways are not ours. Yet in Byzantium too there was also doctrine – *filioque* and so on – on the one hand, and policy – taxation, or the defeat of the Bulgars – on the other.

It is vulgar and regrettable that important historical crises should be decided by personal ambition, but it is also, unfortunately, true. Soviet sources themselves are perfectly explicit about the role played by personal ambition and malice in the struggle for power, though naturally only on the part of the defeated. After accusing the 'anti-party group' of the egoism and love of power, Kuusinen, in his speech to the 22nd Congress, said: 'The main effort of the group was to remove from the Presidium of the Central Committee Comrade Nikita Sergeyevich Khrushchev.' Or again, 'Although the gingerbread was poisonous, Bulganin, being dissatisfied with his position in the party, nevertheless ran after it when it was promised to him' (S. D. Ignatiev at the December 1958 Plenum).

Policy is bound to enter in, if only for the reason that a struggle for power cannot be conducted openly on the programme 'We want your posts because we want to rule'. Doctrine is an element by which power can get a purchase. Stalin would have been thought a moderate at the time of the struggle against the Left Opposition, and was doubtless praised as such in the Western press. Having destroyed them, he was in a position to steal their policies and use them against the Right. Similarly, Khrushchev ensured Malenkov's first defeat by sponsorship of 'left' policies, and then turned right himself. The struggle with the anti-party group in 1957 has almost always been misrepresented. In fact both the victorious and the defeated factions contained right- and left-wing elements. The tactics they objected to in Khrushchev were ones of style rather than policy proper: 'The anti-party group – Malenkov, Kaganovich, Molotov, Bulganin and Shepilov – accused our party's Central Committee and also Comrade N. S. Khrushchev of practicism and of being too engulfed in the practical tasks of economic construction. As is known, such accusations were also raised by the Yugoslav revisionists (I. I. Kuzmin at the 21st Congress, *Pravda*, 5 February 1959). A viewpoint shared by Molotov and Tito is scarcely one of policy.

This also reminds us that, since, as we have said, the group contained the 'liberal' Malenkov and Shepilov as well as the 'reactionary' Molotov and Kaganovich, it could be attacked in connection with almost any policy which later became popular. Malenkov headed the list at first, and Molotov was transferred to top spot when, and only when, Khrushchev was directing his main fire against remaining 'conservative' elements within the party.

Another important deduction from this way of looking at things is that there is no necessary connection between policies. During the height of Khrushchev's 'liberalisation' at home, in 1962, we get the

Cuban adventure, a far riskier piece of 'forward' policy than anything of Stalin's – and understandably condemned, even by the Chinese, as 'adventurism'. What linked Khrushchev's policies was their 'style', as the Russians say – large, risky initiatives, looking as if they could bring big results on the cheap. Temper, or personality, rather than coherent views, seems the common factor – a curious conclusion about a man who was widely taken as primarily just the locus of social forces. It may remind us of Canning's 'Away with the cant of measures not men! – the idle supposition that it is the harness and not the horses that draw the chariot along'. This is to put it very strongly; yet in politics, in the area in which the actual decisions are taken that will determine the Russian future, does anyone imagine that things would have been the same if Molotov had come to power? And does anyone think that his accession to power was impossible, under some Law of History? Politics proper, moreover, is the realm of the accidental, the run of bad luck, the chance concatenation. The death of Hugh Gaitskell transformed British politics. So it has always gone, from the assassination of Lincoln to Kozlov's heart attack. Accident is unpredictable, but its effects may not be. To put it at its lowest, if we neglect the elements of this level of Soviet phenomena, we will not understand the rest.

No one would deny that there are other drives than mere power in the Soviet politician's motivations. Indeed, (as I wrote) in any struggle of this sort, 'idealism, conviction, careerism, and factiousness form an inextricable blend'. And again: 'it is virtually impossible to clarify how far the Communist leaders, or particular ones among them, are motivated by *odium theologicum* and how far by ambition, even in the struggle for power itself. This is more a psychological question than a political one.' We do not need to discover the extent to which the other motivations are psychological 'justification'. What we can say is that these qualifications apply to *all* political societies, but that the power motive is more obviously compelling or less adequately sublimated in some cases than in others. Napoleon had it worse than Lincoln, and Stalin than Attlee. And under Stalin, in the USSR, by a process of unnatural selection (as I also wrote), 'a hypertrophied type has been bred in which the motives that are sufficiently frenetic even in a wild Western office or university have become a full-time, consuming passion.'

Kremlinology may be thought of, *mutatis mutandis*, as the Namierism of Soviet political history. In Namier's special period of eighteenth century England the political nation consisted of a limited number of men – those members of the nobility, the merchant and intellectual classes, and the squirearchy, who were interested in politics. He was able to revolutionize a study previously based on generalizations by examining the particular moods and opinions of numbers of those concerned. Similarly, in the USSR, the *pays légal* is a limited one. Until recently only the actions of very few people at the centre needed to be considered, and the bare record of the allegiances of minor figures was adequate. It is now suggested (for example, by Edward Crankshaw) that, since a larger number of people are perhaps being admitted to the oligarchy, the method is no longer applicable. The contrary appears to be true: what is now required is large-scale research into the background of the lower-level repositories of power.

For in speaking of Kremlinology as a sort of Namierism we must unfortunately qualify this by saying that on the whole it is an inadequately resolved Namierism. There is still too much that we do not know but could know with a good deal more effort. To take a single point: Namier got his results by investigating the politics and the political weight of comparatively large numbers of people forming at least a reasonable cross-section of the entire *pays légal* of eighteenth-century Britain. My book and most of the others in the field seldom descend, and never fully or effectively, below the Presidium, or at most the Central Committee. The provincial secretary level and lower, and even the detailed backgrounds of all the Central Committee membership, are simply impossible without far greater and more widespread time, effort and facilities.

When it comes to talk about Russian politics there is really no such thing as a non-Kremlinologist. Whoever remarked that the man who says he is not a philosopher is simply a bad philosopher was making a point which may perhaps be taken as applying in this case to the study of Soviet politics. But can results be obtained within the field itself? Yes. It was possible to give what proved to be a sound account of the June 1957 crisis before confirmation came with later revelations. Even without much in the way of deduction and extrapolation, assembly of known facts and statements often provides a clear enough picture of events, and one which sometimes goes usefully against false preconception, giving a desirable shock to lazy assumptions that Soviet politics are not so different from our own. It is true, indeed, that deduction – or even speculation, if carefully controlled – can give good results, and in any case better ones than those based on conservative assumptions about harmonious development. As to simple deduction, I may quote one of several cases from my own book. With no 'inside' information, but simply working from facts and probabilities of their interpretation, I wrote of the circumstances of Khrushchev's Secret Speech:

> The impression remains strong that, although some sort of intention to disavow the purges had developed some weeks before the congress, the precise tactics had not been decided on up to the last moment . . . all this confusion and hesitation followed by a decision must have taken place within the presidium . . . a group determined to press the issue regardless could possibly have threatened to appeal to the Central Committee, or even the Congress, with facts which the others were in no position to deny, and the Secret Speech, unopposed, may represent a very reluctant compromise.

Five years later, Khrushchev, reporting to the 22nd Congress, said:

> Comrade-delegates, I want to tell the congress how the anti-party group reacted to the proposal to raise the question of abuses of power in the period of the cult of the individual at the 20th congress. The proposal was violently resisted by Molotov, Kaganovich, Malenkov, Voroshilov and others. We told them in reply to their objections that if they resisted consideration of this question, we would put the matter to the congress delegates. We had no doubt that the congress would express itself in favour of the consideration of this question. Only then did they agree, and the question of the cult of the individual was reported on at the 20th Congress.

Is this really to be regarded as having been either obvious or unimportant?

Everything that we read among the revelations about the struggle tells us something, begins to define the nature of the Soviet polity: it is one where a police chief plans a *coup d'état*; where an army leader is accused of 'Bonapartist aspirations towards a single-handed seizure of power'; where a Prime Minister throws his armed guards round the presidium; where gross insults are hurled between leading figures; where policies are launched not on their merits but to secure a power advantage, and condemned not on their demerits but in theological terms; where one former terror operative can charge his fallen opponents with terrorism – but not secure their expulsion from the party; where the very party history is altered decisively from edition to edition. Kremlinology is an attempt to obtain now, when it can be most useful, the information about Soviet politics which is thought to be essential when it comes to writing a history of earlier years. If an adequate account of the past is found impossible without it, how can it be imagined that an account of the present can dispense with it? Without this information our interpretation of events is certain to be defective at best. It is true that we may not always be able to get enough data for our purpose, but surely we are bound not to reject the attempt to do so.

For the essential importance of Kremlinology is this. We do not know enough about Soviet politics. We do not know the alignments, the political forces and motivations which produce the great policy decisions and lead to the enormous and important shifts, reversals, initiatives of the regime. We can all predicate, more or less, the choices open to the Soviet government in a given field, but we have little idea of what will decide the final real action.

It is not that we can seek any finality, any data on which certain prophecy can be based. No more can we in any other country; but in most other capitals we can at least meaningfully discuss the forces at work, the party and factional alignments, the personal affiliations. In fact most political comment about the rest of the world is in such terms. When we attempt it for the USSR, we must either *call* ourselves non-Kremlinologists and just guess or intuit, or we must go to Kremlinology, which is merely the assertion that faction and divergence exist in Russia as in every polity, and the formal determination to discover or deduce as much as possible about it by a conscientious study of the relevant evidence.

1962

A Degenerate Dynasty: Michel Tatu

Michel Tatu is uniquely qualified among analysts of the Soviet scene. His reports to *Le Monde* during the period 1957–64 were the undoubted high-point of Moscow-based journalism in that period, with their reliability as to fact and perceptiveness as to political nuance. He was deservedly lucky: the dates, it will be seen, cover almost precisely the period during which a skilled reporter could find, practically as in a civilized country, at least a few sources who would tell or hint some of the truth of what was actually going on. Better still, Tatu was able to send it out without the certain risk of expulsion (even when he recounted the proceedings of the disgusting writers' meetings at which Pasternak was vilified by a group of what one might well call, in the old Stalinist phrase, 'literary hyenas'). A few years later such freedom was inconceivable.

This was only one of the ways in which the Khrushchev interlude, however inadequate it appeared at the time, must now be looked back on as, comparatively speaking, a veritable Camelot. Tatu in his *Power in the Kremlin*, covering the period 1960–7, records its decline and fall and the establishment on its ruins of the narrower and nastier successor regime. It is by far the most impressive work in the field for many years.

It is, of course, true, as M. Tatu says, that more information will eventually be forthcoming. As he puts it, 'this reconstruction is only tentative. Some day, we may hope, archives will be opened – those of the Politburo and the Central Committee. The classic methods of historiography can then be applied and the present author for one will be delighted.' For the foreseeable future, however, the 'Kremlinological' method is the only way of approaching the problem of the relation between power and policy in the Soviet state. 'At present,' Mr Tatu remarks, 'there is in fact no other way of understanding what is going on in the centres of Soviet power'; indeed, he adds, the term 'Kremlinology' is in itself 'an unconscious tribute' to the method of detection, interpretation and deduction on which researchers must rely.

Mr Tatu has both of the qualities required for the task. On the one hand he has patiently sought out the fine detail of evidence. But, even more important, he has handled it with the skill and judgement, the open-minded boldness and the equally necessary refusal to jump to premature conclusions which mark the real master.

He has observed the substance, not the formalities, of scholarship. He has not cluttered up his book with references, but it is almost always clear from the narrative where to turn for additional data or analysis. I might note, parenthetically, that the question of 'scholarship' is a much muddled one. Nor is this the only field where a certain decadence in current notions of it need to be remedied by a good deal of back-pedalling. If one had to point to one central fault in modern academic attitudes, it is surely the attempt to import into areas where they are not suitable the discipline of the physical sciences, or the abstract generality of philosophy. As a result, we are beset with pretentious pseudo-sciences, or at best premature sciences (in the fields of sociology, psychology and literary criticism in particular), where a more modest and tentative approach might provide real insights.

To say that this is the best political history of the USSR in the 1960s is not to pay much of a compliment, since there are no others that rate the label. But, in addition to being unique, *Power in the Kremlin* is in itself a work of the highest excellence – a fact that does not have to be validated by comparison. It was time we had such a history. It was also time we were reminded once again of the dominating role of power in Soviet politics. In the author's words: 'Experience has in fact shown that the importance of objective problems frequently depends on their relevance to power relationships.' To compare Tatu's account with the majority of the works written during the Khrushchev period, which were based so frequently on the assumption that the First Secretary was in full control and meeting with no opposition (apart from a certain amount of friendly criticism on the part of his colleagues), is almost like comparing two different countries or epochs.

There is scarcely an area in which the author does not contribute illuminatingly to our knowledge. He shows clearly that – contrary to the analyses of so many experts – the CPSU Central Committee did *not* play a decisive role either in the 1957 or in the 1964 crisis. At first sight his microscopic examination of Soviet internal politics – that is to say of the struggle among the handful which constitutes all the live politics there is in the Soviet Union – may in itself appear a specialized interest, like entomology. But the conduct and motives of this limited fauna do, as it happens, connect with the gravest world problems. Tatu establishes the backgrounds and careers of the present leaders with exemplary skill, and follows the (often muffled) controversies which have marked the period in the clearest fashion. The fine detail itself is illuminating. We see, for example, that among the main groups struggling for power were two based respectively on the party machines in Dniepropetrovsk and Kharkov – as if the USA were a plum disputed by the power groups of a couple of Californian towns (San Diego, say, and Sacramento). Such are the reasons for the promotion of fourth-raters like Trapeznikov, head of the Science Department of the Central Committee (and attacked as such by academician Sakharov), dredged up by Brezhnev from petty bullying on the 'dull Moldavian steppe'.

Scraping the barrel for optimism, one is reduced to noting that rumour, the more credible because it was contrary to the natural guess, said of the decision to invade Czechoslovakia that it was undertaken against the advice of Suslov and Kosygin. However that may be, these are men who, though notorious for dull dogmatism in the Stalin and post-Stalin periods, were still bright in comparison with their colleagues – not necessarily less hostile in principle to democracy, even Czechoslovak style, but at least able to react not simply in Pavlovian slaverings and jerkings. Such men, with all their faults, are at least not quite extrusions of the lowest-common-denominator feelings of the baser grades of the New Class, ecoplasm of the *apparat*.

But, even allowing for these, it is remarkable how little individuality emerges in the later rulers. Malenkov, Beria, Molotov, Khrushchev were all colourful personalities, even if the colours were sometimes rather ghastly ones. They had standing with the population and party. They had definite policies. They were a leadership to be taken more or less seriously. In the later phase, a Russian writer commented: 'Khrushchev is a total empiricist, a dull man, entirely engrossed in his immediate affairs'; but 'as for the other leaders, Brezhnev is a lecherous toady, Suslov an anonymous illiterate'.

After the Second World War, Litvinov used to take foreign diplomats and correspondents aside and warn them that Stalin and his colleagues were thoroughly ignorant of the outside world, and that this constituted a terrible danger. But ignorance is a relative term.

Later rulers were almost literally deprived of any genuine notion of 'outside'. Nor should we be misled by the fact that Soviet moves are explained and justified in Marxist language. It is a fairly easy routine to pick up, and the rulers employ 'ideologists' fairly skilled in word-play, who bear about as much relation to Marx as a gangland lawyer drafting legal wrangles for a hoodlum does to Blackstone.

Brezhnev and his colleagues were the first generation of rulers actually to be the products of the Stalin system. Their predecessors, though they all played murderous roles in the purges, had already risen to positions of influence before the system started. They were at least the manufacturers of terror rather than its products, Franken-steins rather than Monsters. But those who came up in 1930–53 all qualified mainly by the ruthless servility of their denunciations of colleagues. They were, as a close observer noted at the time, 'morally and intellectually crippled'. And so the sequence Lenin-Stalin-Malen-kov-Khrushchev-Brezhnev is like (even physically, though that may be accidental) a chart illustrating the evolution of the hominids, read backwards. If this trend continues, who knows what shambling Dusk-Man awaits us next? The main reflection arising from Tatu's precep-tive work is a gloomy one: that it is difficult to be optimistic about the prospects of peace when vast military power is in the hands of men one could hardly trust with a catapult.

Thus the period that Tatu covers – at least after the fall of Khrush-chev – is in one way less interesting than earlier times. The degener-ation of the Soviet ruling caste had reached the stage in which there were no longer powerful personalities with definite attitudes and programmes, but third-rate, short-view, hidebound petty bureau-crats, concerned only about how best to enjoy the fruits of office. That even these third-raters can here for the first time be seen in a genuine political perspective, in their tensions and disputes, is a major achievement of the author.

The conclusion that seems to arise from the whole Khrushchev interlude is that no ruler can reform Russia, even in a fairly mild use of the word, unless he can crush the old-line *apparat*. Khrushchev made some progress in this direction, but not enough. His schemes went far enough to irritate, but not far enough to subdue the apparat-chiks. Mr Tatu shows in detail how these tactics led to the First Secretary's fall.

One looks to the even slightly more intelligent members of the Politburo in the hope that one or another of them may attempt (or be forced) to defend himself and fight for power by once again turning to the weapon of anti-Stalinism. Thus far, to be sure, we can only detect the merest catspaws of such a wind, hardly stirring the sluggish surface on the Soviet political waters. In the long run, however, progress can come only with some contender for power using anti-Stalinism against his opponents, as Khrushchev did against the 'anti-party group' in 1957.

It may be argued, of course, that (unless as a result of a complete breakdown of authority) genuine reforms in Russia can be carried out only by an autocrat like Peter the Great or Alexander II, able to face down the opposition of his own ruling class. However that may be, the country is now stuck in a situation in which revolutionary change is called for by all the social, economic and intellectual forces, and opposed and aborted only by a political machine specially constructed for the purpose. It is a highly artificial situation, resembling that of Mr Waldemar in Poe's story. In the very long run, Mr Tatu expects an eventual liberalization of the Soviet system and the emergence of a true parliamentary form of government. Meanwhile, he thinks the country will experience various swings, including a possible reversion to one-man dictatorship and even police coups and military coups: 'things are probably doomed to get worse before they get better.' The one thing he believes certain is that the rule of the current morocrats is 'drawing to an end'. This book is more of a monument than they deserve, but it is indispensable to anyone wishing to understand contemporary Soviet history.

1969

Pseudo-history 1: Isaac Deutscher

It was as a biographer that Isaac Deutscher established his reputation. His trilogy on Trotsky is a striking and valuable work. It was
a theme which fitted perfectly with his virtues and made no call on
his vices. For biography, and in particular the biography of a highly
histrionic and self-dramatizing character like Trotsky, fits almost
perfectly with his unshakeable notion of history as a Great Drama.
The biography of Stalin is less impressive, but it has its merits.

The trouble is that Deutscher wishes to be more than a historical
dramatist (within the Unities, or rather Trinities, laid down by that
bearded old Boileau of the British Museum). Men with one gift often
waste it on unsuitable enterprises: it is no reflection on Engels's real
talent that his writings on science are almost worthless. The temptation to set up as a general seer is none the less unfortunate. In
Deutscher's case this is accompanied, as so often, by an unbecoming
touchiness and asperity, with the frequent implication that personal
malignity is at work against him.

In *Ironies of History* he has rather mistakenly included the material
of a speech on Vietnam which he delivered in Washington in 1965.
In it he argues that following the Second World War Russia would
for long 'not be able to wage any major war', and that therefore
NATO was based on an unreal scare. Pro or con, it is at least clear
that the whole purpose of NATO was precisely to face Stalin with
the prospect of a major war if he tried to expand his empire further.
Without NATO, he could have expanded *without* facing a major war.
Such is the state of Deutscher's major premise on this point. But it
is when we come to the evidence supporting the anti-Western view
that the real trouble starts. 'It was only after the Communists had
been ejected from the French and Italian governments that Stalin
began to eject the anti-Communists from the Eastern European

governments.' In fact, it was in January 1945 that Vyshinsky's ulti-
matum secured the expulsion of Maniu and the democratic parties
from the Romanian government. Petkov and the Bulgarian equivalents were out by that summer. In East Germany the Social Democrats were destroyed in April 1946. Mikolajczyk and his Peasant
Party had been excluded from the Polish government by February
1947; and in the same month the Smallholder leadership in Hungary
had been accused of conspiracy, and their Secretary-General was
under arrest. It was in May 1947 that the Communist ministers left
the governments of Italy and France.

In various other contexts, his view of history can be seen to lead
to this tidying-up of reality. Deutscher even omits, in a long dramatiz-
ation of Bolshevism's well-deserved and foreordained triumph over
Menshevism, that telling – though perhaps in the wrong way – last
scene: the fake Menshevik Trial of 1931, of which neither Trotsky
nor any other communist expressed disapproval. The same approach
is the be noted, too, in his reconstructions, in *oratio recta*, of entirely
hypothetical discussions in the Presidium, or between foreign states-
men; and in the curious attempt, based entirely on gossip, to present
Marshal Rokossovsky as a keen anti-Stalinist. It is hard, in that case,
to account for his signature on a reactionary letter to several Soviet
papers in April 1966 attacking as an attempt to 'defame' heroic
traditions *Novy Mir*'s cry for the elimination of 'shoddy untruths' from
party history.

Critics of Mr Deutscher have several times given laborious chapter
and verse on his mistakes in the analysis of Soviet politics, and his
failures in prediction. The past, at least, already exists, with much
material of use to the historical dramatist; to write the drama of the
future is trickier, since we are always catching up on it. Sometimes,
particularly when he has made several contradictory forecasts on the
same point, he turns out to have scored some hits, and he makes the
most of these. When he is right *with* the main body of commentators,
as he often is, he contrives an impression of solitary insight by arguing
against straw men of his own creation or inflation. Where he is wrong
against the main body of commentators, as with his confident assertion
in October 1964 that the new Soviet leaders 'will certainly go to
Peking on a pilgrimage of penance and reconciliation', he omits the
prediction.

Mr Deutscher's views are not clear-cut, and to some degree they
lack coherence. He has to postulate that the 1956 Hungarian movement was anti-socialist – and he even asserted at the time that it had
fallen into the hands of Cardinal Mindszenty, a non-fact of which

Sartre wrote that 'only Stalinist paranoia' could lead to such a mistake. Mr Deutscher is tetchy about opponents he understands to be speaking of him as a mere apologist for Stalinism. And, of course, he is no such thing. He sees the 'barbarism' of Stalinism, even of Khrushchevism, embedded in the present Soviet scene. But when it comes to action he invariably urges political restraint upon the liberal forces in the bloc – a line which has even involved him in sharp interchanges with the revisionists in Warsaw. He is often illuminating about Stalinism and about the partial nature of 'de-Stalinization'. But somehow none of this is essential. Behind the 'accidents' he sees, like some medieval philosopher, 'substance' unaffected by them. He is not a 'Trotskyite' or a 'Stalinist'. But he still remains in general, though touched by hopes of a limited degree of liberal progress, within the scope of the monopolistic political idea behind both of them. He once expressed the hope that a future Russia would have public statues to both Stalin and Trotsky. Better neither than either, or both.

1983

Pseudo-history 2: G. D. H. Cole

We may take a single incident to show both the distinction, (some-times blurred by Professor Cole in his *Communism and Social Democracy 1914–1931*) between communist and non-communist habits of mind, and at the same time the slightly slap-happy nature of Cole's methods of scholarship on sensitive points. In 1925 several hundred leading Bulgarians were killed when Sofia Cathedral was blown up. In his *Selected Articles*, published in English in London in 1951 we find Georgi Dimitrov saying two different things. In 1933, he claims that it 'was not organized by the Bulgarian Communist Party . . . That act of provocation, the blowing up of Sofia Cathedral, was actually organ-ized by the Bulgarian police.' In 1948, now safely in power, he admits 'the desperate actions of the leaders of the Party's military organization, culminating in the attempt at Sofia Cathedral'. Pro-fessor Cole is able to say, 'It never became fully clear who was behind this outrage.' He also gets the date wrong.

Professor Cole is inclined to argue that what anti-communist social-ists mainly object to in communism is that it comes to power by violence. But the objection to the Bolsheviks is much less their taking power by force than their later dissolution of the properly elected Constituent Assembly, with its great socialist, though anti-Bolshevik, majority. Professor Cole's democrat who rejects the use of violent methods against a tyranny is a myth. What is rightly detested is the use of violent methods against the *people*, converted into a permanent method of rule. Lenin was not just a sort of socialist Garibaldi. And Professor Cole sees this part of the time. He makes the points against Soviet 'centralized bureaucracy' which he sees to be 'destructive of personal liberty and freedom of thought and action'. But he largely discounts them on the grounds of the 'brutalizing social and econ-omic' effects of capitalism. His theme is that communist rule is fine socially and economically because it is non-capitalist. But it is a country organized in what Professor Cole regards as a socialist manner, Poland, whose economy is officially declared at intervals to be in a state of 'disintegration'. It has been in 'socialist' countries that the working class, which Professor Cole believes to benefit from Soviet-type rule, has turned in desperation to the weapon of the general strike – in East Germany, Hungary and Poland. Even with political liberty there may be economic injustice; without it, it is inevitable.

This fourth volume of the author's *A History of Socialist Thought* is devoted to such fetishism of the formal economic structure, with the accompanying thesis that communism, though in many ways reprehensible, is a sort of socialism. And he seems besotted with the idea that, historically speaking, Bolshevism emerged from the social-ist movement and *therefore* remains part of it. The political genealogy is correct: but this is like saying that Cordelia and Goneril are two of a kind because they are sisters. The occasional slip-up on the facts is hardly relevant. For this is not history but exegesis. To take a minor but ineluctably factual point – the dates of death, to which the brief preface makes special reference: for example, Lozovsky is given as dying in '194?' (*sic*), whereas it has long since been officially confirmed that he was shot in 1952. Nor ought it to be difficult to tell us whether the leading Russian social democrat, R. Abramovich, an active and accessible figure in New York, is alive or not. Again, how is it possible even to sketch the history of Polish socialism and communism in the twenties without more than passing reference at all to the Marchlewski puppet government? In fact, throughout, the theme comes first and the facts must fit in as best they can – a sort of socialist Toynbeeism. And it should be remembered that we are writing of a man of enormous repute on the British Left and in British academe.

1958

Pseudo-history 3: The Revisionist Mind

It might be argued that the books we now deal with are not worth the powder and shot. Intrinsically, this is true enough. But as phenomena, representative of much printed material disinformative of the West, they are after all significant.

D. F. Fleming's *The Cold War and Its Origins 1917–1960* for example, would be of no interest at all except that it was heartily welcomed by a large fringe here and in the USA as a sort of seminal work. So it has some significance, as an indication of the intellectual and political standards of such people. 'Bible', even if one takes it in terms of some crackpot sect, is not quite the right description. Dr Fleming's method is rather that of the crackpot pseudo-sciences – the assembly of a vast amount of ephemeral and uncritical quotation from non-authorities which supports his views. In fact, he gives the effect of scholarship by endless references from, in the main, journalism which happens to suit the thesis and, far from strengthening it, weakens it. It was precisely in this way that similar tomes proved the Baconian theory, or the existence of flying saucers. In fact, it is political pseudo-science, related to political science proper as those fads are to the relevant genuine disciplines.

The book purports to be an account of the contest between the Soviet and Western blocs and runs to more than 1100 pages. But it is a curious history of the 'Cold War' which accepts (on such a basis) Stalin's good intentions towards Eastern Europe; contrives not to mention that the Balkan Peace Treaties guaranteed the freedom of operation of all anti-fascist parties; maintains that the Smallholders Party in Hungary was an agency of 'dispossessed landlords'; that the opposition to communism in Greece in 1944–5 came from 'the Greek officer class'; that the revolting Bierut regime in Poland was 'popular'; and so on. The author says that 'the American police state, conjured up during a wave of hysteria to combat a non-existent inundation by the Soviet police state, which Khrushchev has since very largely dismantled, still grinds away. Our Communist "enemy" has proved that it can largely purge itself of such practices. Is a great democracy helpless to do so?'

The book, relying on the sources it does, of course teems with factual errors, and it is extraordinarily badly written. But this is nothing compared with the animus shown in the sentence just quoted. One would imagine, reading it, that opposition parties flourished and anti-communist books could be bought in the Soviet Union while in the United States a one-party regime prevented the sale of anti-capitalist literature. I can buy *Pravda* in 42nd Street, I can get Sholokhov in any paperback store. In Moscow I cannot even buy Pasternak, let alone the *Wall Street Journal*.

Dr Fleming is not so much pro-Soviet as anti-American. But his attitude to Russia is fantastic throughout. For instance, he opposes Kissinger's idea that it might be possible in a nuclear war to declare open cities. There are arguments against this proposal, but the adjective Dr Fleming uses is a little curious when he comments that the idea would be unacceptable to 'the Kremlin or any other spirited government'.

In 1945 Stalin assured Harry Hopkins, Roosevelt's representative, that he did not want Poland to be sovietized. Dr Fleming asks, 'was Stalin merely pulling the wool over Hopkins' eyes?' After all, 'he spoke these words to his friend Harry Hopkins . . . after Roosevelt's death Hopkins was the man in all the West whom Stalin had least reason to hoodwink.' So Dr Fleming concludes, as indeed he does of all other pronouncements by Stalin, that Stalin was perfectly sincere and only changed his line because of Western wickedness! Instances of Stalin consciously deceiving those with whom he came in contact are thick on the ground from the earliest moment of his political career. As for Harry Hopkins being Stalin's 'friend', he seems to have taken particular pleasure in sending much closer friends to the execution cellars on false charges. But how is it that this even needs to be said?

In America one sees a vast output of anti-American books, but there are pro-American books to balance them. In Britain, by an invidious process of selection, we get practically nothing but the anti-American stuff, reinforced by local output on the same lines – the political equivalent of Auden's

Enormous novels by co-eds

> Rain down on our defenceless heads
> Till our teeth chatter.

Vulnerable minds are often persuaded by this method of the most unlikely propositions – that Oswald did not kill Kennedy, for example.

There are cants and cants, and each country produces its own variety. One of the American-style importations – perhaps based on all that is most third-rate in American university thesis-writing – is this taste for ream after ream of pseudo-documentation. Another example is David Horowitz's *The Free World Colossus*. It is fairly clear that the author believes 'Colossus' to be a derogatory word – perhaps he is thinking of Juggernaut or some cliché different from the one employed. At least the standard of thought implies something of the sort. Its style of thesis is that Britain and America support 'reactionaries' all round the world. We have Greece, for example, listed as a 'dictatorship' in the years 1946–61!

The method is simple. For instance – to take the Greek example again – you wish to support the loathsome Zachariades and the victory of the communists in the post-war struggle. You prove that it was solely in the interests of reaction that the British intervened against them by quoting another leftist, Mr Howard Smith, on our wish to install 'the discredited monarchy and its blindly vengeful Rightist supporters'. Add a footnote referring one to 'loc. cit.', and follow with a good deal of 'ibid.'-ing through the chapter. You then make a lot of assertions about Greek poverty: Greece had at this time in fact, one of the highest rates of increase in productivity in the world. Even more to the point, the alternative offered, as practised north of the Rodopi, was a reduction to sweated poverty. The Karamanlis 'dictatorship' held free elections resulting in a change of government. Even under right-wing rule one could see crowded communist meetings in the middle of Athens; in Sofia, the social democrats were destroyed and no voice but that of the government permitted.

Foreign politics have deep moral implications. Yet it will hardly be denied that there are ways of moralizing about it which amount to smug cant. If a man takes an extreme, absolutist moral view – the equivalent of Kant holding that it would be wrong to tell a lie even to divert a murderer from his victim – we may shrug our shoulders impatiently but yet have a certain respect for the argument and the arguer. When someone points out the slightest deviation from a proposed set of standards on the part of democracies, holding that immoral action by their opponents does not justify their replying in kind, any more than the police should use criminal methods, again we may feel that the rigour is excessive, but respect the argument.

What we get in practice is something different. The excesses of the totalitarian regimes are palliated or excused. It is not said: 'Oh, one cannot expect any better of them, but we should not follow their example.' On the contrary, their aggressions and atrocities are spoken of almost with affection.

A young socialist once said to me that, though he personally fully agreed with the defence of the Western democratic culture (where socialists are allowed) against the totalitarian communist culture (where they are not), he often found himself in difficulties when arguing the detail against, for example, those who maintained the humanism of Hanoi or Havana. He knew that the facts and arguments they produced were not based on knowledge, but were obtained wholesale. But still he did not have the counter-arguments to hand.

In reality, the true facts in every field are available. We are not in the position – as we were to some extent in the thirties – of lacking a core of serious students of the communist countries. It is possible to read and study their work. What is missing is any highly organized system, or party machine, for transmitting the results, such as is available to the falsifiers.

But this is always the case with the comparative advocacy of truth and falsehood. It requires much more effort and 'proof' to show that black is white than that black is black. The anti-Western argument, being against good sense and common knowledge, needs this sort of special pleading.

Even in more rigorous spheres, it is common enough that the ideas which sweep the half-baked are not those of, say, scholarly medicine, but acupuncture or the molasses diet. Nor is the nub of the matter affected by the occasional serious student on the crank side who sometimes lends its case a little colour (just as the communists got a genuine British major to prove that the Red Army's 1939–40 campaign in Finland was a brilliant triumph – a view long since abandoned in the Soviet military press).

George Orwell writes in 'Such Were the Joys', his story of his schooldays, that when he was ten years old he knew more facts about sex than he had done when he was six or seven; but that, basically, he knew less about it – for he had forgotten the essential point that it was enjoyable. One finds intellectuals who know more 'facts' (many of them, indeed, as dubious as the facts about sex known to a ten-year-old boy) about totalitarianism. But, basically, they know less about it than the man in the street – for they have forgotten, as he has not, that it is not enjoyable.

The argument is sometimes overtly anti-Western. Sometimes (as with Mr Horowitz) it is an attempt to save the West by the modest proposal that we should, on the whole, support our opponents. As the author regretfully admits, progressives like Stevenson and Kennedy, Humphrey and Johnson did not share his views – and one might add Attlee and Gaitskell, Wilson and Callaghan. It is not a question of left or right, but of sense or silliness. The material we have dealt with here illustrates a psychological rather than an intellectual phenomenon. There seems little prospect of any cessation of its products. But at least one can be on guard against their unique combination of tediousness and gullibility.

1961/1967

Pseudo-history 4: Anti-Anti-Stalinism

In addition to the traditional psuedo-historians of the whole Stalin and post-Stalin period, a new group of 'revisionists' raised their heads in the 1980s. Their main themes were that not much of a terror took place, that 'social' change and political restructuring were of more interest, and that unofficial evidence was prejudiced and otherwise unsatisfactory.

They argue that hitherto two versions of the 1933–8 period have existed. The first, the official Stalinist account, is untrue. The second, put forward by Westerners and dissidents, is equally or almost equally misleading, with its theme that Stalin had Kirov murdered, and from then on built up an increasing terror; and that his motives were to secure his own power by installing an absolute despotism.

This Western approach is, moreover, invalidated by its supposedly relying on a 'totalitarian model' or a 'Great Man model', and by its implying a belief in the high efficiency of the Soviet bureaucracy and Stalin's total control over events. Perhaps there are historians, caught in a simplistic political science, who entertain such views; but it is hard to think of any.

All this is typified in *Origins of the Great Purge*, by J. Arch Getty. For the author the 'Western' version is not merely misleading: it distracts attention from more significant events. He regards 'structural, institutional and ideological' matters as the important ones, and in particular holds that not the purges as a whole but the 'structural and factional' struggle within the party, and especially the series of official party expulsions of 1933–7, are the central feature of the period, with the rise of a new leadership stratum. But the administrative changes of the period did not take place in a vacuum. The circumstances of the replacement of one ruling stratum by another were decisive as to the whole nature of the new selection. As the physicist Alexander Weissberg noted (of the new generation of factory managers in the Ukraine, but the point applies generally), 'they had not even the normal advantages of youth in their favour, for the choosing had been a very negative one. They were the men who had denounced others on innumerable occasions. They had bowed the knee whenever they had come up against higher authority. They were morally and intellectually crippled.' 'Subjective'?: yes, and confirmed by hundreds of other observers, Soviet and non-soviet, up to the present day. The author deduces from the official press that there were 'radicals' and 'moderates' among the leadership, by which he means that those actually in charge of industry sought lower production targets than those concerned with ideology. Since men of both types perished in the purges, this distinction hardly seems decisive to the understanding of the period. But nor should the public moves anyhow be taken at face value. For instance, Karl Bauman is labelled a 'radical', and 'seems to have been held responsible for the extremist policy towards the kulak in 1929–1930'. But Bauman's demotion was not because he advocated 'radical' policies different from Stalin's but because it was better to blame him than Stalin for their failure – and it was not anyhow a matter of kulaks, but of the crash collectivization of non-kulaks.

Getty believes that truths unobtainable from defectors and such are to be sought primarily in Soviet *speeches* of the period. Stalin's famous speech to Red Army graduates on 14 May 1935, on the importance of a sensitive attitude to human life, came when he had chalked up his first 10-million-odd corpses, and was ready to start on the second 10 million! Nor is this misapprehension a new one. Sidney and Beatrice Webb, in their absurd *Soviet Communism: A New Civilization*, wrote of Stalin's 'historic' speech of 23 June 1931, in which he condemned 'specialist-baiting', that it was a 'Magna Carta for the intelligentsia'. But they had to add, with some confusion, that 'renewed outbursts of persecution of the intelligentsia almost immediately recurred'.

It will be seen that Getty's approach is somewhat narrower in scope than that of previous studies of the period. And he restricts himself, in principle, to 'primary' sources, by which he means official sources (rather as if one based a study of Hitler's Germany on the *Völkische Beobachter* and the archives of the Baden NSDAP). By these means, he considers, he has avoided the 'Manichaean' aberration common to both Stalinist and non-Stalinist writing, and been able to achieve 'objectivity'.

Anyone who had not yet developed severe qualms about the

author's notions about history would certainly have them at this point.

It is a delusion, and a fairly primitive one at that, to believe that historical 'objectivity' can be achieved by some mechanical methodology which eliminates opinion. Such devices merely conceal opinion. It is the frank admission by the historian that he indeed holds specific views which forces him to treat the evidence as objectively as possible. As G. M. Trevelyan says in *Clio, A Muse* (surely a fairly basic text): 'The dispassionateness of the historian is a quality which it is easy to value too highly, and it should not be confused with the really indispensable qualities of accuracy and good faith.'

John Morris noted that all the leading historians from Thucydides on have put forward their own beliefs, and that it is the 'more pedestrian writers' in the field who 'are less aware of their own bias . . . we must be especially wary of the man who claims to set down objective truth free from bias, for the closer he comes to his ideal, the more he is enslaved to the passing prejudice of his own day.'

Moreover, Getty constantly imputes bad faith to those who do not follow his line. Anti-Stalinists, even Khrushchev, are 'self-interested'. 'Cold War' and 'the McCarthyite period' have distorted the facts. But this last ploy is impossible to maintain even at its own low level: one of Getty's main targets is Roy Medvedev, to whom it cannot conceivably apply; while another 'Manichaean', Stephen F. Cohen, is one of the leading critics of so-called 'Cold War' attitudes, without this affecting his realistic view of the Stalin period.

It becomes even plainer that the author has no idea of what history is about when we look at his idea of its 'sources'. He seeks, in his own words, 'internal records of the participants' rather than those of 'exogenous victims of the process'; and, as we have said, describes the former as 'primary' and therefore to be used exclusively or almost exclusively (though, of course, accounts by victims are equally 'primary', at least as regards their own experiences).

Now, first of all, the official record is (to put it mildly) heavily falsified; and even the lower confidential documents at the Smolensk level now in the West are also of limited use, being almost equally encrypted into Stalinese. Relying on such records, indeed, one would remain ignorant of such vast events as the terror-famine of 1933, in which millions perished. How easy the writing of history would be if such a simple method of validating research material were indeed available. But in fact, especially in the Soviet case, it leads to accepting both falsification and restriction.

In the many areas of history where usable evidence is hard to come by, researchers have always had recourse to sources which are not 'primary' in Getty's sense. His knowledge of the past is apparently limited to those rare cultures whose public documents are generally speaking both comprehensive and reliable; though, even with these, his method would be shaky and incomplete.

The trouble about revising the main matters of the period is that they are solidly established. The weak spot, as Getty sees it, is that the evidence is various and difficult. All the unofficial, often second- or third-hand reports which historians of the Stalin period have hitherto used are dismissed as unreliable. But of course all sources are, in one way or another, imperfect, and whoever seeks this sort of reliability seeks 'what ne'er was, nor is, nor e'er shall be'. That a source may be erroneous or unreliable on certain points does not automatically invalidate all its evidence. As Gibbon says, a historian may use such material without making himself 'answerable . . . for all the circumjacent errors of inconsistencies of the authors whom he has quoted'.

Getty is free with words like 'dubious' for sources of which he disapproves. But, as John Morris wrote, the historian 'may not insinuate like an advocate, whose plea that the evidence falls short of absolute proof covertly invites his hearers to disbelieve the evidence', and again 'falsehood must be demonstrated as carefully as accuracy, and may not be casually implied by labelling a statement "dubious" without argument'. The author complains of 'the leading expert on the great purges' (the present writer) that he has said that 'truth can thus only percolate in the form of hearsay'. My point of course was not that other material should be neglected but that, in Soviet conditions, we would very seldom get proper information about the more crucial political decisions or events except at second or third hand, something so obvious that it hardly needs defending.

Getty constantly attacks defector 'raconteurs' and 'second hand accounts', and suggests that such work as that of Medvedev and myself 'are uniformly based on memoir sources . . . rely almost exclusively on personal accounts'. This is quite untrue, as anyone looking at the notes to both our books will see immediately.

What is true is that unofficial sources, like official ones, have to be handled carefully. The author prefers simply to dismiss such material as Nicolaevsky's 'Letter of an Old Bolshevik' and Alexander Orlov's book – both the particular objects of his criticism. Of course they have their defects, and these have been noted for decades by earlier historians. The whole matter, on these two and others, is gone into at length in the Bibliographical Note to my *The Great Terror*, originally published in 1968, where, for example, it is made clear that Nicolaevsky could not have learnt from Bukharin about events later than the spring of 1936, and that Orlov's access to information tails off. Getty notes that Orlov was not in the USSR for more than a few days after 1936. This is true, but it is truth told to imply something untrue – that Orlov did not have closest contact with old colleagues who knew the inner secrets of the NKVD. This is not the place to consider Orlov fully; but since I wrote his evidence has stood up well to that provided independently by *samizdat* sources, and even by Khrushchev. To call it 'corridor gossip' is especially misleading, since such highly confidential information is seldom given out round the water-cooler. The 'Letter of an Old Bolshevik' Getty simply announced to be 'spurious'. This is merely abuse. It is clear, as I have said, that it is a compendium of reports and rumours and that these must be treated with care. But its matter up to March 1936, or that part of it evidently provided or confirmed by Bukharin, is of high quality, and much of it has since been confirmed. Nicolaevsky was not some oddball exile. He had been head of the Marx-Engels Institute in Moscow; he was Rykov's brother-in-law. And it is absurd for Getty to tell us dismissively, for example about Politburo votes on such matters as the Ryutin affair, that 'the only way for Bukharin to have found out about Politburo debates and votes . . . would have been for someone else to have told him'. He was a member of the Central Committee constantly meeting those in the Politburo, so even at second hand his account would be of high quality. But in fact, in the words of Khrushchev (a firsthand source!), at this time, 'members of the Central Committee who happened to be in Moscow were entitled to attend Politburo meetings'!

Roy Medvedev's *Let History Judge* appeared after my own and similar works, and relies on quite different sources. These too are of no value to Getty: 'none of Medvedev's informants was close enough to the centre to be of real use.' Well, Medvedev uses the Petrovsky archives. It is true that these were given him by Petrovsky's grandson, but surely, what with Petrovsky's candidate membership of the Politburo and survival until 1958, the source is 'close enough'? And when Medvedev lengthily quotes a (this time quite firsthand!) communication from Yakubovich, the only survivor of his sentence, on how the Menshevik Trial was set up, this obviously makes all the tons of official publications on the subject kick the beam.

Medvedev, though comparatively rarely, quotes 'MS by S—'. Getty censures him for this as typifying his material, though in fact

Medvedev lists twenty-one memoir sources by name, some of them firsthand, as to quite important matters, and quotes several others. But Getty then speaks (for example) of a 'rumour' reported by Medvedev about Stalin's final attack on Yezhov at the Senioren Konvent of the 18th Congress in March 1939, where Medvedev gives his source by name: E. G. Feldman, a delegate from Odessa who figures as such in the congress report, and who was – once more – an eyewitness!

But Getty's ability to get Medvedev wrong is uncanny. For example, he writes that Medvedev in *Let History Judge* (p. 218) reports that anti-Bolshevik political parties continued to exist underground in Russia in the thirties. what Medvedev actually says is that Communist Parties outside the Soviet Union were mostly underground, so that many of *their* leaders were in Moscow (in fact Medvedev elsewhere specifically notes that no Menshevik underground existed in the USSR)!

We are none of us immune from such bloomers, though those making exceptionally high claims to rigour should perhaps be more careful. However, the rigour itself is, after all, not quite up to the claims. For example, the author does indeed use 'memoir' sources (such as Svetlanin and Tokaev), where it suits his own argument. And at the same time, and for the same reasons, he is always ready (as we have seen) to dismiss a firsthand account he doesn't like: thus he refutes Djilas's eyewitness description of the behaviour of the Politburo in Stalin's presence – by a footnote referring to a Western economics writer who does not accept it. The impression given, perhaps unfairly, is that the author rather fails to live up even to the standards he set himself.

The refractory art of Soviet history consists of wringing the truth out of materials all of which, official and unofficial, present inadequacies and difficulties. As Jacques Barzun and Henry F. Graff tell us in their *The Modern Researcher*, the process of historical verification is 'conducted on many planes, and its technique is not fixed. It relies on attention to detail, on common-sense reasoning, on a developed "feel" for history and chronology, on familiarity with human behaviour, and one ever enlarging stores of information.' And, they conclude, 'No interesting or important question . . . can be settled without detailed knowledge, solid judgement, lively imagination and ability to think straight. What to do and how to go about it come with practice; to enumerate rules would be endless and of little use.' This is, in fact, the crux: that 'judgement' is needed, that it is a delicate matter, and that no mechanical criteria of validating or rejecting evidence exists. They also note that the sort of judgement which is in the end the crux of the historian's equipment is in all essentials the same as that needed in matters of everyday life, where error and falsehood equally have to be coped with. Some of the delicacy of such operations is to be seen in Gibbon, when he tells us that testimonies are often 'imperfect and partial' but that 'as it is unreasonable to expect that each of them should vouch for the whole, so it would be impossible to define the boundaries of their respective property'.

So far we have dealt with the question of method in history, and expressed doubt at the validity (and at the consistency) of the author's approach. Let us now see how it works out in practice. For though he eliminates much of the potential evidence, and regards comparatively petty themes as more significant than is perhaps usual, he might nevertheless have presented a picture which, while neither wholly true nor particularly interesting, added something to our knowledge and understanding.

We may get a fair impression of the author's performance if we consider his chapter on the Yezhov period. For this, according to him, we have little but 'impressionistic data' – a way of saying that previous historians have relied on unofficial sources. But there is enough official material for the author to work on, and his use of it is instructive.

First, he explains Yagoda's fall, and Yezhov's appointment to the (or rather a) Kemerovo mine explosion which had taken place a few days earlier. This is *post hoc ergo propter hoc*: pure, though not illegitimate, speculation. All the evidence points against it – the phrasing of the Stalin telegram, the date of the arrest of Radek, the general ignoring of similar disasters. And incidentally it is not the case that *Pravda* Sept 26 [it should be 27 September] 1936 provides the only official biographical information on Yezhov': it is a re-edited version of an earlier article in the *Small Soviet Encyclopaedia*, omitting one important appointment.

Then we are told that when Yezhov removed Yagoda's men he staffed the NKVD with 'his people'. In fact (as Medvedev has pointed out, though it can anyhow be seen in the official record) only half a dozen such can be found in high or fairly high posts. Every one of the fifteen men identifiable as NKVD heads in the union republics (and the Far East) over 1937–8 was a veteran, as of course were Yezhov's chief deputies Frinovsky and Zakovsky.

On the Yezhov team's first triumph, the suppression of the supposed Tukhachevsky plot, Getty is particularly perverse. He claims that its existence or otherwise is a moot point. But since the officers were all rehabilitated in the late 1950s, and all Soviet sources now agree that it was a frame-up, as do all serious outside commentators, some fairly strong evidence is required to support the contrary, and all Getty does is produce two sources, both of the reprobated 'memoir' variety, which in fact tell of different possible conspiracies by different officers!

Getty sees the 'height of the Yezhovshchina' in late 1937, though survivors speak of September–October 1938 as the worst period. At any rate, the author sees Stalin as dissatisfied with Yezhov and the NKVD at the end of 1937 – not appearing at the NKVD decennial meeting, though there at the musical performance afterwards. This, together with supposedly inadequate reporting of a Yezhov speech, is represented as 'Yezhov was in trouble and was probably being blamed for excessive repression'.

The supporting evidence Getty adduces is that Deputy NKVD People's Commissar Matvei Berman was transferred to be Commissar for Communications and Deputy NKVD People's Commissar M. I. Ryzhov to be Commissar for Forestry in January 1938. But in fact Berman's transfer had taken place the previous August, while Ryzhov was anyhow replaced by one of Yezhov's very closest clients, Z. B. Zhukovsky. Moreover January and February are precisely the moment when two more of Yezhov's clients finally get key posts – as NKVD chiefs in Moscow and Leningrad, while his secretary is soon afterwards promoted to be head of one of the key GUGB departments.

It is clear that, if Stalin was dissatisfied, it was not with Yezhov. It is equally clear that any dissatisfaction was due not to excessive repression but to its opposite; and Zakovsky's arrival at the centre in January marked the beginning of a fresh wave of terror and, at last, the successful production of the Bukharin Trial. This error of Getty's is again not in itself an improper speculation, though tenuously and inaccurately supported even by Kremlinological standards. But if one makes this sort of estimate, one should check all the easily accessible official information relevant to it.

There are a number of other erroneous speculations over the period – for example that from April 1938 Yezhov concerned himself almost entirely with the Commissariat of Water Transport (at which, in fact, he seldom appeared). And Getty also has a passing swipe at high figures given by previous annalists for victims of the Yezhovshchina – partly because he cannot reconcile remarks by Roy Medvedev and myself to the effect that the Party suffered most severely, but that many more victims were ordinary people. It is simple: about half the

Party perished, and only about a tenth or a twelfth of the remaining adult population. Getty indeed strongly condemns Stalin for the use of terror – though only to imprison 'many thousands' of innocent people, and execute 'thousands'. Since millions were certainly imprisoned, and as a minimum hundreds of thousands shot, even here one can see a tilting of the balance in Stalin's favour (as with, for example, 'One must express one's horror at the Holocaust, in which thousands of Jews perished').

The crux of the period is, of course, the Kirov murder. It is a striking and revealing oddity of Getty's book that he devotes a special appendix to denying the evidence against Stalin. He is concerned to establish first that the murder did not lead directly to the Yezhovshchina; second that there is no evidence of any dispute between Kirov and Stalin; and third that Stalin did not procure the murder. The first words of Evgenia Ginzburg's *Into The Whirlwind* are 'The year 1937 really began on the 1st December 1934' – the date of Kirov's death; and most historians agree, though noting that Stalin had to manoeuvre, in his usual devious way, before the result followed. Getty parlays these manoeuvres into a lack of real connection. In this uncalled-for decoupling of the phases he again falls into factual error. He says that the decree of 1 December 1934 was not the basis of later charges, which came under Article 58 of the penal code. But the December decree was not penal but procedural; so the point is anyhow misconceived. And, in fact, later cases *were* tried under the 1 December 1934 procedures: for instance it is cited in the verdict on Tukhachevsky and his colleagues, and in all other known cases except the three set piece Moscow Trials.

Again, he asserts that the NKVD officers sentenced to short terms on 23 January 1935 for negligence in protecting Kirov were tried by 'their fellows on an NKVD board' – thus apparently removing the police aspect from the high political arena. In fact they were tried, like all other major cases, by the Military Collegium of the Supreme Court under Ulrikh. But even apart from such mistakes, the notion of discontinuity in Stalin's general strategy, as against steps forward and back, has the advantage (as with so much of the author's schematism) only of novelty, if advantage it be.

Readers interested in the matter are referred to p.128–133 of my *Stalin and the Kirov Murder* (1989) in which I show that Getty's other points are equally dismissive of the evidence; that there is massive and long-standing (even official) testimony to Stalin's bad relations with Kirov; and that all the rest of the many points urged in favour of Stalin's non-complicity in the assassination are without substance.

The Kirov case, though interesting and important, is only one event in the huge and terrible human drama of the Stalin purges. It is clear that Getty's historical standards are untenable; and that he has departed even from these when it suited his argument. But all that is minor compared with his concurrent reduction of the whole fantastic alien scene largely to petty matters of administration and rational economic disputes. As Orwell said, to understand the Soviet Union needs an effort of the imagination as well as of the intellect. What is missing here, and in the similar writings now occasionally obtruding themselves, is above all any sense of exotic and primitive despotism or of the ambience of a strange millenarian sect. Stalin and his followers are seen to commit cruelties and falsifications, but any feeling for the drives and motivations, the wholly alien culture incarnate in them, is absent.

One of the tests of a scholar is that he knows not only his chosen field, and that in great and often reconsidered detail, but also much in other fields peripheral to it or illuminative of it. Indeed, without some perspective on other times and other cultures, on the generally static 'pre-critical' societies of the ancient empires or the destructive conquering regimes of mediaeval Asia, on the psychology of the millenarian sects of ancient Alexandria or mediaeval Germany, he is hobbled.

Such knowledge is not available to this school, who hold that there was not, there could not have been much of a terror. One of its adherents argues that not everyone was terrified all the time. Two others – demographers – apply to the period tables derived from quite different societies and conclude from this circular argument that losses were low. Another maintains that peasant deaths in the collectivisation terror could not have been as high as what is readily deducible. What they share, in fact, is devotion to the notion of a level of death and imprisonment contradicting what all the evidence requires.

Parochialism, limited vision, and ignorance of the nature of historical (or other) evidence: these are fundamentally destructive of the study of history. The central error, as Joseph Brodsky has pointed out, is that such commentators are unable to believe that Stalin's acts were possible. They make conscious or unconscious assumptions which do not admit certain types of reality. The accompanying inconsistencies, omissions and misrepresentations are no more than the natural product of such a substantially shaky approach. Heaven knows, even the soundest principles do not prevent us from making mistakes or arriving at misconceptions. But without them error is inevitable, and likely to be on a grand scale.

It is true that, by an agreeable irony, this stuff is sooner or later refuted by Soviet revelations. Still, we can hardly afford to have so much misinformation and misdirection in a field where the truth is so vital to an understanding of the central issues facing the human mind today.

1985/1989

Postscript: Since the above was written Soviet sources by the score have, of course, confirmed the numbers of those killed and of those sent to labour camps as as high as, or higher than, those proposed by myself and others. They have similarly noted the devastating effect of the terror on the population, and the 'negative selection' of a new ruling caste which accompanied it, as the major results for the country of the whole Stalinist experience. And they have written that they find it hard to understand Westerners who have stated the opposite. So do I.

EPILOGUE

The Whole Man: Solzhenitsyn

1

The appearance of Solzhenitsyn in English and the other Western languages has been an enormously different phenomenon from the mere 'translation' of a 'writer' in the ordinary sense. For the barrier between ourselves and the Russia of the present day is not merely linguistic or literary. It is a matter of witness being borne about a culture, a political culture, which is from our point of view almost unbelievably strange; a culture which we can only begin to understand by a constant effort of the imagination.

Work like Solzhenitsyn's which helps us, or even forces us, into that understanding is therefore crucial to our real grasp of the world today, of the very springs of policy – in fact of the preservation of our own future.

He is first a witness for the dead – the tens of millions of innocent and helpless victims of the regime. Secondly, he is witness for truth against what Pasternak described as 'the inhuman power of the lie'. The whole experience – the greatest trauma that has shaken Russia – remains a moral albatross around the necks of the men in the Kremlin. Solzhenitsyn insists that this is intolerable. So it is. Until rulers can be relied on to allow the truth to be told about their past they are hardly to be trusted in any sphere whatever.

Solzhenitsyn had hardly emerged in the West before it became clear that many people here were finding him an awkward customer. He had stood magnificently for liberty, and faced down the most powerful group of despots in the world by sheer force of courage and personality. That could not be denied: but it soon became only too obvious that he was not a nice, obedient projection of the comfortable notions of Western 'liberals'.

And so . . . the process of chipping away at this colossus started. Every method was used: from KGB-sponsored slanders about his private life to smarmy expositions of the theme 'he is such a wonderful man, what a pity that . . .' His intervention, openly criticizing aspects not merely of the West, but specifically of Britain, led to a concentrated outburst of spite from the hosts of Lilliput.

It is true that his critics contradicted each other. Yet we can distinguish the various methods which came into use for pretending that he does not really exist much.

The method of excited abuse, as employed by the *Daily Mirror*, was perhaps effective with people who knew nothing of what he has really said. All one had to do is ask 'Does Solzhenitsyn want to turn us into a mirror-image of Russia'? The true answer is of course: No. But the moragogic implication is the opposite, taking us right back to the days when people were telling us we could not fight fascism without becoming fascists ourselves. One can go on from this to suggest 'Does Solzhenitsyn want' – an arms race, Cold War, Hot War?

The minimum, and commonest assertion is that he advocates a return to the Cold War. No he doesn't. He is saying that we are in the middle of a Cold War, (with elements of Hot, as when Russian tanks and guns blast away in Africa, Indo-China and the Middle East). And that pretending otherwise will not do much good. He aggravates this offence by stressing the view that devoted enemies in principle of everything we stand for are not best coped with by giving them whatever they want in return for an occasional polite remark. History, one would think, tends to be on Solzhenitsyn's side. So in addition to misrepresenting his views, one must ignore history.

The next effort is to describe him as a Slavophile or a Russian Nationalist. This is based on the fact that he likes Russia and the Russian people, is of the orthodox faith, and so forth. The implication – that he stands for an aggressive expansionist Right-wing Russia – is absolutely false. In fact he publicly urges the withdrawal of Russia from the colonial territories of the non-Slavic portions of Soviet Europe and Asia. This point must therefore be evaded, or misrepresented.

Being a Slavophile goes with his being a 'reactionary'. It can certainly be shown that Solzhenitsyn is opposed to many things regarded as 'progressive'. To some degree, he is even an offender against the curious notion that 'you can't turn the clock back'. You can, of course, turn the clock back, and it has often been done with beneficent effect – as in Germany in 1945. Solzhenitsyn certainly believes that the half-century before the Russian Revolution, when a civic and judicial order was being gradually built up, was preferable to the post-1917 period, whose main achievement has been the extirpation of this promise – a 'turning the clock back', if you like, in a much nastier sense, to something resembling the time of Nicholas the First. This too can be rebutted by ignorance of history, and loud noises about progress.

Solzhenitsyn naturally, gave offence to a lot of people who thought of themselves as Socialists, by his remark that 'Socialist democracy' was an expression of the same type as 'boiling ice'.

On any usual definition of Socialism proper, State Socialism, Solzhenitsyn has the advantage of first being right in logic – in that a democracy cannot be Socialist because that deprives it of its democratic right to be non-Socialist if and when it wishes. Second, he is empirically in the right to the extent that every State whose economy can be defined as Socialist is, in fact, a thorough-going tyranny. In this field a particularly sturdy ignoring of fact and logic must serve.

We are then told that Solzhenitsyn does not understand the West. This is belied to quite a fair extent by the nature of some of the attacks on him and his principles, which resemble nothing more than carefully contrived proofs of his allegation that all too many Westerners resent being told what it is like out in the cruel hard world. All the same, it is naturally the case that Solzhenitsyn knows less about Britain or America than he does about Russia. Mr Bernard Levin commented on the BBC, I think rightly, that Solzhenitsyn underestimated the reserves of moral strength in the country; though the mere fact of his addressing us is in itself an appeal to such qualities. But, paradoxically, if he has made our position out to be even worse than it really is, this would be due to his having unavoidably gained most of his impressions from the Press, especially the liberal Press. Indeed, it is surprising that he doesn't go a good deal further in a diagnosis of extreme decadence, if he has relied on most of our supposed leaders of opinion.

On his major theme, in any case, the precise degree of decadence we have reached is not really the point. A doctor, a cholera expert, coming here from a cholera-infected country, pointing out that the plague is sweeping westward, and recommending measures which could protect us, would hardly be thought to have been refuted by someone noting that he had misunderstood a few details about the inefficiency of our Health Service. On the contrary, we would queue to accept his cholera shots, however painful.

Chekhov once wrote that 'great writers engage in politics only in so far as it is necessary to defend people against politics'. Nowadays, in the Communist countries, and so in those countries under threat of Communism too, it is very necessary. And it is in this sense, and this sense only, that Solzhenitsyn's talent and drive are political.

As a witness his moral power has often been remarked on. The astonishing thing, to my mind, is less the moral part than the power part – the way he was able as a single determined individual to face and outface the most powerful rulers on earth. The lesson he teaches, with the other bold novelists, historians, poets, and philosophers of the Soviet dissidence, is that force and dogma are vulnerable to the free mind. The world needs the knowledge that he, and others in similar case, provide. It also needs the example of the power of the human spirit which they have, often at immense personal cost, given to us all. That 'hideous strength' with which they have contended is one which faces all of us everywhere today.

Nevertheless there are many in the West who prefer to close their eyes in the hope that the danger will go away. And, if not, that the bearer of uncomfortable news will vanish.

1980

2

It was, in fact, clearly the hope of the Soviet establishment too that Solzhenitsyn's impact would die away. And by the early 1980s, as he lived quietly in Vermont working at his novels, it did seem as though his time had passed. He was almost never 'in the news' in the West, and was almost unmentioned in the USSR. The calculation of the Brezhnevite regime that exile would lead to oblivion seemed to have been accurate.

But appearances proved wrong: the progress of glasnost led in the autumn of 1988 to his once more becoming an epicentre of the moral and intellectual earthquakes shaking his country. In February 1987, Sergei Zalygin, the editor of *Novy Mir*, had hinted that Solzhenitsyn might be published in Moscow. Official circles strongly repudiated the idea. A few months later another *Novy Mir* editor, Anatoly Strely-any, said at a meeting that if *Novy Mir* did not publish Solzhenitsyn other journals would. He was soon removed from the board. In January 1988 yet a third member of *Novy Mir*'s board, who had also been fired, wrote in *Literaturnaya Ucheba* of the contributions of emigre writers to Russian literature, and for the first time mentioned Solzhenitsyn's name in print. In June *Novy Mir* printed selections from Varlam Shalamov's fine labour camp stories, *Kolyma Tales*. Shalamov's introduction to these mentioned Solzhenitsyn in the same breath as Tolstoy, and a review of them in the main literary weekly *Literaturnaya Gazeta* spoke of Solzhenitsyn twice. In July several mentions appeared. And on Soviet television the leading writer Viktor Astafiev told of a pilgrimage he had paid to the grave of another Russian Nobel Prizewinner for literature who had died in exile, and how he had asked Bunin to 'forgive us . . . forgive your poor motherland . . .', predicting that his own grandchildren would some day utter the same words at Solzhenitsyn's grave.

In August, Zalygin wrote in so many words that Solzhenitsyn might be published in *Novy Mir*; and the critic Elena Chukovskaya published an article 'Return USSR Citizenship to Solzhenitsyn', in *Knizhnoe Obozrenie*. Over the next weeks, other well known writers heaped praise on him. Vyacheslav Kondratiev wrote, 'Solzhenitsyn is needed by Russia and by all of us not only as a writer of enormous talent, but as a *personality*. One has only to imagine what strength, what courage it took for a writer to enter into combat, alone, with a powerful and cruel administrative system which could crush a man with a single wave of the hand'. He ended 'We do not now have in Russia a writer of his stature. Aleksandr Isaevich should be here with us'. And now, as it seemed, the dam broke. Dozens of letters from well known intellectual figures were published. And when an 'Advisory Committee to Oversee the Creation of a Monument to the Victims of Illegality and Repression was formed, it voted to ask Solzhenitsyn to join it. (He thanked them for the honour, but said he had already celebrated their memory in *Gulag Archipelago*, and in any case was unable to return to the Soviet Union). But the invitation showed two things. First, that he had been right. And second, that his testimony, perhaps regarded as out of date in some Western circles, retains its immediacy and its validity.

In September *Novy Mir* officially decided to print the *First Circle* and *Cancer Ward* and parts of *Gulag Archipelago*. Solzhenitsyn agreed, stipulating that he should select the *Gulag* chapters, and that they should appear first. A million and a half copies of the October issue were run off, announcing this on the back cover. But in mid-October the authorities had the issue withdrawn and the announcement cancelled, while the Politburo's cultural spokesman Vadim Medvedev, in an unpublished but unofficially taped speech, attacked the writer for *Gulag Archipelago*, as anti-Leninist, and 'undermining the basis of our life'.

As I write early in 1989 this is how things rest. As to the future, we shall see. But it is striking, for example, that the most liberal of the official cultural bodies, the Union of Soviet Film Makers, announced that it had set up a commission of a hundred leading figures to protect 'professional rights and personal freedom' and that its first act was to request the Presidium of the Supreme Soviet to review the legality of Solzhenitsyn's expulsion, especially in view of his 'huge role' in exposing repression. More important yet, it was not only sympathizers with Solzhenitsyn's position who spoke up, but also cultural figures who have criticized and even attacked him. The well known writer Yuri Koryakin said, 'Let him be an anti-Communist. So was Dostoevsky. Is *he* an enemy? . . . we can't fail to enter into debate with such a person, just as we came to debate with Andrei Dmitryevich Sakharov'. The historian Ya Etinger made the same point. Writing that Solzhenitsyn and Sakharov 'personified the spirit of opposition presented by the healthy and democratic forces in Soviet society against Stalinism and Brezhnevism', he added that, 'it is time to put right the injustice in the case of A. I. Solzhenitsyn also. In the whole civilized world he has long been rightly considered one of the greatest Russian writers of the twentieth century. One can argue or disagree with his ideological and philosophical views as a writer, but he belongs to Russia, of which he has been an ardent patriot all his complex, tragic life'. V. I. Lakshin, too, said they should discuss his books 'on the basis of full knowledge of their content', and 'exchange polemics with the author, whose strong, almost painful love for his homeland and his people cannot be gainsaid'.

In fact Solzhenitsyn's position as a writer has been resoundingly reaffirmed by hundreds of his literary colleagues of all opinions. And his case has once again become a central issue for the moral and intellectual development of Russia.

The leadership may not yet (or in the worst case might never) be ready to come to terms with him. Politically and philosophically they are very reluctant to face the idea of tolerating the strong exponent of views so different from their own. Yet until this barrier is down, there can be no true civic society in the USSR. And without that, as both orthodox and unorthodox Soviet thinkers know, there can be no social or even economic progress. But progressive sentiment also waits his return for another reason. He represents, is the voice of, Russian traditions and patriotism. The new nationalist trends in Russian include elements that may legitimately be called fascist – xenophobic, anti-semitic, expansionist. Solzhenitsyn's patriotism totally rejects all that. The great mutual respect between him and Andrei Sakharov, covering a range of different opinion but excluding

all radical extremes, draws the broad limits of consensus for a freer
Russia.

3

Moreover, time is indeed ripe, or overripe, for Moscow's political
leadership to consider the advice Solzhenitsyn gave in his *Letter to
Soviet Leaders* which he sent to them while he was still in the Soviet
Union, on 5 September 1973. Its central message, neglected at the
time even in the West, is now widely recognized as the only workable
agenda for the immediate future. He asked of them not that they
abandon power but that they withdraw the autocracy to the realm
of political rule only, allowing an autonomous civic, legal, economic
and intellectual life to their citizens; and that they renounce their
expansionist world mission. These ideas are now being publicly
accepted and urged by a wide range of lawyers, economists, sociologists and other members of the Soviet intelligentsia.

The huge organism of falsehood is now in its death-throes. It is
not yet dead, indeed; and death-throes can be long and dangerous.
Solzhenitsyn was not only responsible, with others I have covered in
this book, for bringing down this fearful monster: he also showed the
best way forward for a return to reason and reality, to prosperity and
peace in Russia, and hence in the world.

1989

INDEX

ABOUT THE AUTHOR

Robert Conquest is the author of numerous books on the Soviet Union and foreign policy, and has also published poetry, fiction and criticism. He received his M.A. and D.Litt. from Oxford University and has held posts at Columbia University, the London School of Economics and elsewhere. He is currently a Senior Research Fellow and Scholar-Curator of the East European Collection at the Hoover Institution, Stanford University.